Windows® XP™ Home Networking

Paul Thurrott

M&T Books

Best-Selling Books • Digital Downloads • e-Books • Answer Networks
e-Newsletters • Branded Web Sites • e-Learning

New York, NY • Cleveland, OH • Indianapolis, IN

Windows® XP™ Home Networking

Published by
Wiley Publishing, Inc.
909 Third Avenue
New York, NY 10022
www.wiley.com

Copyright © 2002 by Wiley Publishing, Inc., Indianapolis, Indiana

Library of Congress Control Number: 2002108092

ISBN: 0-7645-3675-3

Manufactured in the United States of America.

10 9 8 7 6 5 4 3 2 1

1O/RV/QX/QS/IN

Published simultaneously in Canada

Credits

ACQUISITIONS EDITOR
Terri Varveris

PROJECT EDITOR
Pat O'Brien

TECHNICAL EDITOR
Greg Guntle

COPY EDITOR
Kim Darosett

EDITORIAL MANAGERS
Kyle Looper
Mary Beth Wakefield

SENIOR VICE PRESIDENT, TECHNICAL PUBLISHING
Richard Swadley

VICE PRESIDENT AND PUBLISHER
Mary Bednarek

PROJECT COORDINATOR
Maridee Ennis

GRAPHICS AND PRODUCTION SPECIALISTS
Stephanie D. Jumper
Gabrielle McCann
Laurie Petrone
Jeremey Unger

QUALITY CONTROL TECHNICIANS
Laura Albert
John Greenough

PROOFREADING AND INDEXING
TECHBOOKS Production Services

About the Author

Paul Thurrott is a recognized Windows expert with over 10 years of Windows experience. Paul is the author of over a dozen books about Windows, Web and software development, and other computing topics. His SuperSite for Windows (www.winsupersite.com) is dedicated to providing all of the information you need to evaluate Microsoft's upcoming Windows operating system technologies.

This book is dedicated to my daughter, Kelly. I love you.

Preface

Windows XP Home Networking gives you everything you need to set up an Internet connection that can be safely and securely shared with other PCs and devices in your home. Home Networking is cool—especially wireless networking—and if you set it up right, you'll wonder how you ever got along without it. In that way, it's kind of like indoor plumbing, or electricity.

This book is written for real people. Normal people. People who don't want to spend an entire week wiring their homes or configuring bizarre technical settings just to get things working. I'd considered writing networking titles in the past, but Windows XP is the first operating system that makes this technology truly available to everyone. So if you're just getting started with XP, you made the right choice. And if you're wondering whether XP is worth the upgrade hassle, hopefully this book will prove that yes, it sure is.

That's the magic of XP, really: It makes previously difficult tasks easier to complete. So any discussion of XP home networking really has to start at the beginning of that product's life cycle.

Sometimes It All Comes Together

On October 25, 2001, I attended the Windows XP launch event in New York's Times Square, which ended up being an unfortunately boring affair, despite the general excitement over Microsoft's most impressive—and consumer friendly—operating system product ever. Microsoft Chairman and Chief Software Architect Bill Gates presided over the monotonous procession, which featured highlights such as the "death of DOS," a lot of product demonstrations, a goofy "Who Wants to Be a Millionaire" bit with Regis Philbin, and some general back-slapping. I was almost falling asleep by the time the launch event came to a close, when Gates suddenly started wrapping things up. A PowerPoint slide filled the massive video screens behind him, and my eyes refocused, and a smile came to my face. Gates was talking about the best features in Windows XP, and listed on the slide above him were the following bullet points:

- Real-time communications
- Mobile Computing
- Help and support
- Digital photography
- Digital music
- Digital video
- Home networking

I was smiling because I had just proposed the book you're now reading to Hungry Minds, which has since become part of the Wiley family. Hungry Minds had also published my previous book, *Great Windows XP Digital Media* (http://www. xpdigitalmedia.com), which covers about half of the topics on the Gates slide mentioned above. This book, *Windows XP Home Networking*, neatly covers the other half.

I love it when a plan comes together.

Even Bill Gates himself apparently agrees that the digital media and networking technologies in Windows XP are the best reasons to upgrade. And that, really, is what this is all about. You can create home networks (and work with various digital media technologies) with previous Windows versions, but it isn't as good. It isn't as fun. And it certainly isn't as easy. The further you go back in time, in fact, the harder and more technical these tasks become.

And *technical* means boring. If you have to know how to manually assign IP address and DNS settings, perform port forwarding, or configure technologies with bizarre names like NAT, then the topic we're discussing is for experts only. And frankly, experts don't need or want a book about home networking anyway. They're weenies.

I used to write books for weenies. Heck, I used to be a weenie. But part of maturing and growing up is that you learn to put things in perspective. And my current perspective is that technology isn't the reason I write about these topics. No, I write about these topics because of what the technology *enables*.

Let me give you an example. Since adding wireless networking to my home, my wife and I can browse the Web, read email, or do anything else that we used to do from a desktop computer, using a wireless-enabled laptop or Tablet PC. The difference is, we can do it from the couch, or from bed, or from the back yard. We could even use it from the bathroom if we want, though no one is owning up to that particular scenario. The point here isn't that wireless technology cool. The good part is what you can do with it.

Here's another example. Let's say you want to share photos with family members on the opposite coast. In the past, you might have ordered double prints and sent them via snail mail when the pictures came back from the photo developer. Today, you can hook your digital camera to the PC, acquire the images, resize them if needed, email select pictures to your family, and use Windows Messenger to chat about them in real time. And it all happens nearly simultaneously. Again, the technology itself isn't what's cool. It's what you do with that technology that makes it worthwhile.

Simple networking is changing the computer from an office-based productivity tool to a more pervasive, life-enhancing phenomenon.

Remember, it's all in how you look at it.

How to Read This Book (Don't Skip This Part!)

You don't have to read this book from beginning to end, in order, unless you really want to, but we do follow a logical sequence. There are plenty of cross-references for more information, so if you decide to skip around, you won't be penalized (heavily) for it.

Some sections, naturally, include chapters that build on each other. And some chapters, like chapters 3 and 4 are mutually exclusive. For example, if you need to set up the modem-based connection discussed in Chapter 3, you probably don't need to set up the broadband-based connection discussed in Chapter 4, and vice versa.

A Little about This Book's Structure

This book is divided into four parts, with each part annoyingly containing a different number of chapters. As with other books I've written, the original goal was to create something very logical, but things change during the writing process, ideas get worked on and overhauled, and then the end result bears only a rough resemblance to the original vision. I mean, it's still about XP home networking. That was always the goal. So in that sense, the book is a huge success.

Here's what you can expect to see as you progress through this book.

Part 1: Getting Connected

In Part I, you learn the basics, including Windows XP home networking features, networking in general, and connecting to the Internet via modem and broadband accounts. It's the meat and potato background stuff that you need before you can start a home network.

Part II: Home Networking

This part shows you how to design and set up a home network, share your Internet connection, work with users and passwords, secure shared network resources, upgrade to wireless networking, and other advanced home networking features.

Part III: Internet

This part explores XP's many Internet-oriented features, including .NET integration, browsing and searching the Web, using Email and newsgroups, chatting with Windows Messenger, and publishing to the Web.

Part IV: Remote Access

In Part IV you will learn about some advanced XP features, including Remote Assistance—for getting help—and Remote Desktop, a Windows XP Professional-only feature that lets you access your desktop PC remotely (thus the name).

Part V: Device Connections

This part covers some of the cool devices you can use with a Windows XP-based PC, including Palm OS-based handheld, Windows CE-based Pocket PCs, laptops, and other devices.

Web site

This book comes with a Web site: http://www.xphomenetworking.com. This way, you can stay up to date on Windows XP and home networking topics. Best of all, it's free. That's right, we're not trying to grease you for any more money: You buy the book, visit the site regularly, and we start a little relationship. No, you can't come to my kid's birthday parties; it's not that kind of relationship. But if you need advice about home networking, or have a book-related question, click on the *Contact Paul* link, and I'll write you back. I promise.

Icons Used in This Book

This book contains a few icons to help point out important information to you. This, apparently, is because words are too hard to understand. Here are some of the icons you can expect to see.

This icon gives you information that could cause planning, implementation, or functionality problems. I use these only when necessary, so pay attention to them.

This icon points the way to useful information in other locations in the book. In general, this is required because of the slipshod nature in which books are created, but the reality is that most topics are hard to explain in a linear fashion. And frankly, those that aren't are often boring anyway.

This icon gives you some additional information about the subject at hand, including reminding you when information applies only to either XP Home or XP Pro.

This is a piece of friendly advice, like "don't run with scissors" and "don't give Paul your credit card number. Seriously."

Acknowledgments

I would like to thank Debra Williams Cauley for pushing to have this book published. Special thanks, too, must be given to Terri Varveris for putting up with me, my complicated schedule, and various delays; Terri was a calming force (which sounds contradictory, but isn't) throughout the development of this project and though I've come to expect things to never turn out the way I might have hoped, Terri quietly and gently pushed things along to fruition. Thank you.

Thanks to Nate Bucholz and Lindsey Orcutt , my friends at Waggener Edstrom, for always putting me in touch with the right people at Microsoft when I needed help. In my day job as a tech reporter, I've come to discover that the right people often make all the difference. And Nate and Lindsey have certainly made a huge, and positive, difference in the way that I regularly deal with Microsoft.

Very special thanks must be given, of course, to my family. My wife Stephanie still manages to put up with all the time I spend, troll-like, hiding in the office, my pale skin lit only by the glow of an LCD screen. And shortly before the start of this project, my son Mark was joined by a beautiful sister, Kelly. Mark's obvious joy at having a little sister he can boss around represents a new and interesting form of networking in the Thurrott household, and one that will last well beyond the lifetime of Windows XP.

Contents

Part I

Getting Connected

Chapter 1

Windows XP and Home Networking

IN THIS CHAPTER

- ◆ Understand the history of Windows XP and why it is needed

- ◆ Learn the features of Windows XP Home Edition

- ◆ See the difference between Windows XP Home Edition and Windows XP Professional

WE'RE TAKING PART in a revolution. Look around you, and you might not see it. You may not even realize that it's happening. But it is. And if you're reading this book, you're part of it.

The revolution began with the release of Windows XP, a shot across the bow of desktop computing complacency. Thanks to this stable, reliable, and powerful platform, the world will be connected, and computing – indeed, our very lifestyles – will be dramatically altered in the days ahead.

It's not farfetched. Simply by releasing a new Windows version, Microsoft can affect the lives of hundreds of millions of people. But XP isn't just any Windows release. It's built with a rock-solid technological foundation and designed to interact with a new generation of connected services and devices. It's a Windows for the future.

Previous Windows releases offered various improvements, but XP is the first to combine the technologies Microsoft first developed for businesses with those aimed at consumers. It could have been disastrous, a Frankenstein monster-like mishmash of incompatibilities and problems. Fortunately, that's not what happened.

This chapter takes a quick look at XP and then examines the home networking technologies that make this Windows version something special.

Introducing Windows XP

Technologically, Windows XP is the successor to Windows 2000 and the latest version of what was once called the Windows NT product family. Internally, XP is NT 5.1. Windows 2000 was NT 5.0, so you might think of XP as a minor upgrade. XP is indeed a minor upgrade when compared to Windows 2000.

For home users, XP is much, much more than a minor upgrade. Home users have been stuck with a series of products – Windows 9.x/Millennium Edition (Me) – that were based on Microsoft DOS (MS-DOS), the company's first operating system (released in 1983). DOS and non-NT Windows versions suffered from a number of technological deficiencies. To people using these systems, the results were bizarre, with application and operating system crashes, and constant rebooting.

A Little History

Microsoft's decision to continue the DOS code base for so long wasn't an effort to hurt customers. Instead, the company realized that application and hardware compatibility were key customer demands, and these needs made it hard for Microsoft to make a big leap beyond DOS.

However, an enterprise operating system project that began in the early 1990s held some promise. Hiring the Digital Equipment Corporation (DEC) engineer that spearheaded the development of Digital's VMS operating system, Microsoft began a new operating system project called NT ("new technology") that would compete with the leading enterprise operating systems of the day. NT would specifically overcome the limitations of the DOS platform and scale beyond the limited Intel-compatible hardware platforms on which DOS and Windows relied.

It bombed. Big time.

Early versions of NT – soon renamed Windows NT and modified to incorporate a user interface virtually identical to that of the DOS-based versions of Windows – didn't exactly take the world by storm. But these NT versions featured integrated networking capabilities, security features, and cross-platform compatibility (they could run on non-Intel chips) that far-outstripped Windows.

Early NT versions were also performance dogs that required far more processing and memory power than Windows. So Microsoft went back to the drawing board and fine-tuned the product. Subsequent releases refined performance and, in 1996, added the famous Windows 95 user interface that had taken the world by storm. By the release of this NT version – Windows NT 4.0 – Microsoft finally had an unqualified hit on its hands. And the company began talking about an eventual convergence, where its two product lines – NT and Windows – would combine into one. It was only a matter of time.

SPEED BUMP ON THE ROAD TO UNITY

Combining two incompatible products is no easy task. The efforts began with the release of Windows 95, which incorporated the underlying 32-bit NT programming interfaces (Win32) into its 16-bit core and added new interfaces of its own. In this way, Windows 95 and subsequent Windows 9.x products were hybrids of 16-bit DOS and 32-bit Windows technologies, and this was the reason for both their problems and successes: Thanks to their continued use of the 16-bit DOS core, Windows 9.x operating systems were still backwards compatible with previous hardware and software, but that same code also meant the inefficiencies and bugs in a 1980s-era product perpetuated for two decades.

Interestingly, both Windows and NT had various benefits and deficiencies, and throughout the latter half of the 1990s, Microsoft ironed out these differences. Windows 2000 (NT 5.0) incorporated a number of the important ease-of-use features that users expected from Windows, including true Plug and Play support, advanced power management, DirectX gaming capabilities, and the like. Meanwhile, the Windows 9x line was heading toward extinction: The last version of that product line, Windows Me, increased its reliability by removing some core 16-bit DOS features and included new home networking and digital media functionality. The stage was set for a new, combined Windows version based on NT, not DOS.

WELCOME TO WHISTLER

The new combined Windows version, like NT itself, got off to a rocky start. Originally, two groups at Microsoft were working on what would eventually be called Windows XP. The first was comprised largely of the people who had engineered Windows Me. They were working on a product code-named *Neptune,* which would appeal to consumers. A second group, made up of ex–Windows 2000 team members, was working on a business-oriented successor to Windows 2000 Professional, code-named *Odyssey.*

Just before the end of 1999, word came down from on high that the teams would be combined, as would the projects, which were consolidated into a new project called *Whistler.* The new Whistler team would deliver a family of operating systems based on the NT/2000 kernel that would replace both Windows 9x/Me and NT/2000. Both consumer and business versions would be available.

The consolidation was more than an internal political ploy. By creating a single product family, Microsoft could ensure that consumers receive the exact same underlying technology as business customers. The business version could be a true superset of the home version, offering enterprise- and mobile-oriented improvements that wouldn't make sense in a home environment.

Throughout 2000 and early 2001, this product was fine-tuned and heavily tested both inside and outside of Microsoft. There were obvious surface improvements – such as a colorful new user interface – and subtle (but arguably more important) architectural changes, including new self-healing and recoverability features, deep-rooted integration with digital media tasks such as photos, music, and movies, and thousands of application compatibility program fixes aimed at answering a couple of the major complains. Why doesn't my Windows 9x/Me game work under NT/2000 and Why doesn't Windows NT/2000 run my older business applications?

It would have been easy and understandable if Whistler had overpromised and underdelivered, given the heady number of improvements the company planned for this release. But Microsoft did something fairly rare in its 25-year history: It hit a home run.

The Case for Windows XP

This book deals almost exclusively with the home networking and connected features in Windows XP, but there are more reasons that consumers would want to upgrade to this product.

SECURITY

Windows XP is the most secure product Microsoft has ever built. Windows XP is built on the NT code base and features many security improvements over previous NT versions.

Don't believe sensationalistic news stories: Contrary to reports, the automatic updating features in XP have protected millions of consumers from security exploits without requiring them to manually find and install patches. XP is the most secure operating system you can buy for use at home.

A new firewall feature, shown in Figure 1-1, automatically protects users from common Internet attacks.

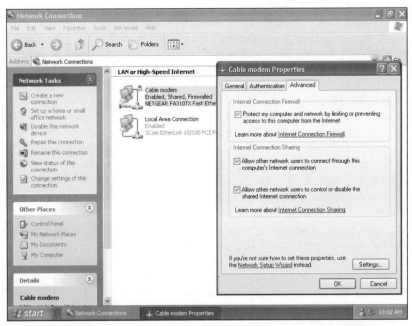

Figure 1-1: XP supports modern security features such as a firewall on in-bound network connections.

RELIABILITY

Windows 9.x users understand the pain of constant reboots, planned or not. When an application crashes in such an operating system, it can often bring down the entire system, sometimes resulting in the infamous "blue screen." XP is far more resilient than previous Windows versions, and it includes features that protect users, even from themselves: Install an errant device driver, for example, and XP lets you uninstall it (or "roll it back" in Microsoft parlance) – as shown in Figure 1-2. If you do something that causes a system instability, you can restore Windows XP to a previous point in time. XP is the most reliable operating system you can buy for the home.

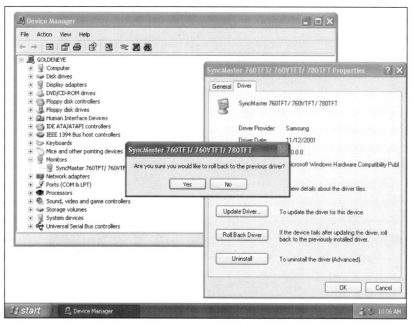

Figure 1-2: Device driver rollback can prevent driver problems from ruining an otherwise stable system.

COMPATIBILITY

Despite being based on NT/2000, XP actually works with most Windows 9x hardware and software, so you get the best of both worlds. If you find a recalcitrant application, you can run the Program Compatibility Wizard and fool the app into thinking it's running on Windows 95 or 98. And Microsoft releases compatibility updates on a regular basis through the Windows Update Web site, improving the compatibility picture continually. This means that many legacy applications – including some DOS games – will actually run in Windows XP. In Figure 1-3, a Windows 3.1 entertainment package is being installed on XP.

FUN!

Are you a game player or digital media enthusiast? If so, Windows XP is the place to be. In addition to being compatible with the most popular games and multimedia software titles on the planet, XP is also the most stable and reliable system on which you can play these games and manage digital media content. So you can stay up all night, competing with players from around the globe in your favorite online game, and never worry about the system going down. And XP's digital media features make working with digital music, photos, and even movies, a snap, giving consumers an obvious and simple way to work with these exciting features, as shown in Figure 1-4. I'm so excited about XP digital media that I wrote a book about it — *Great Windows XP Digital Media* (Wiley). You can find out more about this at the book's Web site: www.xpdigitalmedia.com.

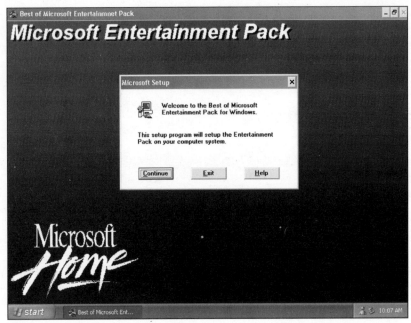

Figure 1-3: Windows 3.1 games on NT? Impossible. But with XP, the compatibility shims often come through in a pinch.

POWER

XP is a multi-threaded, preemptively multitasking, protected-memory, multiuser operating system that supports the latest computing technologies. Geeky stuff, yes, but it makes XP a viable platform for the future. Because XP is a fully 32-bit operating system, it takes full advantage of modern microprocessors such as the Intel Pentium 4 and the AMD Athlon XP. And a 64-bit XP version, creatively titled Windows XP 64-bit Edition, runs on Intel's high-end Itanium hardware, which may very well be the computing platform of choice five years from now. In Figure 1-5, you can see the Task Manager, which presents a technical view of the various processes in the system. Unlike in Windows 9*x*, a crashed application cannot bring down the system.

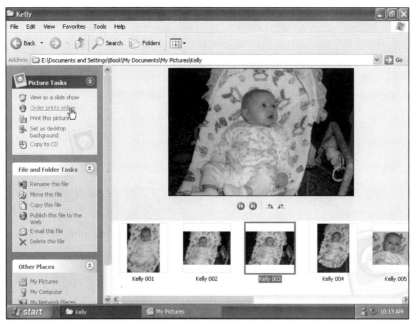

Figure 1-4: Windows XP includes built-in features for handling digital music, movies, and, shown here, digital photos.

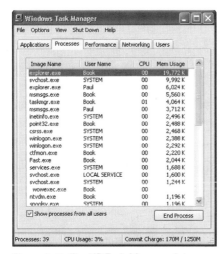

Figure 1-5: The XP Task Manager lets you manage processes, system and networking performance, and even users.

COOL STUFF

XP includes cool end-user features such as a colorful new user interface (shown in Figure 1-6) that takes advantage of the latest video hardware, a Windows Media Player that features a skinnable interface and vibrant visualizations, and other fun features that may just make you smile the first time you run into them. You can configure your user account with your own photo, for example, and view slide shows of your photos. You can make your own movies and burn audio CDs for use in your car or home stereo. The list goes on and on, but the end result is that XP is less about technology than it is about making a statement: Computers can be – and should be – fun.

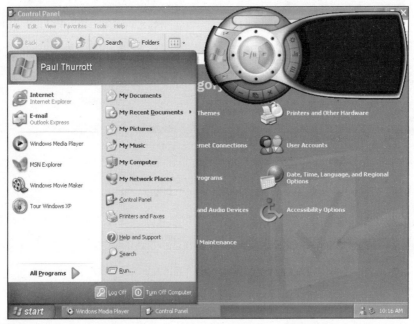

Figure 1-6: Windows XP features a modern, colorful user interface that takes full advantage of current 3-D video hardware.

EXTENSIBILITY

Windows XP is the platform of the future, and as such, it will instead be upgraded over time. Even when XP first shipped in October 2001, for example, Microsoft also released a slew of free, Internet-based updates, giving users new versions of

Windows Movie Maker and Windows Messenger, new compatibility updates, new device drivers, and other updates. And since that time, the company has shipped free add-ons and updates. Unlike other operating systems, XP isn't stuck in sand the moment it ships on CD. XP is a dynamic, constantly evolving product. Some updates are automatic, while others can be downloaded from Windows Update, as shown in Figure 1-7.

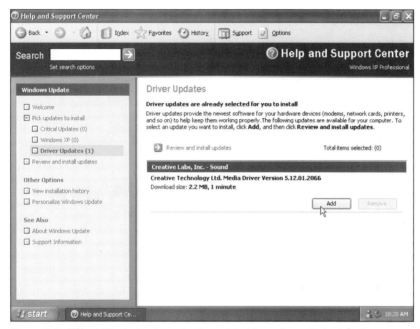

Figure 1-7: XP's ability to be dynamically updated is, perhaps, its best feature.

CONNECTIVITY

XP isn't an island on its own, unaware of the outside world. Instead, it is the center, or hub if you will, of your connected world. With XP, you can easily get online, connect with other PCs in a home network (see Figure 1-8), work with portable devices, connect to non-PC home-based devices, and interact with others across the globe. XP's connected features are exciting, and they're the reason I'm writing this book. Check out the next section for a closer look at the XP features that let you reach out and touch someone.

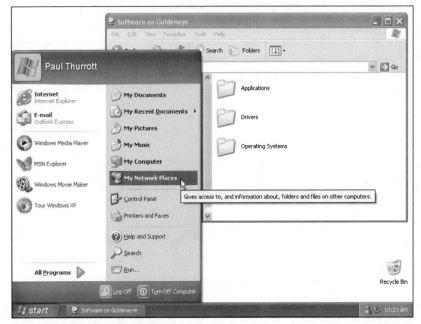

Figure 1-8: XP's home networking capabilities make it easy to connect with other PCs and share files, printers, and Internet connections.

Windows XP Features

Like you, perhaps, I've always been enthusiastic about computers. I can recall spending hours and hours with PCs over the years, staying up late at night doing who-knows-what. What I can't remember is how I passed this time in the years before the Internet. My overall computer usage probably hasn't increased dramatically since the rise of the Internet, but in the intervening years, I can at least point to the Web and e-mail and understand that these features are both time-consuming and beneficial. I can't imagine life without them.

XP takes advantage of connections, whether internal networking – wireless, wired, whatever – or external, through broadband (cable, DSL, satellite) or modem. It lets you communicate with others through e-mail, text chats, and audio- and videoconferencing. You can request help with your PC and enable a friend or family member to access your XP machine remotely. You can collaborate interactively, in real time, with others, and publish and backup to the Web. And you can work with an emerging generation of connected devices, including Pocket PCs and other PDAs, set-top boxes and home gateways, digital audio players and audio CD players, and more.

If this sounds exciting, you're in the right place.

Easy and Secure Home Networking

In the past, users upgrading to new PCs replaced their existing machines with the new ones. Today, that's no longer true, largely because PCs become obsolete much more slowly. So people are augmenting their current rigs with a new PC and pawning off the existing PC on another family member. When you have two or more PCs in a home, it's possible to connect, or *network,* them together to share resources. For example, you probably already have a printer on one machine. Wouldn't it be nice to use that printer from the second PC? With home networking, there's no need for the "floppy shuffle" or installing application software to make this happen.

Of course, you can network PCs many different ways, and XP takes advantage of them all. Traditional Ethernet networking involves running 10 or 100 Mbps (Megabytes Per Second) cabling between PCs, which can be expensive and unsightly (especially if the PCs are in different rooms). But there are alternatives, including power-line networking, phone-line networking, and wireless networking. Wireless networking is emerging as the number one solution as prices drop and speeds improve.

Historically, home networking has been painful for most users, because it involves complex and technical concepts and products. With XP, home networking has never been easier, thanks to clever wizards that can auto-detect network settings and friendlier UI pieces that remove the guesswork. It's not perfect — indeed, a mid-2002 XP upgrade focused solely on fine-tuning its home networking features — but XP, out of the box, offers the simplest networking features of any operating system.

Networking is of little use if the technology allows hackers free reign over your personal data files. So XP includes all the great security features from previous NT/2000 versions, including per-user authentication, while adding new features such as a software firewall. You can create special user accounts for your children and ensure that they can never accidentally delete your files. And you can prevent hackers from even seeing that your PC is connected to the Internet (what they don't know can't hurt *you*).

Complete Internet Integration

The Internet isn't just a buzzword anymore; it's a crucial information infrastructure for consumers, students, and businesses. Although Microsoft's decision to bundle Internet functionality into Windows was controversial just a few years ago, it's inconceivable that any company would build an operating system today that didn't include such functionality (and people say Microsoft doesn't innovate). Even most *applications* today have Internet connectivity features, and the software industry is moving to a Web services-based software subscription model that will one day supplant the shrink-wrapped software we're all used to. And yes, XP is ready for that change, too.

XP's Internet integration features are more pervasive than those of any other operating system. In addition to the obvious Internet-oriented applications such as Internet Explorer, Outlook Express, and Windows Messenger, Microsoft has implemented Internet functionality into just about every facet of XP. Here are a few examples:

◆ Applications such as Windows Media Player, Windows Movie Maker, and even the photo wizards integrate with the Internet.

◆ The operating system can update itself with critical security patches automatically, over the Internet, ensuring that you're always up-to-date and safe.

In short, if Internet connectivity is your forte, XP is the place to be.

Communication, Collaboration, and Publishing

After you've established a connection with the outside world, the possibilities are endless. You can communicate with others via e-mail, Usenet newsgroups, and text, audio, and video chat. You can collaborate interactively, in real time, with friends, family, and coworkers across the Internet on documents. And you can connect to remote servers, accessing them as if they were shared resources on the local network.

These capabilities mean that you're not alone. You can find other people who share your interests, regardless of their physical location; they could be across the street, in the next town, or in a small hamlet in South Africa, Australia, wherever. PCs used to be solitary devices, attractive only to geeky loners, but this is most definitely no longer the case.

Interested in self-publishing? XP makes it easy to set up and connect to your own Web site. So you can get the word out, using simple operating system–based tools.

Optimized for the Home

Previously, Microsoft's enterprise-savvy operating systems, such as NT and 2000, were inappropriate for the home, though certain technical users dealt with their compatibility limitations to take advantage of their better security, reliability, and networking features. With XP, the compromises are over, and you no longer have to choose between the lesser of two evils.

Windows XP is available in two mainstream editions:

◆ **Home Edition:** This edition obviously is aimed at consumers and is the version that ships with most new XP-based PCs.

◆ **Professional Edition:** A true superset of Home Edition, Professional Edition offers mostly business-oriented improvements over its little brother.

I discuss the differences between the two editions in the section "Windows XP Pro Extras," later in this chapter, but it's worth noting here that either version is appropriate for home use. XP is, by and large, a consumer-oriented release.

Intelligent Device Connections

One of the coolest things about XP is that it integrates so well with non-PC devices, such as digital audio players, residential gateways, digital assistants such as Pocket PC devices, various home stereo components include SonicBlue Rio receivers and the like, and a whole host of upcoming hardware devices based on the Universal Plug and Play (UPnP) standard. At the time of this writing, UPnP devices are just appearing, but many existing devices connect with XP using standard computer ports, such as USB 1.*x* and 2.0 and FireWire (IEEE-1394); UPnP devices typically are connected via a home network.

Windows XP Pro Extras

Windows XP Home Edition is designed as a consumer-oriented upgrade to Windows 9.*x*/Me (indeed, Windows NT/2000 users cannot even upgrade to Home Edition). As such, it includes an easier to use security system when compared to XP Professional Edition and fewer user groups. The Home Edition security is aimed at protecting a home computer instead of trying to protect against all the security opportunities under a Professional or business computer.

Some other important XP Professional-only features include:

◆ **Remote desktop:** XP Professional provides a one-user version of the Terminal Services feature that debuted in Windows NT 4.0 Terminal Server Edition.

◆ **Multiple processor support:** XP Pro supports up to two processors, whereas XP Home supports only one.

◆ **Automated System Recovery (ASR):** In XP Pro, the Backup utility has been enhanced with a system state recovery tool called ASR. In XP Home, ASR is missing, and you have to install Backup manually from the Setup CD.

◆ **Web server:** XP Pro ships with Internet Information Services (IIS) 5.1, the latest version of Microsoft's Web server software; XP Home does not.

◆ **Security features:** XP Pro supports encryption in the file system and file-level access control.

- **Enterprise features:** XP Pro machines can join an Active Directory (AD) domain and support other enterprise-oriented features such as Group Policies, IntelliMirror, and Roaming Profiles. XP Pro can also be deployed more quickly using automated installations through SysPrep and the Remote Installation Services (RIS).

- **Advanced networking features:** XP Home does not support certain networking features that are available in XP Professional, including IPSec, SNMP, Client Services for NetWare, and client-side caching.

 For more information about the differences between XP Home and Pro, please visit my SuperSite for Windows: www.winsupersite.com.

Home Edition is going to be just about right for most people. So how do you choose between Home and Pro?

- Consider the price. Professional Edition usually runs about twice as expensive as Home Edition.

- Look over the list of Pro-only features and determine whether you can live without all of them. If not, go with Pro.

 Most topics in this book apply to both Home and Professional Editions. When topics relate only to Professional Edition (such as Remote Desktop), they are marked obviously.

Chapter 2

Introduction to Networking

IN THIS CHAPTER

- ◆ Learn the Basic Networking of PCs and Users
- ◆ Understand what is required and how to physically connect computers
- ◆ Use software to allow the computers to talk to one another

ANYTIME YOU CONNECT two or more computers together in some fashion, (physically through a wire or wirelessly) you have created a computer network (or just *network)*. Although setting up a network might seem like a horribly technical task, it's actually gotten much easier over the past few years, and the options for connecting computers have grown exponentially. Likewise, the cost has come down dramatically as well, and you should be able to find affordable solutions for almost any home networking need.

So why would you want to network? In the past, computers were isolated islands of functionality. Although that might have been satisfying in certain ways, the real power of a PC becomes revealed when it is connected, in some way, to other PCs. For example, in a simple scenario, you might share a single printer between two PCs. Or perhaps one PC has a large hard drive on which you've stored a digital music collection. If you wanted to access that music from another PC without networking, you might have to re-create it, a time-consuming and possibly costly endeavor. But with networking, you don't need to duplicate the collection: If you share it from the first PC, it's available to the other PCs in the network.

With more homes having two or more PCs, the single biggest reason to network is to share an Internet connection, preferably a broadband connection such as cable or DSL. Regardless of how they connect to the Internet, most people have a single connection coming into the house; if that connection isn't shared, you have to manually connect to the Internet from each PC at different times.

Another common rationale for networking is security. For various reasons, many people shield their PCs from a direct connection to the Internet because of a perceived security vulnerability. These people often purchase hardware devices (called *routers* or *residential gateways*) that separate their PCs from a cable or DSL connection but allow the Internet connection through networking technology.

17

Whatever your reason – and I explore many such reasons throughout this book – networking unleashes the hidden strengths of your PC. And it opens up a new world of functionality, some aspects of which might not be immediately obvious. In this chapter, I examine some of the basic networking topics and how they relate to Windows XP.

Connecting Users and PCs

In the United States especially, since the late 1990s there has been a dramatic turnaround in the way people purchase home computers. Previously, new PCs typically replaced existing units, which were usually pawned off on less discerning family members, friends, or coworkers. But as computers have become more sophisticated, they've tended to age better. A three-year-old PC is no longer an obsolete piece of junk.

As a result, more and more people are holding on to their old PCs when they get new ones. And the old computers often end up in a child's room or a corner office where another person in the household can use it. This has resulted in a large potential market for home networking hardware, a situation that companies such as Linksys, D-Link, and NETGEAR have taken advantage of. Today, you can buy networking solutions that were previously quite expensive and geared solely toward businesses.

Networking PCs is all about connections. The idea is to connect at least two PCs by using a wired or wireless solution. After this connection is made and both computers can "see" each other, the fun begins, and you can share files, folders, and printers. But just making this connection is often quite difficult, though it's gotten much easier recently.

Understandably, networking began as a business-oriented task. Originally, there were numerous, often-incompatible ways to connect various computer systems. Over the years, several industry standards governing hardware connections, devices, wire protocols, and related technologies have ironed out interoperability issues. Sadly, some legacy networking issues still play a role in Windows networking today, and I deal with those when appropriate. But Windows XP is good about exorcising these ghosts from the past or shielding you from them when appropriate. There's never been a better time to get into home networking: If you're working with new hardware, many networking functions will work as soon as the hardware is installed.

Networking Methodologies

In large- and medium-sized businesses, various networking methodologies govern the architecture and installation of networks. For example, you may have heard the term *client-server*. In networking, a client-server setup establishes relationships between powerful server computers, which provide services to desktop PCs and other devices, collectively referred to as *clients*. Typically, people don't sit at a server and use its resources interactively, as they work with a home PC. Instead, servers store massive amounts of data or complex data-processing services that can handle queries from clients and then return the appropriate results. For example, when you apply for a loan at a bank branch, the person who enters your loan information in the computer is probably using an application that remotely accesses a number of servers. These servers valid the data entered, then processes the request by sending the completed form to a Manager's work queue. The Manager can grant or deny your loan based on information and other criteria that's possibly stored in different servers all over the world. It's a typical, if complex, client-server scenario. Figure 2-1 shows the basics of how this process works.

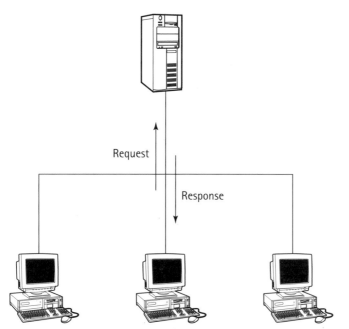

Figure 2-1: In a client-server setup, clients (typically PCs or thin client, browser-based machines) request services from servers.

At home, a client-server setup rarely makes sense. When the computers in a network are all *peers* and are used interactively by users in a more typical manner, you typically set up a *peer-to-peer network*. Microsoft calls this type of network a *workgroup*, but don't be confused by the terminology — both names mean the same thing. In a workgroup (or peer-to-peer network), each PC is an equal. Management is localized (on a per-PC basis), not centralized like a more complex network (such as a client-server network). Figure 2-2 shows how a typical home network can be set up. Each machine equally shares services.

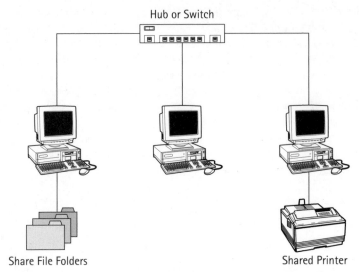

Figure 2-2: In a workgroup such as a home network, each PC is an equal and can share resources.

Localized management is both a boon and a curse. In a workgroup, each PC is in control of itself. If you want to share files and printers or set up user accounts, you must do so, individually, at each PC. These tasks are fairly easy (and you may only have to do them once), so unless you have more than 5 or 6 PCs in your home, peer-to-peer is definitely the way to go with a home network. And if you have more than five or six PCs at home, you're not exactly in the target market for this book anyway, are you?

Designing a Home Network

The process of creating your home network is covered in a later chapter, but you need to consider a number of issues before you head out to CompuSaveALot and plop down your hard-earned money. Here they are, along with chapter references when appropriate:

- ◆ **Internet connection:** Your connection to the outside world always comes first. What type of Internet connection (broadband, satellite, modem) do you use and how will you bridge your internal network to the outside world? For example, you can use a PC to connect your home network to an Internet connection, but this PC will require a modem and network interface card (NIC) for a modem connection or two NICs for a broadband connection. Or perhaps you'd prefer a hardware gateway/router device instead. These topics are discussed in Chapters 3 (modems) and 4 (broadband), but Figure 2-3 identifies some of the key ways your home network might connect to the Internet.

◆ **Type of network:** The type of network you choose depends on cost and personal needs. If you have two or more PCs, and they're in the same room or in close physical proximity, you might opt for a wired networking solution, such as 10 or 100 Mbps (megabits per second, where 1 Mbps is about 1,000 times faster than 1 Kbps, or kilobits per second) Ethernet, along with a hub, router, or switch if required. Other solutions can bridge longer distances without requiring you to specially wire your house, but they tend to be slower than Ethernet: You can choose between phone-line-based networking (which uses the existing phone jacks in your home but doesn't disrupt voice calls), power-line networking (which uses the existing power plugs in your home), or various wireless networking solutions, for example. Phone and power-line networking are covered in Chapter 5. Wireless networking is becoming so popular that it gets its own coverage in Chapter 9.

◆ **Sharing your Internet connection:** After you establish an Internet connection and a home network, it's time to get all of your PCs online, using the one connection. This topic is covered in Chapter 6.

◆ **Letting others use the network:** It's unlikely that you created a home network just for yourself. If you'd like other family members or friends to access only certain network resources and not harm your personal files, find out how in Chapters 7 and 8.

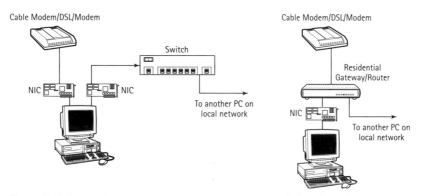

Figure 2-3: Internet connections come in many shapes and sizes; here, I compare some of the common ones.

However you proceed, be sure to evaluate your current situation along with any foreseeable future upgrades. Remember, you can mix and match. For example, you can use wired Ethernet for computers in a home office, and wireless for laptops that can roam anywhere in your home. My setup, incidentally, is pretty complicated. It looks like Figure 2-4.

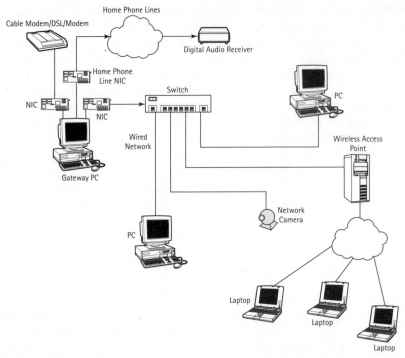

Figure 2-4: My home network isn't necessarily typical, but it shows what's possible if you want to mix and match networking types to meet particular needs.

Networking Hardware

Network connections require a range of hardware, based on your requirements. You may need to exchange files and share printers between two PCs. Or you may have several PCs and a shared Internet connection. Depending on your current and future needs, you can select a networking solution that balances cost, capability, and complication.

PC to PC

There are a couple of simple, inexpensive hardware options for sharing files and printers between two PCs.

You can use more capable networking hardware than these options to connect two PCs. That gives you the option of expanding your network later without completely replacing your system.

DIRECT CABLE CONNECTION

This is the bare-bones option for connecting two PCs, perhaps to share files. If the PCs are located close together, you can actually make the connection using a single cable and your existing serial or parallel ports through a *direct cable connection*. It's slow and generally not enticing. But it works, and at least one commercial product – LapLink – made quite a market for itself offering this very capability.

NETWORK INTERFACE CARDS

For convenient networking, you need more capable hardware than a direct cable connection. Even a very simple wired or wireless network requires two *network cards* (NICs), one card for each PC. A wired network also requires at least one *cross-over* cable. This setup is fine if you only have two PCs and will never upgrade beyond that. Wired network cards are very cheap, as is the cable, though you need to be careful to purchase a cross-over cable, not a normal Ethernet cable. Wireless network cards, meanwhile, are relatively cheap (under $100 for desktop PC versions).

Both wired and wireless network interface cards require you to open your PC (see Figure 2-5), unless you purchase more expensive external USB versions. I prefer internal cards (or PC Card versions for laptops), because they don't tie up the precious, shared bandwidth on your USB. But USB NICs are easier to install.

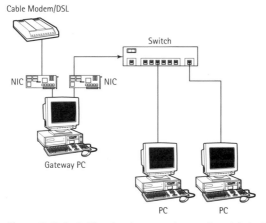

Figure 2-5: Installing hardware such as network interface cards often requires you to get down and dirty with your PC. If you're not into cracking open the case, consider external expansion via USB instead.

Multiple Connections

If you have more than two PCs, or two PCs and a gateway/router to share your Internet connection, you need more powerful hardware to connect your system.

HUBS

The cheapest setup for linking more than two PCs involves a hardware device called a *hub,* which can run at speeds of up to 100 Mbps (see Figure 2-6). Hubs typically include at least five *ports,* or connectors, into which Ethernet cabling (10 or 100 Mbps) can be plugged. So the hub sits, logically and physically, in the center of your home network, and you connect each PC's NIC to the hub using normal (not cross-over) Ethernet cable. Though extremely inexpensive, hubs are somewhat limited bandwidth-wise, in that they share the network bandwidth between whatever PCs are connected. So a 100 Mbps hub can only use 100 Mbps: If you have five PCs connected, they might only get 20 Mbps or less per PC.

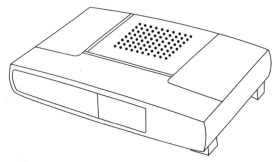

Figure 2-6: Hubs are a cheap way to extend a network
beyond two PCs, but better solutions are available.

SWITCHES

For more speed than a hub connection, you can use a 100 Mbps *switch,* like the one shown in Figure 2-7. A switch is a hub-like device that offers the full 100 Mbps bandwidth to each connected PC, resulting in much speedier network connections. You'll see a dramatic difference when transferring many files or larger files across such a network. Switch/router prices have come down dramatically in recent years, so there's little reason to skimp in this area. I strongly recommend a switch over a hub.

WIRELESS ACCESS POINTS

If you want to connect more than two PCs wirelessly, you need a wireless access point (WAP). These devices plug into an open port on a hub or switch/router if you have a wired network, or a residential gateway, if you don't.

WAPs have fallen in price dramatically: I recently picked one up for less than $100.

Although WAP security has improved, it's still unclear whether any wireless network can truly be secured from the outside world. Wireless security issues are explored in more detail in Chapter 9.

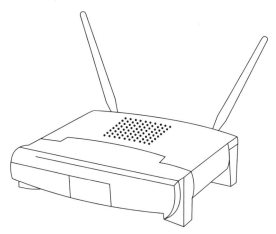

Figure 2-7: Switches offer far greater network speeds than hubs. Switches used to be prohibitively expensive, but that's no longer the case.

I take a closer look at networking hardware in the appropriate chapters, but your cash outlay for a home network will likely be pretty small. Most PCs come with some form of networking hardware these days, and it's generally not expensive to upgrade them if they don't.

Networking Software

Before Windows 95, networking PCs generally required users to choose and install third-party networking software. This was a messy undertaking for several reasons, the most obvious being cost and compatibility. With Windows 95, Microsoft provided users with a mainstream Windows version that included modern networking software that actually worked and interoperated with the outside world. What a concept.

Various networking software types have made the rounds over the years, but aside from historical curiosity, most of them aren't very interesting today. In this section, you find out about TCP/IP (the only networking software that really matters), a historical oddity called *NetBIOS* (which you may need from time to time), and other XP networking software issues.

Using TCP/IP

Network *protocols* establish the technical *conventions,* or rules, for sending information over a network. The most popular networking protocol is the *Transmission Control Protocol/Internet Protocol* (TCP/IP). It makes the Internet possible. In Windows XP, TCP/IP connects to the Internet, but it's also used on internal networks, like your home network, to exchange information between PCs. XP uses TCP/IP for many of its internal networking services, such as logon and file and printer sharing. For these reasons, it is installed by default on all XP machines.

UNDERSTANDING TCP/IP

Without getting into the geeky details too much, TCP/IP is a *suite* of protocols, not a single protocol. The main components of this protocol suite include the *transport layer* (TCP) and the *Internet layer* (IP). These layers sit in the middle of a conceptual four-layer model.

- The *applications layer* is at the top of the TCP/IP model. The applications layer includes TCP/IP applications, utilities, and services. These are such Internet standbys as FTP, Telnet, and PING.

- The *network interface layer* at the bottom of the TCP/IP model deals with the hardware connection that transfers data across the wire.

Using TCP/IP, each TCP/IP host gets a unique 32-bit numeric *IP address* that identifies that host. These addresses take the form xxx.xxx.xxx.xxx where each xxx is a number between 0 and 255. A typical address is 192.168.0.123.

The first three segments of the IP address are called the *network ID;* this identifies the network on which the host resides. The last segment, or 123 above, is the host ID; this identifies the actual host.

TIP   Though you may think of a host as a particular PC, this is not truly accurate. Each PC can have more than one NIC, each with its own unique address. And some hosts aren't NICs at all: A residential gateway or broadband router is a host, too, because it is assigned a unique IP address. For home networking, a host is generally just a PC.

If this was all there was to TCP/IP addressing, most people would probably be able to wrap their minds around this concept pretty quickly. Sadly, that's not all there is to it, and if you're not a mathematically inclined individual, it's going to start getting difficult now. In addition to the IP address, each host has an associated *subnet mask*, another 32-bit numeric address that identifies the subnet in which the host resides. Subnets divide large networks into smaller, more digestible chunks where each subnet is physically separated from the rest of the network by a router. The subnet mask — such as 255.255.255.0 — makes IP addressing possible by identifying whether network requests need to be routed to the local network or a remote network.

With a few exceptions for true power users, all the PCs in your home network will be on the same subnet (so they can "see" each other), and each host (typically a PC) will have its own, unique IP address. In addition, one host is the *default gateway*.

This default gateway is the physical link between your internal network and the outside world, and it is responsible for routing network traffic between the local and remote networks. The default gateway could be a PC – if it's connected directly to a modem or broadband connection – or a residential gateway-type device. If it's a PC, the NIC that's not connected to your Internet connection, but rather to your internal network, is considered the default gateway.

TCP/IP ADDRESSING AND HOME NETWORKS

If you compute the possible number of unique IP addresses in the 32-bit IP addressing system, you'll find that it's not a very big number and couldn't possibly handle all the possible Internet hosts out there. The people who came up with this scheme – I believe they're beings of pure energy, if I understand the story correctly – thought of this, and came up with two fixes, one temporary and one permanent. The temporary fix is the one we're concerned with here (the permanent fix, *IPv6* – Internet Protocol version 6, will open up more addresses because it uses a 128-bit addressing scheme).

Because many networks will be internal only and will not directly connect to the outside world, the TCP/IP architects set aside certain IP address ranges to be used solely in local, or *private,* networks. These private IP addresses can be used in any home network (or corporate network for that matter) as long as the machines using them do not directly connect to an outside network, such as the Internet. In this sense, they're safe for internal use only.

By default, the types of networks you'll generally use at home will use the private IP address range of 169.254.0.1 through 169.254.255.254, with a subnet mask of 255.255.0.0. In such a network, the default gateway is typically 169.254.0.1, though you can technically change this if you'd like.

XP AND AUTOMATIC ADDRESSING

Because of the commonality of private IP use, Microsoft added *automatic IP addressing* to XP. This feature kicks in when an XP machine boots up and can't find a *DHCP server* to assign IP addresses on a network. In corporate settings, DHCP servers are common, they are also used by every ISP (internet service providers), and they allow administrators to specify how IP addresses are doled out. At home, DHCP servers are superfluous because XP machines can generate their own IP addresses.

 DHCP stands for Dynamic Host Configuration Protocol.

Say you've got a home network, and you're using the default settings: The gateway is 169.254.0.1, and it's connected to the outside world using a broadband or modem connection. When an XP machine (also using the default settings) boots up while connected to such a network, it scans the network and looks for a DHCP server. If it can't find one, it simply generates a unique IP address for itself and keeps booting. That IP address then identifies the XP machine (more correctly, the XP machine's NIC) as a host on the local network.

The beauty of this feature is that it's enabled by default. Most of the time, you can just plug an XP box into a network and boot it up. It's a very handy feature.

There's another benefit to automatic IP addressing, and this is why I believe that you should leave this setting alone and let XP do the addressing: In addition to assigning a unique identifier pair (IP address and subnet mask) to each machine, automatic IP addressing also passes along IP address resolution server information from the default gateway. On the Internet, *DNS servers* provide routing information so that browser URLs such as www.apple.com can be resolved into IP addresses (and vice versa).

 DNS stands for Domain Name System.

When you manually configure an IP address, you generally need to enter DNS server address information as well. But because this information is automatically passed along from your Internet connection when you use automatic IP addressing, it's often more difficult to resolve Internet IP addresses when you don't use this feature. So again, it's generally easier to let XP do its thing.

XP AND STATIC ADDRESSING

If you're the anal-retentive type, you might want to control which addresses are given to particular hosts. This is called *static IP addressing* because you manually assign IP addresses to individual hosts. This requires you to sit at each PC, look up the properties for each network connection, and manually type IP address, subnet mask, default gateway, and sometimes DNS server information.

Working with Legacy Networking Protocols

Before the Internet and TCP/IP came along, Microsoft was pushing its own networking schemes. Some date back to its early work on OS/2, an operating system the company collaborated on with IBM back in the late 1980s. Primitive though the work seems now, Microsoft still needs to address some key issues that apply to TCP/IP: Each host on a network needs to be uniquely identified in some way, and there has to be some way to move information along the wire. Compared to the elegance of TCP/IP, Microsoft and IBM's solution was somewhat ham-handed: *NetBIOS* (Network Basic Input Output System).

NetBIOS is a protocol, like TCP/IP, that adds local area network functionality to operating systems such as DOS, OS/2, and Windows. However, NetBIOS is limited in so many ways that it's almost not worth mentioning, except for one key issue: Because of its pervasiveness in the Windows world, many existing local networks are based on NetBIOS. If you have a NetBEUI network and consider the XP upgrade, heed these warnings:

◆ You must change your networking software so it uses TCP/IP before you upgrade. XP doesn't natively support *NetBEUI* (NetBIOS Enhanced User Interface), the enhanced NetBIOS version that most Windows networks currently work with. In fact, Microsoft planned to drop NetBEUI altogether in XP (NetBEUI was in previous Windows versions), but customer complaints resulted in a compromise. NetBEUI is on the XP CD-ROM, if you look hard enough.

◆ NetBEUI isn't a routable protocol such as TCP/IP. You can't use most of XP's best networking features with NetBEUI. You can't share Internet connections, for example.

NetBEUI is on the way out. So avoid it.

I don't discuss NetBEUI, NetBIOS, or OS/2 elsewhere in this book. If you're using these, you're in a completely different world anyway.

Technically, you can't actually escape from NetBIOS-related technologies in XP. All Windows machines use a message format called *Server Message Block* (SMB) to share files, folders, and other resources on a network. But SMB can run over TCP/IP, and that's the way it runs in XP.

Why You Want to Be a Client for Microsoft Networks

If TCP/IP sounds like a one-stop shop for all your networking needs, you've almost got it. But TCP/IP can't do everything. If you're using private IP addressing, most of the hosts in your local network aren't visible on the public Internet and therefore will not have fully qualified domain names (such as `paul.apple.com`). They need to be addressed via IP address (such as `169.254.0.2`) when accessing local resources, like shared files and printers.

Fortunately, there's a solution to this problem. Microsoft installs a networking service called *Client for Microsoft Networks*. This service allows XP machines and other Windows hosts to identify themselves and others on the network with simple names. The service also allows sharing resources and accessing other shares. So you might name a system *Paul* or *Big-Dell* instead of using a hard-to-remember IP address.

The Client for Microsoft Networks service is installed by default, so you shouldn't need to do anything to configure it. Just don't uninstall it, or all the good stuff I cover in this book will be unavailable.

Sharing Files and Printers

Assuming you have left the default settings alone, it's now possible to share resources on your local system and access shared resources, across the network, from other systems. Shareable resources include file folders and printers.

You can share network resources in a variety of ways, and this is somewhat determined by how you've set up a new XP Professional feature called *Simple File Sharing.* Simple File Sharing works the same way in both XP Professional and in XP Home Edition. Simple File Sharing can only be customized two ways: what folders to share and whether or not users can change files in those shared folders. So, if Simple File Sharing is on and you share a folder or printer, that resource is available to anyone on the network. Simple, right?

Not really. This approach is fraught with all kinds of problems, including the possibility that Internet hackers could access these shares. I discuss this more in Chapter 8, along with the way in which you can turn off this feature in XP Pro, or at least better secure your system if you're stuck with Home Edition.

But assuming you've properly secured your network, sharing resources is where it's at. If you have a powerful HP LaserJet on your spouse's system, there's no reason you shouldn't be able to print on it from your own system or from a wirelessly connected laptop.

Resource sharing lets you take better advantage of the hardware you've got — especially hard drives and printers — regardless of where they're connected. I'll be looking at this topic more throughout the book.

From Theory to Reality

Okay, enough networking theory. One could write an entire book just about TCP/IP addressing and the like, but you don't need it for your XP home network. The next few chapters look at various ways in which you can set up Internet connections, and then move into the actual creation of your home network and how to share the Internet connection. From that point, the possibilities are wide open, so have some fun with it.

XREF   If you're dying for more technical details about TCP/IP and networking theory, I've collected a wide range of online and printed resources and published them on the Web site for this book.

Chapter 3

Life in the Slow Lane: Connecting with a Modem

IN THIS CHAPTER

- ◆ Understanding how a modem works

- ◆ Using the Modem Wizard to configure and connect your modem to the Internet

- ◆ Learn how to manually manage your modem connections; making copies, renaming, and configuring

DESPITE MARKETING PUSHES from telecommunications companies, cable companies, and computer industry giants such as Microsoft, broadband Internet access still hasn't taken off. Though broadband usage is expected to increase dramatically over the next few years, most people still access the Internet using a standard dial-up telephone account and a modem.

Modem speeds have pretty much topped out at today's 53 Kbps, so modem technology is mature and stable. You can get a nice modem very cheaply these days, and even broadband users should consider the purchase, if only as a backup for a broadband service outage.

For laptop users, modems are still a necessity, especially for frequent business travelers. Though hotels, airports, and other locations offer high-speed wired and wireless LANs in many cases, most locations force you to connect via modem. Chances are good that you'll be forced to deal with dial-up accounts and modems some time. If this if your primary Internet connection, perhaps because of cost or location issues, you'll want to be well versed in how Windows XP establishes these connections. So I take a close look at modems and dial-up connections in this chapter.

A Quick Look at Modems

Standard telephone lines are *analog* data carriers for sounds. Before you can access a phone line from your PC, which communicates *digital* data, you must use a device that can convert between the analog sounds in the phone line and the digital data issued and received by the PC. This device is called a *modem* (MOdulator/ DEModulator).

Whichever style of modem you choose, the technology is the same. Modems come in two typical configurations:

♦ Internal — a card that must be placed in a PCI slot inside your PC.

♦ External — the electronic components sit outside your PC in a separate box with end-user-accessible controls.

   For most home users, internal units are more desirable. They do not require any extra power outlets, they have no other cables or cords, and they're the least expensive.

Modems are able to dial telephone numbers when connected and then interact, or *negotiate,* an Internet connection with another modem at your Internet service provider (ISP). This negotiation results in the familiar screeching sound we've all heard, like ancient beasts circling each other before a fight. But if the screeching (excuse me, negotiation) is successful (the proper credentials are received and accepted by the remote modem), you'll be online.

Modem Speeds

Dial-up modems offer relatively slow connection speeds. In the early days, these speeds could be as low as 150 bps (bit per second) or 300 bps. Over the years, the speeds have increased dramatically, though they never touch the blistering speeds of the cable modem and Digital Subscriber Line (DSL) technology discussed in Chapter 4. Today, speeds of 28.8, 33.6, and 56 Kbps (really, 53 Kbps due to limits of the phone lines) are common.

But these speeds are even slower than they seem because modems are constantly converting signal types and must use bizarre error-checking routines to ensure that data is transmitted properly. They do this because phone lines are hit or miss: Some recently installed lines are "clean" and can transmit data efficiently. But many phone lines have been in place for decades and have deteriorated over time. And if even one such line is between your modem and your ISP, your connection speed suffers dramatically. This is the true weakness of a dial-up Internet connection.

Modem speeds are generally fine for e-mail (unless you get large attachments) and simple Web browsing. However, modern Web sites with lots of graphics can bring a dial-up connection to its knees.

If you want to download pages faster on a dial-up connection, consider configuring your Web browser to only download text automatically. You'll get the words, and blank spaces for pictures. If you read the page and decide you want to see a certain picture, right-click where the picture goes and select Show Picture from a popup menu.

Choosing a Modem

So how do you decide on a modem? Honestly, it's not a huge decision: I recommend just getting the cheapest version that explicitly advertises compatibility with Windows XP. If you're concerned about occupying a precious PCI card in your system, an external modem is an option, but I wouldn't personally spend the extra money unless I had to.

In many cases, of course, new PCs simply come with a modem installed, and this is even more likely with a new laptop. If you need a modem, simply shop for the best price.

TIP   CNET's excellent Shopper.com Web site is a great place to visit to get prices on modems and many other electronic devices. Of course, you already need to be connected to the Internet to access this site.

Using New Connection Wizard with a Modem

You can make a modem connection in Windows XP a variety of ways, but the simplest and best is the New Connection Wizard. This wizard offers a step-by-step, handholding experience. Don't feel patronized, though; it's good stuff.

TIP   If you have a setup CD for AOL, or another ISP, insert the CD into your computer and follow its instructions. You don't need the New Connection Wizard.

Oddly, finding the wizard is fairly complicated. But the easiest way is through the Control Panel. Here's how you launch the wizard:

1. Choose Start→Control Panel. The Control Panel window opens.

2. Click Network and Internet Connections. The Network and Internet Connections portion of the Control Panel appears, as shown in Figure 3-1.

3. Click the Set Up or Change Your Internet Connection option under Pick a Task. The Connections tab of the Internet Properties dialog box appears, as shown in Figure 3-2.

4. Click the Setup button to launch the New Connection Wizard, which is shown in Figure 3-3. Note that the Internet Properties dialog box closes when you click this button.

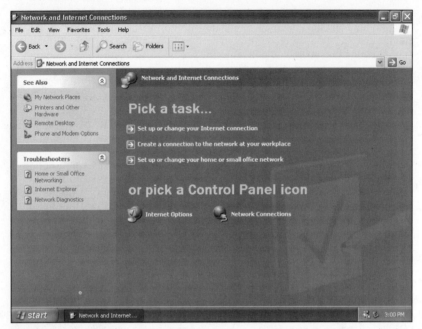

Figure 3-1: The Network and Internet Connections allows you to configure your options for the modem.

Figure 3-2: The Internet Properties dialog box showing all your dial-up connections.

Figure 3-3: The Welcome screen for the New Connection Wizard, which helps you configure your modem.

As with most XP-related tasks, there are many ways to access the New Connection Wizard. A slightly quicker way is to right-click My Network Places in the Start menu and choose Properties. Then choose Create a New Connection under Network Tasks in the window's task pane.

Now you're ready to go forward and configure your connection.

Configuring a New Connection

When the New Connection Wizard launches, it's time to get busy and configure your connection. Here's how:

1. Click Next to move to the second step of the wizard, where you choose the Network Connection type, as shown in Figure 3-4. As you can see, you have numerous choices here. Some choices are for Internet access and some are more generic network connections.

2. Select Connect to the Internet (the default choice) and then click Next. The wizard progresses to the Getting Ready stage, shown in Figure 3-5. Here, you need to choose one of the following options for connecting to the Internet:

   ■ **Choose From A List Of Internet Service Providers (ISPs):** Choose this option if you don't already have an ISP and would like to select a new ISP from a list provided by Microsoft. Then move ahead to the next section titled "Choosing a New Internet Service Provider (ISP)."

- **Set Up My Connection Manually:** Choose this option if you already have an ISP and know your connection settings – user name, password, and access phone number.

- **Use The CD I Got From An ISP:** Although I won't be covering this option explicitly here, it's straightforward. You don't need to use this wizard if you have such a CD. If you choose this option and click Finish, the New Connection Wizard exits, and the Online Services folder is displayed.

  Move ahead to the section titled "Connecting to an Existing ISP," later in this chapter.

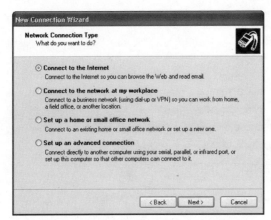

Figure 3-4: Choosing the type of modem connection for this configuration.

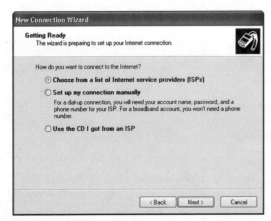

Figure 3-5: Choose how you want to make the connection to the Internet.

Choosing a New Internet Service Provider (ISP)

If you chose to view a list of ISPs so you could create a new Internet connection, the wizard now resembles Figure 3-6. You can choose The Microsoft Network (MSN, Microsoft's online service) or select from a list of other ISPs. Your choice should be based on your needs.

- ◆ If you travel a lot, look for a national ISP, such as MSN or AOL. You can access national services from local phone numbers all over the country without paying long-distance charges.

- ◆ If you don't travel, shop around for the best price that doesn't require a long-distance call. You might need to experiment with ISPs to find a service that works well for you, but try the cheapest first.

TIP National ISPs like MSN and AOL tend to be more expensive than local ISPs.

Figure 3-6: The connection wizard can help you choose a new ISP.

The next two sections examine the experience you'll have based on the ISP choice you make here.

GET ONLINE WITH MSN

If you select Get Online with MSN and click Finish, the New Connection Wizard exits, and you are prompted by the MSN message box shown in Figure 3-7. The choice you make here will dramatically affect your online experience, so proceed carefully.

♦ If you click No, you will get a standard POP3 e-mail account, which can be used with any e-mail client, including Outlook Express.

♦ If you click Yes, MSN Explorer will be your primary Internet client. For all but the most unsophisticated users, I do not recommend this option because it will create a Web-based version of your new e-mail account, which isn't necessarily what you want. You can learn more about MSN Explorer in Chapter 12 and decide for yourself whether this is the route you'd like to go. If it is, you can reconfigure your connection at any time to use this client. So click No here and continue. That is the choice I assume for this book.

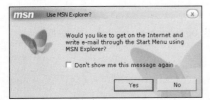

Figure 3-7: Configuring MSN Explorer and your email.

 When you click No, the MSN Wizard appears with a Welcome to MSN Explorer message, as shown in Figure 3-8. Don't be put off by this. MSN sort of assumes that you'll want to use its client, but it's not required (though MSN makes it really hard to not use MSN Explorer). For now, I'll show you how to set up an MSN account, and I'll decommission MSN Explorer later.

Follow these steps to continue setting up the MSN account:

1. After clicking Continue, MSN proceeds to dial the appropriate local number as shown in Figure 3-8. The MSN Wizard progresses.

2. Choose your country/region location (for example, United States) from the drop-down list and click Continue.

3. In the next stage of the wizard, shown in Figure 3-9, you must choose whether you want to use

■ A new MSN e-mail account

If you don't have a free Hotmail or MSN e-mail account, select this.

- Your existing free Hotmail or MSN e-mail account

  If you already have a free Hotmail or MSN e-mail account, you can associate that existing account with your new MSN connection.

- MSN Explorer with your existing connection. I'll skip over this choice, of course.

Figure 3-8: The MSN Explorer client window.

Figure 3-9: Choosing a standard email product or creating a new email account.

Preexisting Hotmail or MSN e-mail accounts will work just fine with your new connection, regardless of your choice here.

4. Click Continue, and you're presented with dialing options. In a home scenario, you probably won't need to change these settings. You can

- Enter a number that needs to be dialed to reach an outside line

- Enter a code to disable call waiting

- Select non–touch tone service if needed

5. Click Continue. The wizard dials a toll-free number at MSN, connects, and authenticates you so the sign-up process can commence. If this takes a while, remember that modem connections are often slow.

6. Enter your first and last name.

7. Enter your birth date and occupation so that MSN can give you the correct type of account. If we understand the rationale here, MSN is really just trying to determine that you're an adult who can legally sign up for an account that will require a regular credit card charge.

8. Enter your address and phone number information.

9. Choose a plan that's right for you. If MSN Broadband – a DSL connection – is available, you'll see that listed. Otherwise, your only choice is Dial-up Internet Access. Select that and click Continue.

10. The wizard presents its recommended local access numbers. You generally see several choices, unless you live in a remote area; I recommend checking all local-call numbers because the connection you're creating will automatically dial a new number if the current one is busy.

Be sure that none of the access numbers are toll calls in your area. You don't want to pay long distance charges while you access the Internet.

11. Enter the email name you wish to use as shown in Figure 3-10. If another person is already using the name you want, the wizard presents choices based on your name, as shown in Figure 3-11. Common names like *paul*, *bob*, and *thurrott* were taken a long time ago, so you might have to get a bit creative here.

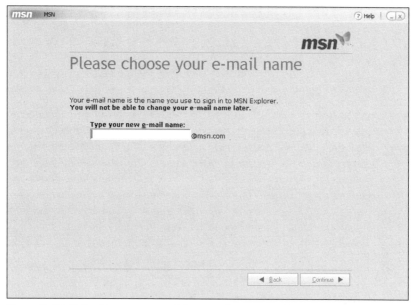

Figure 3-10: Enter the name you wish to use for your email address.

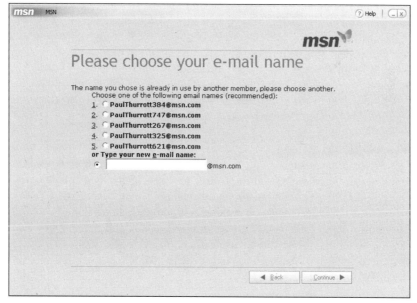

Figure 3-11: If the name you wish to use is already taken, MSN shows you a list of options that it recommends based on the name you would like to use.

12. Choose your password (which must be at least eight characters long) and a secret question/answer combination that MSN support will use if you ever call for help. Your password should include a mixture of mixed-case letters and numbers for better security. Don't choose anything obvious like your children's names or your birth date. Your password is your first line of defense against hackers and other troublemakers, so make it a good one.

13. Enter your credit card information so MSN can bill you for Internet access. This section of the wizard also includes a seemingly innocuous little choice called *Please Create a Passport Wallet for Me So That I Can Use Express Purchase on the Internet.* I cover the Passport Wallet more closely in Chapter 11, but the Express Purchase feature lets you associate credit card information with your e-mail account so that you can more easily purchase goods on secure Web sites that are compatible with Microsoft's Passport service. I recommend leaving this check box unchecked; you can associate this information easily enough at a later time if you'd like.

14. Finally, you agree to the MSN Internet Access Subscriber Agreement and certify that you are at least 18 years of age. Then the wizard finishes, and your MSN account is available. If you decline, the wizard cancels, and your account is not created.

MSN makes a couple of changes to your system when you create an account. If you open up your Network Connections (right-click My Network Places and choose Properties), you see the MSN Explorer connection listed under the new Connection Manager section, for example. You can create a shortcut to this connection on your desktop if you'd like a quick way to launch it manually. But it also shows up in your Start menu: Choose Start→Connect To to access this connection.

For information on using this new account, jump forward to the section titled "Configuring Modem Connections."

SELECT FROM A LIST OF OTHER ISPS

If you choose the Select from a List of Other ISPs option and click Finish, the New Connection Wizard exits, and the Online Services folder is displayed, as shown in Figure 3-12. This folder is typically located in `C:\Program Files\Online Services`, so you can always navigate to it manually as well.

Avoiding Microsoft's final attempt at signing you up for MSN, you can double-click the Refer Me to More Internet Service Providers shortcut, which launches the mysterious Internet Connection Wizard (ICW), which Microsoft told me was not part of Windows XP. Curious!

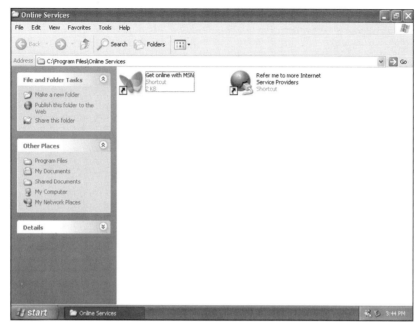

Figure 3-12: This folder maintains a list of other ISPs available.

Here's how you set up a different ISP account in Windows XP:

1. When the ICW launches, it dials Microsoft's Internet Referral Service and retrieves a list of the ISPs that are in your area. This is a toll-free call. When the connection is established, the ISP list is downloaded, and the first step of the wizard appears, as shown in Figure 3-13. This screen displays a list of ISPs, with associated costs and special features. After reviewing the options, pick an ISP and click Next.

2. In Step 2, enter your name, address, and phone number. Then click Next to continue.

3. Though it's not listed as a new step, the next window provides ISP-specific information about billing options. If the ISP offers multiple billing options, you can choose one here.

4. Enter billing information, such as your credit card number and expiration date. Click Next to continue.

5. The ICW then connects to the ISP using a toll-free number so that your connection can be configured. In the next step, choose your e-mail and account name and password. Note that you only enter your password once here, so be sure you enter it correctly the first time.

6. Choose the local access number that is closest to you. You generally have several choices, unless you live in a remote area. But be sure that the number you choose is not a toll call in your area. You don't want to be needlessly charged to access the Internet, and long distance charges can add up.

7. Agree to or decline the ISP's customer agreement. If you decline the agreement, the wizard quits, and your connection is not established. If you agree, your account is created. The wizard then moves to Step 3, and your connection is created.

   Now if you navigate to Network Connections, you see a new Internet connection listed. You can also access this account by choosing Start→ Connect To.

For information on using this new account, jump forward to the section titled "Configuring Modem Connections."

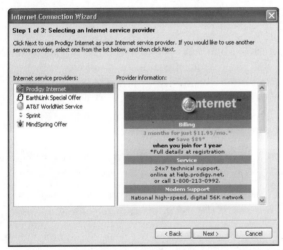

Figure 3-13: List of available ISPs if you do not want to use MSN.

Connecting to an Existing ISP

If you already have an existing Internet account, you can manually make a connection to that account using the New Connection Wizard. To launch the wizard, choose Start→Connect To→Show All Connections. Then choose Create a New Connection from the Network Tasks section of that window's task list.

Follow these steps to configure your account manually:

1. In the Network Connection Type phase of the wizard, choose Connect to the Internet and click Next.

2. Select Set Up a Connection Manually and click Next.

3. In the next phase, Internet Connection, choose Connect Using a Dial-up Modem and then click Next.

4. Give the connection a name. This can be a plain English name of your choosing, such as My Internet Connection, MSN Connection, or whatever. Click Next when you're finished.

5. Enter the phone number for the connection, using the dialing rules for your location. For example, in some areas, you must dial 1 plus the area code before the usual seven-digit phone number, but other areas do not require this. Again, click Next when you're finished.

6. Enter your user name and password, as supplied by your ISP. You have the option to automatically use this connection anytime an application or user needs to connect to the Internet, to make this the default Internet connection, and to enable the Internet Connection Firewall (ICF) for this connection – this feature is handy if you're going to share your connection with other PCs on your home network (see Chapter 6 for more information). Make your choices and then click Next to continue.

7. Now the wizard completes, and you are given an option to place a shortcut to this connection on your desktop. (You can delete the shortcut later if you decide you don't want it.) Click Finish to exit the wizard.

At this point, the Connect dialog box for your new connection appears automatically, as shown in Figure 3-14. You can click the Dial button to attempt a connection, but first, you may want to check out the section titled "Connecting and Disconnecting," later in this chapter, for detailed information about this dialog box and its many options.

Configuring Modem Connections

After you've created a modem connection, you can configure the connection somewhat to ensure it behaves as you'd like, and you can configure certain aspects of the modem.

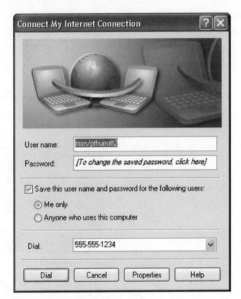

Figure 3-14: Ready to test your new connection.

Managing Connection Properties

First, choose Start→Connect To→Show All Connections to display the Network Connections window. Here, you see icons called *connectoids* that represent each of your modem or LAN connections. In Figure 3-15, two dial-up modems and three LAN connections are visible.

To configure a modem connection, select the connectoid and choose Change Settings of This Connection in the Network Tasks section of the Tasks list for that window. This displays the Properties dialog box for that connection. For modem connections, this dialog box is split into five pages, which you access from the tabs at the top of the window. These pages include:

◆ **General:** Here, you configure the modem used to make the connection (which is handy if you have multiple modems for some reason) and the phone number(s) you use to access your ISP. Windows XP lets you alternate between multiple phone numbers for any given connection. It will automatically try to dial numbers with which it has been successful before those numbers with which it has been unsuccessful. When you click the Alternate button, you see the Alternate Phone Numbers dialog box, where you configure this list of numbers (see Figure 3-16).

The General tab lets you configure whether it uses the system's dialing rules. You find out more about this feature in "Managing a Modem," later in this chapter.

You can determine whether an icon is shown in the tray notification area next to the clock when this connection is established. I recommend leaving this on for modem connections because it gives you a visual cue that the connection is established.

◆ **Options:** The Options tab includes dialing and redialing options. For example, you can configure the connection to redial several times if the connection attempts fail, and redial if the connection is lost. Both of these features are enabled by default, so you shouldn't need to mess with this tab unless you have specific needs.

◆ **Security:** Most dial-up connections use standard security settings, but in some rare cases, you might need to configure a connection to use data encryption or various secure protocols. These features — available through the Advanced Security Settings dialog box, shown in Figure 3-17 — cannot be applied to a standard dial-up account, if you're somehow interested in more security. Your ISP will specify these features if they're necessary.

◆ **Networking:** The Networking tab resembles the General tab of a LAN connection properties dialog box, which is covered in Chapter 4. Unlike a LAN connection, it's unlikely that you'll ever need to manually configure such features as TCP/IP settings or File and Printer Sharing for Microsoft Networks; instead, your dial-up connections will typically use PPP (the Point-to-Point Protocol) and be configured automatically. I don't recommend changing these settings.

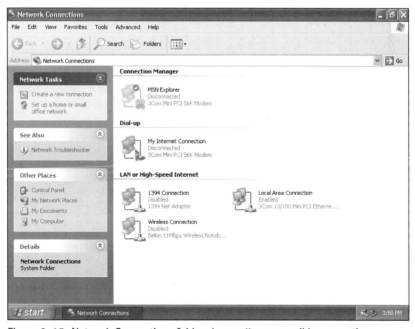

Figure 3-15: Network Connections folder shows all your possible connections.

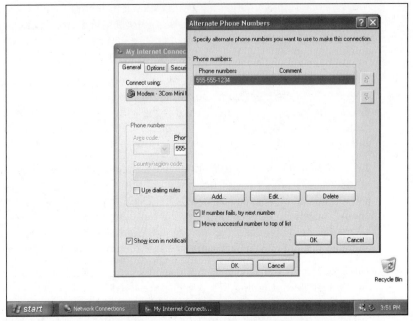

Figure 3-16: Stores alternate phone numbers for dialing into your ISP.

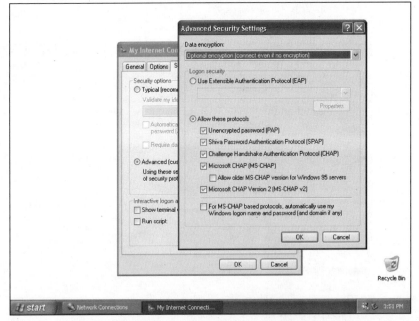

Figure 3-17: Configuring your dialup account to be more secured.

◆ **Advanced:** You can determine whether the connection uses the *ICF* or *ICS* features. These topics are broad enough that I cover them in their own chapter, so check Chapter 6 if you'd like to work with ICF or ICS.

Managing a Modem

In addition to the connection itself, you might want to configure the modem so that you can manage dialing rules and even the modem's volume. Modem configuration occurs through the Modem Control Panel. Here's how to find it and configure the modem hardware:

1. Choose Start→Control Panel. The Control Panel window appears.

2. Select Printers and Other Hardware, and the Control Panel display changes to show this subset.

3. Under the section titled Or Pick a Control Panel Icon, click Phone and Modem Options. This displays the Phone and Modem Options dialog box, shown in Figure 3-18.

   This dialog box contains three pages, which correspond to the three basic modem-related tasks you might want to configure:

   ■ **Dialing Rules:** Here, you configure the locations from which you might dial the modem. This isn't too critical for a desktop PC, which usually sits in a single physical location, but it could be critical on a laptop, which you can take with you traveling anywhere in the country or the world, for that matter. By default, XP creates a location called *New Location* that is configured with your area code. If you click the Edit button, you can configure this location in the Edit Location dialog box, shown in Figure 3-19. Here, you can rename the location and specify various dialing rules. For example, perhaps you need to dial a number to access an outside line, as you might at an office or in a hotel. You can also disable call waiting or specify tone or pulse dialing.

   If you travel, you might specify a new location that includes dialing rules that are different from the rules you'd use at home.

   ■ **Modems:** On the Modems tab, you can access the hardware-related properties for any modems you might have connected, or add and remove modems. To view the modem properties, select the modem and click the Properties button. This displays the Modem Properties dialog box, shown in Figure 3-20.

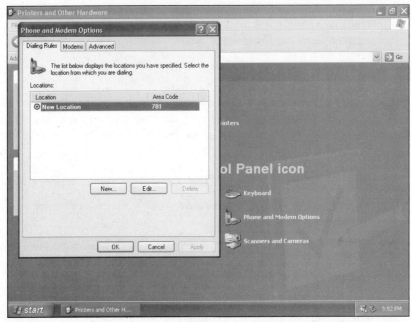

Figure 3-18: Phone and Modem Options for configuring and testing your modem.

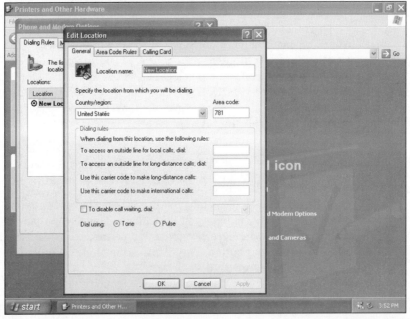

Figure 3-19: Editing your location settings for configuring how your modem should dial.

There's a lot of technical information here, but three options stand out. On the Modem tab, you can configure the modem's speaker volume, from mute to high volume, though some modems might not support this feature. If you suspect that the modem is misbehaving, access the Diagnostics tab to have XP poll the modem and see how it responds; click the Query Modem button to do this. Finally, the Power Management tab lets you set power management–related options, depending on your modem and PC. If this is your primary Internet connection on a desktop PC, you might consider letting the modem bring the PC out of Standby mode.

- **Advanced:** This tab isn't generally of interest, but it allows you to configure various telephony service providers, which are low-level services that can be transmitted over low-bandwidth networks like a dial-up connection.

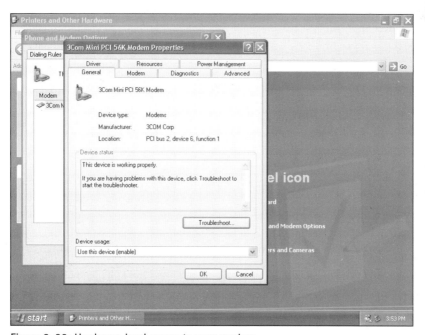

Figure 3-20: Hardware-level access to your modem.

Connecting and Disconnecting

If you've been reading along since the beginning of the chapter, you've gone through a lot of preparatory work, and it's probably time for a little payoff. For modems, that payoff is the actual connection, though again, in light of recent developments with high-speed broadband connections, even this might seem like a bit of a rip-off. But it is what it is, and no connection is worth a thing unless you can actually connect with it.

So let's do it.

Connecting with a Modem

However you created your connection in XP, you can access that connection directly from the Start menu. Simply choose Start→Connect To and then the name of your connection. This displays the Connect dialog box, shown back in Figure 3-14. If it's configured correctly, you can just click Dial to connect, but you can also access the properties for the connection if you'd like.

When you click Dial, the modem attempts to make a connection. If it works, a small yellow balloon help window appears at the lower right of the screen, as shown in Figure 3-21. This window notes that the connection was successful and displays the speed of the connection (40 Kbps, 33 Kbps, or whatever — the faster the better).

Figure 3-21: Windows XP displaying the connection information after a successful modem connection to your ISP.

While your connection is active, you see a small icon in the system tray. If you hover the mouse cursor over this icon, as shown in Figure 3-22, you will see a small tooltip window with the name of the connection, its speed, and the amount of bytes that have been transferred in and out of the connection.

Figure 3-22: By placing the mouse over the small icon, you can see the basic connection information.

When you click this icon once, a Status dialog box displays, as shown in Figure 3-23. This dialog box lets you access the connection properties and disable (that is, disconnect) the connection if you want.

If your connection doesn't succeed, you might see an error message like the one shown in Figure 3-24. Connections fail for a variety of reasons: Perhaps the phone line isn't connected, or someone is using the phone to make a voice call. Check your connections and try, try again.

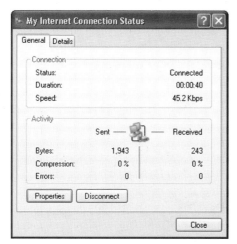

Figure 3-23: Status dialog box where you can
see more details about your connection as well
as disconnect from your provider.

Figure 3-24: Typical error message displays
the problem with dialing the ISP.

Likewise, dial-up connections often fail after they've been established. If you
configure your connection properly, it will automatically redial and reconnect if it
gets disconnected.

Disconnecting a Modem

Disconnecting a modem is simple: You can right-click the connection's system tray
icon and choose Disconnect, or you can single-click the same icon and click the
Disconnect button. When the connection is disconnected, the system tray icon
disappears.

Copying a Modem Connection

Occasionally, you might want to copy a modem connection. Maybe you want to
keep most of the settings but just modify the phone numbers for different cities.

Instead of re-creating a connection from scratch, it's easier to copy it and then just modify the settings you need. Here's how:

1. Choose Start→Connect To→Show All Connections to open the Network Connections window.

2. Right-click the connection you'd like to copy and choose Create Copy. A copy of the connection appears in the Network Connections window, as shown in Figure 3-25.

3. Reconfigure this connection as needed. To rename it, see the next section.

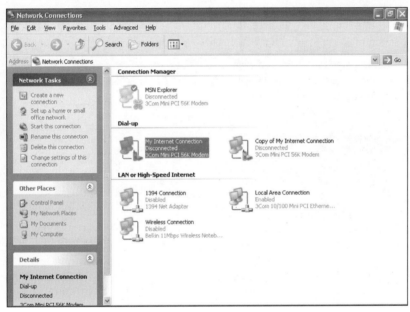

Figure 3-25: Creating a copy of an existing connection is easy.

Renaming Modem Connections

You can rename your modem connections (and indeed, all network connections) to make them more descriptive if you'd like. Renaming a connection is easy: Just select it in the Network Connections window and choose Rename This Connection from the Network Tasks section of the window's task list.

When you do this, the text under the connectoid is highlighted, indicating that you can edit it in place.

Caught Between a Rock and a Hard Place: AOL and Windows XP

In case it's not obvious, at least one major dial-up ISP is missing from Microsoft's list of Internet providers. Because of legal problems between the two companies, Microsoft declined to offer America Online (AOL) a spot in Windows XP, and users interested in this service have to install AOL on their own.

Thanks to AOL's extensive marketing, this won't be difficult: Most homes in America have been supplied with AOL installation CDs through a variety of means, including direct mailings and magazine bundles. Just be sure that you're installing the latest version of AOL's online software: Only AOL 7.0 and newer are technically compatible with Windows XP, though some users report limited success with AOL 6.0.

If you don't have an AOL CD handy, you can download the software from AOL's admittedly confusing Web site. Because the location changes regularly, I can't provide an exact URL, but look for the Download link — currently found at the bottom of AOL's home page (www.aol.com) — and follow the links from there.

Chapter 4

Information Superhighway: Making the Broadband Connection

IN THIS CHAPTER

- ◆ What is broadband
- ◆ How to choose a broadband provider
- ◆ Learn how to configure a connection manually and by using the wizard

To FULLY TAKE ADVANTAGE of today's Internet, you will want to use a *broadband* connection, such as a cable modem, Digital Subscriber Line (DSL), or satellite, rather than a slower dial-up telephone connection. Broadband opens up a wider range of Internet experiences, from online games and streaming video, to remote desktop access that lets you use your PC from a system across the Internet.

Best of all, broadband accounts are also relatively cheap and getting cheaper all the time. For example, a cable modem or DSL account often costs about the same per month as a second phone line and dial-up Internet access account. So if you can get broadband access – any broadband access – I strongly recommend it.

In this chapter, you find out about the three most common broadband connection types and the ways in which you can set up Windows XP to work with them. For the most part, setting up a connection is identical for most broadband account types.

Understanding Broadband

Technically, broadband is any Internet connection that exceeds the speeds possible with a dial-up modem solution. Some experts peg the bottom end of broadband at about 128 kilobits per second (Kbps). In this sense, broadband refers simply to a connection speed, rather than a specific technology, so even early post-modem attempts, such as *ISDN* (Integrated Services Digital Network), might loosely be considered broadband. Despite this, these days it's most common to use the term broadband when referring to such connections as cable modems, DSL, and satellite. And that's what I assume in this book.

Most broadband connections are *always-on,* meaning that the connections are constant, like electricity, and don't need to be dialed-in, like a modem connection. (Sadly, this isn't true of some low-end, consumer-oriented DSL accounts, as I'll soon examine.) Broadband connections are also far more *reliable* than dial-up connections and don't typically need to be restarted.

Given these benefits, it should be obvious that broadband accounts are highly desirable. But broadband has faced slow acceptance in the market, though it finally seems to be taking off. There have been a couple of challenges:

- ◆ Availability is the biggest problem: Like any new communication technology, broadband accounts were first made available in only the most populated areas, leaving millions of people in more rural areas without any options. This situation has improved dramatically over time, to the extent that all but the most remote areas now have a variety of options.

- ◆ Broadband costs more than lesser services. Cable modem connections debuted at about $50 a month in the United States several years back, and DSL was originally even more costly than that. Over the past few years, broadband suppliers have lowered costs in a variety of ways, and most cable markets now offer $30 monthly rates to customers who purchase their own cable modems and subscribe to cable TV services. Comparing this price to the $24 a month that America Online (AOL) now charges for a slow dial-up connection, it's easy to see why broadband is finally starting to catch on.

Available Broadband Solutions

So the big question, of course, is which type of broadband connection you should opt for. In some cases, your choices are limited by where you live; you might only have access to one or two of these solutions. But many areas — such as the suburban Boston neighborhood where I live — have multiple solutions. In fact, I actually have my choice of two cable modem solutions, several DSL solutions, and one satellite-based broadband solution. Choice is good.

Cable Modem

A cable broadband connection utilizes the modern two-way cable infrastructure that's available in most of the United States and typically offers speeds of 500 Kbps to 1 Mbps, though upload bandwidth is often limited to 128 Kbps by the service provider. Cable is always-on, zero-configuration, and usually the least expensive broadband option.

One bit of controversy surrounding cable involves *shared* bandwidth. Proponents of competing solutions, such as DSL, often cite this as a weakness of cable. This is hogwash, however: All broadband Internet connections are shared. Here's the story: Cable suppliers divide their cable modem networks into neighborhood oriented nodes, and each of these nodes has a limited amount of bandwidth that can be shared among all users in the node. If you're home alone during the day, the story goes, you might see much better download speeds than you will that night, when everyone in the neighborhood is home and using the bandwidth.

The reality isn't so dramatic. Cable bandwidth fluctuates – sometimes dramatically – but so does every other kind of Internet connection. The problems are usually behind the cable service provider's network, not your local node. The bandwidth available to neighborhood nodes can be upgraded: If enough people in your area sign up for cable Internet access, node sizes will decrease (that is, the number of nodes will increase), or the available bandwidth per node will be increased.

Overall, cable is the fastest, cheapest, and most widely available broadband choice. It's the one to get if you have a major cable carrier – AT&T, Comcast, AOL Time Warner, or similar. I've had less success with smaller carriers such as RCN, which tend to offer slower connections than the big boys.

Digital Subscriber Line (DSL)

Essentially a cable competitor that uses existing phone line technology, DSL comes in a bewildering array of packages. Many DSL packages are aimed more at businesses than homeowners. But DSL's biggest strength – the pervasive presence of phone lines in virtually every neighborhood – is also its biggest weakness. The problem, of course, is that most phone lines are ancient and not of high enough quality to let DSL attain the highest possible speeds.

So for many people, DSL is a broken promise. Furthering the technical limitations is a requirement that DSL customers be within a certain distance of a signal repeater, meaning that relatively few people have access to this technology despite the ready availability of phone lines.

Within the home, DSL's reliance on phones can also be problematic: Unlike street-side phone lines, which can at least be upgraded when necessary, it's unusual for people to upgrade the lines within their homes, so many older homes might have problems with DSL.

Despite these seemingly insurmountable issues, DSL is finally starting to catch on with consumers, thanks to increasing availability and lowered prices. And the horrendous install episodes of the past are largely behind us thanks to increasingly experienced phone company crews. Best of all, if you're able to get DSL, you have a better chance of getting the promised speeds on a regular basis because the connection sharing occurs much farther down the line than with cable connections.

DSL comes in a variety of speeds. Lower-end offerings require a bizarre pseudo-dial-up scheme, PPPoE, that you should avoid unless you don't have any other broadband choices or money is an issue. (PPPoE is covered later in this chapter.) Higher-end *Asymmetric DSL* (ADSL) brings download speeds of about 1.5 Mbps and upload speeds of about 384 Kbps, though exact speeds can vary by service provider. Pricing is a bit higher than cable, generally, starting at about $40–50 a month.

Even though DSL uses standard phone lines, you can still use a voice telephone at the same time you're connected. That's one of the many obstacles that DSL technology overcomes with this otherwise somewhat-dated technology.

Satellite

With wired solutions such as cable modem and DSL beyond the reach of rural customers, some satellite TV providers have turned to broadband Internet access in an effort to provide more services and bolster their bottom lines. As a result, satellite broadband is an attractive choice for people in areas that would otherwise be forced to stick with dial-up access.

Satellite isn't as quick as cable or DSL, however. Download speeds top out at 150–500 Kbps, and upload speeds are limited to a fraction of that. So online gamers will find satellite to be a non-starter. Satellite is also more expensive, both month-to-month and for installation: It requires a satellite dish, professional installation, and most providers still ask for yearly commitments. Monthly fees are even higher than cable and generally run about $70–75, if you're getting satellite TV access as well; without TV, the price will be slightly higher.

Doesn't sound so great? If satellite is what you can get, you should get it. It is certainly faster than dial-up, a lot faster.

Deciding on a Broadband Solution

In my experience, cable modem is the hands-down winner for consumers seeking a low-cost, highly reliable broadband connection. Cable connections are generally faster than DSL, and much, much easier to set up. If cable is not an option, look into DSL. After that, satellite.

Other broadband options will be available soon, including a variety of wireless solutions based on new 3G technology. None of these technologies are expected to become mainstream during XP's lifetime, however.

Using the New Connection Wizard with a Broadband Connection

Regardless of the type of broadband connection you have, the basics are the same. Instead of a modem, you need a network interface card (NIC) to connect to your broadband connection. If you're using a cable connection, the NIC connects via an

Ethernet cable to the cable modem, which in turn connects via coaxial cable to the street. With a DSL connection, the NIC connects via Ethernet to a DSL modem, which connects via phone line to a standard phone jack. And with satellite, the NIC connects, again via Ethernet, to a satellite modem, which in turn connects to the actual satellite via coaxial cabling.

What this means to you, from a networking perspective, is that establishing a broadband connection is no different from establishing any other network connection. So you'll have an icon in Network Connections corresponding to the NIC or, by extension, the broadband connection. Most broadband suppliers require users to use automated network configurations – a DHCP server on their network provides your IP address dynamically. But some ISPs – usually with DSL accounts – actually provide static IP addresses. Check with your supplier to be sure.

Because of our focus on Windows XP here, I'll assume, for the most part, that your *edge machine* (the machine connecting your internal network to the Internet) is a PC running Windows XP. But it doesn't have to be: Companies such as Linksys and D-Link have made a killing selling hardware devices called *broadband routers* or *gateways,* which allow you to share an Internet connection. Those are covered a bit more in the next chapter, but for now, I'll assume that you're connecting to the broadband account with a Windows XP–based PC.

If your broadband provider supplies dynamic IP addresses, you'll have absolutely no configuration at all: Just plug in the cable and reboot XP (even this step might not be necessary), and you should be online. Load a Web page to be sure.

If this doesn't work, or your broadband account requires a bit more configuration for some reason, XP provides a handy New Connection Wizard that can help you get started. Just follow these steps to use it:

1. Open My Network Places and select View Network Connections from the Network Tasks list in the task pane on the left side of the window. This displays your available network connections, as shown in Figure 4-1.

2. Locate the network connection that corresponds to your broadband connection. If you have just one network interface card, this will be called *Local Area Connection*. Select this connection and click Create a New Connection from the Network Tasks list in the task pane. The New Connection Wizard launches.

TIP

At the end of the chapter, you find out how you can rename your network connections. I strongly recommend this, especially on machines with more than one NIC.

3. When you click Next, the list of choices shown in Figure 4-2 is presented. The default choice, Connect to the Internet, is correct, so click Next to continue.

4. In the next phase, you choose how you want to connect to the Internet. Select Set Up My Connection Manually and then click Next.

5. In the next phase, your choice depends on the type of broadband account you have. Most broadband accounts are always connected, so you will want to choose Connect Using a Broadband Connection that is always on. However, some consumer-level DSL accounts require you to provide a username and password. If you have this type of account – also known as a Point-to-Point Protocol Over Ethernet (PPPoE) account – then check out the next section. Otherwise, click Next to continue.

6. Click Finish. Your always-on broadband account should be configured and working.

Figure 4-1: The Network Connections window displays any network connections, including broadband and dial-up connections, and local network connections of various types.

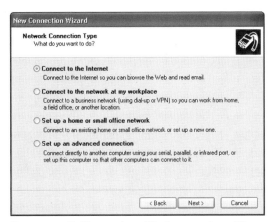

Figure 4-2: Unlike previous Windows versions, XP presents a single unified front for all network types.

Configuring DSL Connection to Use PPPoE

Many home DSL users will need to do a further bit of configuration because these accounts often require you to use PPPoE, a bizarre combination of dial-up networking and Ethernet technologies. PPPoE is only used on the low-end DSL accounts aimed at home users, however, and most DSL suppliers will let you pay more to get faster connection speeds without any need for PPPoE.

But if you're using a PPPoE DSL account, it's easy enough to configure in XP:

1. Follow Steps 1 through 4 for the New Internet Connection wizard in the preceding section. You eventually reach the Internet Connection phase.

2. Here, you choose the type of account you will use. PPPoE users need to choose the Connect Using a Broadband Connection That Requires a User Name and Password option and then click Next.

3. In the next phase, enter your ISP's name, which is used to name the connection icon – called a *connectoid* – in Network Connections, and then click Next.

4. In the next phase, shown in Figure 4-3, enter your username, password, and other related information. For example, you can choose to use this account as the default Internet account, and you can turn on XP's basic firewall, which is described in more detail in Chapter 6. My recommendation is to leave each of the three options you're presented with checked. Then click Next to continue.

   After this, the wizard completes and offers to create a shortcut to your new connection on the desktop.

Figure 4-3: For DSL-based PPPoE users and other broadband accounts that require you to log on, XP offers the ability to configure this information directly into a network connection.

Testing the Connection

Whichever type of connection you create, it's a good idea to test it immediately. The simplest way, of course, is to load a Web page in Internet Explorer. If it comes up, you're looking good. If not, you've got some work to do.

In the old days — back when Windows NT and 2000 were still new — troubleshooting a broadband account would have required you to open up a DOS-like command window and master esoteric command line network utilities. Thankfully, in XP, this is no longer necessary. Instead, you can use simple graphical utilities to ensure that your broadband connection — and other network connections — are working properly.

If your IP address is dynamically provided, the first step is to ensure that you're actually getting an IP address from your ISP. You may recall that XP is smart enough to supply its own IP address if it cannot contact a DHCP server. This IP will be in the 169.254.x.x range, so if you've got such an IP address, then XP generated it internally, and it didn't come from your ISP. Here's how you find out what your IP address is:

1. In Network Connections, double-click the connectoid that corresponds to your broadband account. This displays the Connection's Status dialog box.

2. Navigate to the Support tab, shown in Figure 4-4. This tab displays your IP address, subnet mask, and default gateway configuration information.

If the IP address begins with 169.254 or is otherwise unavailable, then you're not connected to the Internet, and XP was forced to supply its own IP address to the network interface. In this instance, you can attempt to establish a connection with your ISP's DHCP servers and get a proper IP address. To do so, click the Repair button.

Figure 4-4: Command line? Not in XP. Everything you need to configure a network connection is available directly from the GUI.

TIP NT old-timers are probably familiar with the *ipconfig* command line tool, which could be used with the *release* and *renew* parameters, respectively, to provide the same service that XP's Repair functionality provides today. Repair is a lot friendlier and easier to use.

Repair severs the connection's DHCP *lease* and attempts to contact a valid DHCP server to obtain a new IP address. If it's successful, that information is displayed in the Support tab of the connection's Status dialog box. If not, you see an error message.

TIP If you're having problems with a network connection, check the physical connection first. More often than not, a cable is unplugged, or some sort of hardware problem is preventing networking from working correctly.

If the IP address is valid (that is, it isn't in the 169.254.x.x range) but you still can't connect to any Web sites, you can also try to disable and then enable the connection later. This is similar to repairing the connection, but it also lets you put off the DHCP lease renewal if you'd like.

Renaming a Broadband Connection

It's a good idea to rename your network connections, especially if you have more than one. Otherwise, XP gives them names like Local Area Connection, Local Area

Connection 2, and so on, making it difficult to tell them apart. I like to name the connection for my cable modem as Cable Modem Connection, for example.

To rename your broadband connection, select the appropriate connectoid in Network Connections and click Rename This Connection from the Network Tasks list. Then enter a new name for the connection, as shown in Figure 4-5.

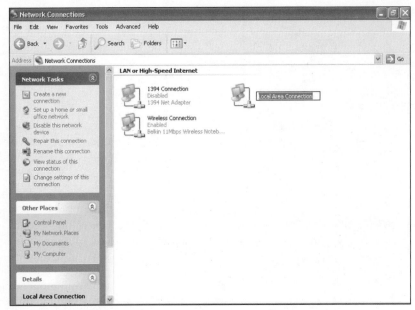

Figure 4-5: With multiple network connections, it's a good idea to rename each connection to reflect what it really is.

Configuring a Broadband Connection

In addition to the connection-related tasks that you see in the task list of the Network Connections window, each connectoid also presents a comprehensive Properties dialog box that lets you configure the related connection. To access this important dialog box, select the appropriate connection and then click Change Settings of This Connection from the Network Tasks list.

General Properties

In the General tab of this dialog box, shown in Figure 4-6, you can configure the network connection hardware and services that are associated with the connection.

Figure 4-6: The General tab of the connection Properties dialog box offers configuration possibilities, including which services and protocols are available to that connection.

To configure the NIC hardware, click the Configure button. This closes the connectoid Properties dialog box and launches the device Properties dialog box, where you can install new drivers and perform other low-level tasks.

In the center of the General tab, you will see installed services and protocols, which Microsoft refers to generically as *items*. Four items are installed by default:

- **Client for Microsoft Networks:** This service allows your PC to act as a client in a Microsoft network and access network resources such as shared folders and printers. This service is crucial for any system in a Windows-based home network.

- **File and Printer Sharing for Microsoft Networks:** This service allows your PC to act as a server in a Microsoft network, sharing its own resources, such as folders and printers. This service is also crucial for any system in a Windows-based home network.

- **Quality of Service (QoS) Packet Scheduler:** The QoS Packet Scheduler debuted in Windows 2000, but in XP, it's a standard feature (so standard, in fact, that removing it here will not actually remove the service). QoS is designed to prevent any one PC on a network from filling up the entire data pipe, so if you're downloading a large movie or whatever, other users on the network can still use the connection. Basically, QoS ensures that at least 20 percent of the available bandwidth is always, well, available to other users. This is configurable. You can actually prevent QoS from stealing any bandwidth. Check out the Web site for this book for details (www.xphomenetworking.com).

◆ **Internet Protocol (TCP/IP):** I hope this is obvious, but TCP/IP is obviously a necessary component of any networked operating system. If you need to configure your connection with a static IP address, select this protocol and click the Properties button.

In addition to these items, you can also choose whether an icon appears in the system tray whenever this connection is active (which should be all the time).

Authentication Options

The Authentication tab is generally not of interest for a broadband connection; it only enables authentication methods over PPP and 802.11-based connections.

Advanced Options

On the Advanced tab, shown in Figure 4-7, you can configure some extremely important technologies, including XP's Internet Connection Firewall (ICF) and Internet Connection Sharing (ICS). These technologies are so important, in fact, that I discuss them in their own chapter, Chapter 6. But I will mention now that any edge connection should have a firewall enabled, so make sure you check the option under Internet Connection Firewall before closing the dialog box.

Figure 4-7: In the Advanced tab, you can configure whether the connection is protected by XP's firewall and if the connection is shared with other PCs on your home network.

Part II

Home Networking

Chapter 5

Creating Your Home Network

IN THIS CHAPTER

◆ Connecting computers together

◆ Understanding the different types of networks that can be easily applied in your home

◆ What are hubs, switches, gateways, routers and how do you use them

◆ Using the networking wizard to manage workgroups

◆ Securing your network

WITH A HOME NETWORK, you can harness the resources of all your PCs without having to physically move from PC to PC. For many users, a home network is the final frontier, that complicated-but-useful albatross that seems harder than it really is.

With Windows XP, home networking is truly easy. XP includes a Networking Setup Wizard that guides you through the process. Even manual home networking configuration is much simpler than you might expect.

The key to setting up a home network is understanding the technical lingo and choosing the right components. XP can interoperate with a variety of hardware and software components to build a home network, as you will learn in this chapter.

Making Computer to Computer Connections

Because a home network technically requires two or more computers, the simplest home network consists of two PCs and some sort of connection between them (usually a kind of wire). Most home networks consist of wired Ethernet or wireless (802.11b, or Wi-Fi, based) networking. You can also create a connection between two PCs by using a parallel cable, a serial cable, a modem, or other similar methods; such a connection is called a *direct cable connection,* but it is technically a network. And if it's in your house, it qualifies as a home network. See, the terminology isn't that difficult!

The Case for Direct Cable Connections

Direct cable connections can't compete with Ethernet-based wired or wireless network performance, but they're simpler to set up. You don't have to install network adapters in any of your PCs. They use existing ports on your PCs. You just purchase a specialized cable.

In previous Windows versions, direct cable connections generally required some configuration. In XP, networking has been dramatically simplified. Any connection in XP – modem, wired network, wireless network, direct cable connection, or whatever – is considered a *network connection.* So you create direct cable connections in XP in the same way that you create any other connection.

For this book, I assume that you're looking for something a little more sophisticated than a simple cable-based connection between two PCs.

Using Infrared

Infrared networking is a relic. It's an early specification for wirelessly exchanging data. Infrared is being squeezed out of the PC market by a new technology called *Bluetooth,* which offers faster speeds, non-directional connection capabilities, and other features.

Infrared connections require two or more PCs or other devices (such as Windows CE devices and printers) that have infrared ports. (Infrared ports are small reddish-black windows.) To connect devices via infrared, the infrared ports of each device need to be lined up. The safest method of ensuring that an infrared connection is connected is to make sure that the infrared port on one of the device is aiming directly at the other device's infrared port. So you can print via infrared from an infrared-equipped laptop to an infrared-equipped printer, but you have to move the laptop over to the printer and do a little finagling first. If you've ever watched two geeks trying to line up two Pocket PCs, doing a contorted device dance in mid-air, they were probably trying to get infrared to work. It can be a bit infuriating.

Like direct cable connections, you set up infrared connections in XP like any other network connection. They're easier now than ever before. But they're also increasingly irrelevant.

Basic Network Types

Powerful home networking technologies are a little complicated, but not really difficult. All modern home networking types are based on TCP/IP, the Transmission Control Protocol/Internet Protocol that makes the Internet possible. (Check out Chapter 2 for more on TCP/IP.) If you're setting up a new home network, you will probably be working with at least one of these network types. Each of these types, described below, requires a single compatible network adapter in each PC. This adapter then interfaces with the network.

Ethernet Networking

The most common networking type is wired Ethernet networking, which typically offers speeds of 10 or 100 Mbps. A more recent version, called Gigabit Ethernet, offers speeds up to 1,000 Mbps (1 Gbps).

In its simplest configuration, two PCs can interface directly by using a single crossover Ethernet cable. However, this setup isn't typical. You normally provide some sort of central hub or switch, a physical device to which Ethernet-equipped PCs connect by using Ethernet cabling.

Wired Ethernet networking is the fastest networking connection available. Its downside is the cabling itself. Ethernet cabling can be unsightly in a home, and hiding the cable in walls can be invasive and expensive. And if you want to network two machines that are physically separated by great distances, Ethernet isn't always a great solution. But when your PCs are all in the same room, it's often the best way to go.

Wi-Fi Wireless Networking

To overcome the physical limitations of wired networking, companies and organizations have been working on wireless networking solutions for the past decade. One of these — *Wi-Fi,* also known as *802.11b* — has been accepted as an industry standard and has been hugely popular in recent years. Wi-Fi offers relatively fast speeds of up to 11 Mbps, though that bandwidth is shared among any devices attached wirelessly. Newer wireless technologies now offer speeds up to 54 Mbps. (Ethernet-based networking is capable of offering each device the full 10, 100, or 1,000 Mbps of bandwidth).

Wireless is so important and popular that this networking technology gets its own chapter. Head over to Chapter 9 for more information.

Home Phoneline Networking

Before wireless networking became affordable to average consumers, other networking technologies were created for consumer needs. One, based on phone line technology, has also grown to offer high-speed solutions that rival Ethernet. This networking type is *HomePNA* (Home Phoneline Networking Alliance).

HomePNA networking adapters look like Ethernet adapters but offer a standard phone jack connector. To network PCs in this manner, you must first install the adapter into your computer (if it is an internal adapter) or connect it to your computer to the USB port (if it is an external adapter). Then plug the phone cable into any available wall jack. Most adapters also offer a second jack connector so that you can connect a telephone; HomePNA networking does not interrupt normal telephone service.

Early versions of HomePNA were relatively slow, offering speeds of just 1 Mbps. In 1999, the specification was updated to 10 Mbps, and then to 100 Mbps in 2002. HomePNA is a practical alternative to Ethernet if you already have phone jacks where you want them.

TIP For more information about HomePNA networking, visit the HomePNA
Web site at www.homepna.org/.

Powerline Networking

Powerline networking takes advantage of a familiar connection in every home: power plugs. Powerline networking uses the electrical wiring in your home to transfer network information. Because such plugs are plentiful in every room, it's fairly simple to set up. It makes sense for those not interested in wireless or in rewiring their homes for Ethernet.

Early powerline solutions were plagued by slow speed and interference problems from electronic devices. However, powerline networking adherents rallied around a single standard called HomePlug. The first version of HomePlug calls for speeds of up to 14 Mbps.

Powerline networking is a technology to watch. Everyone has plenty of power plugs in their homes, and it's likely that a new generation of connected devices will use this technology.

TIP For more information about powerline networking, visit the HomePlug Web
site at www.homeplug.org/.

FireWire-Based Networking

Some newer PCs include an IEEE-1394, or FireWire, port, which was popularized by Apple Macintosh computers. Normally used to connect digital camcorders and external storage, FireWire can also be used for networking purposes (though that particular use is fairly rare). FireWire offers up 400 Mbps of bandwidth, which makes it an excellent networking candidate. A future version of FireWire, dubbed *GigaWire,* will offer much faster speeds.

NOTE Any Windows XP PC with a FireWire port will display a FireWire networking connection in Network Connections, regardless of how the port is used.

Using Hubs and Switches

Wired Ethernet cabling forms the basis of most home networks, though many people also add other networking types—especially wireless—to the mix at some point. The remainder of this chapter assumes that you want to connect two or more PCs by using wired Ethernet.

As mentioned previously, it's possible to use a special type of networking cable called a crossover cable to connect two PCs via Ethernet. However, this type of connection does not allow room for your network to grow. It isn't very flexible or reliable. It's more typical to place a special piece of networking hardware, typically a *hub* or *switch*, at the center of your network. These devices connect two or more PCs and physically form your network. You need one Ethernet cable running between the hub or switch and each network adapter (typically one per PC). So if you want to connect three PCs to the network, you need three Ethernet cables.

Both hubs and switches are plug and play when used with modern operating systems such as Windows XP. Simply make the physical connections and allow XP to use its default networking configuration, and your network will be up and running. The two main reasons to create such a network—to share an Internet connection and to share local resources such as files and printers—are covered in Chapters 6 and 8, respectively. Also, each PC should use the same *workgroup*, which is discussed "Working with Workgroups," later in this chapter.

Hubs and switches offer a range of Ethernet ports. Typically, they use four, five, or eight ports, but other sizes are available, and you can expand your network at any time by adding another hub or switch and by daisy-chaining them.

Working with Hubs

Hubs have historically been much cheaper than switches, but they lack one crucial feature. Instead of providing each PC with the maximum bandwidth afforded by Ethernet (typically 10 or 100 Mbps), hubs share that bandwidth among all the PCs on the network. This can lead to much slower speeds.

A few years ago, hubs made economic sense because they were so inexpensive when compared to switches. This is no longer the case, so if you have the choice, go with a switch.

Using Switches

Switches are basically more advanced hubs. They offer the full Ethernet bandwidth (again, either 10 or 100 Mbps) to each connection, making them more desirable than hubs. And because switch prices have dropped dramatically, there's no compelling reason to choose a hub over a switch.

Note that switches are sometimes marketed as routers or home networking routers.

Residential Gateways and Routers

With more people signing up for broadband Internet access such as cable modem or Digital Subscriber Line (DSL), the market for hardware devices that connect to these connections and create home networks has exploded. Such devices are typically called residential gateways or residential routers. They are designed to interface a home network with the outside world of the Internet. They offer an outbound Ethernet connection for the broadband connection and several Ethernet ports for your home network. They're like switches with additional functionality.

Connecting a Home Network to an External Network

You can connect a home network to an external network like the Internet two ways:

♦ **Using a PC as the gateway:** Your internal home network uses a hub or switch to connect each PC. One PC acts as the Internet gateway and thus has two network adapters, one for the Internet network and one for the broadband (or dial-up) connection. Such a network requires a simple switch, router, or hub.

♦ **Using a residential gateway:** Your internal home network uses a dedicated residential gateway that acts as both the Internet gateway and the internal network hub. The theory is the same as using a PC to do both functions as described above.

The Next Generation: Working with UPnP Devices

Beginning in early 2002, a new generation of residential gateways began appearing. These devices are compatible with Universal Plug and Play (UPnP), a new networking technology that lets devices "announce" themselves on the network to other UPnP-compatible devices, including Windows XP PCs. If you use a Windows XP–based PC as your Internet gateway, it's UPnP-compatible, and the connection can be configured from any other UPnP device, including another XP PC on the network.

Likewise, you can configure UPnP-compatible residential gateways directly from Windows XP PCs. To enable this feature, you have to install UPnP support, which is optional in XP. Here's how you install it:

1. Open the Control Panel and select Add or Remove Programs. The Add or Remove Programs window opens.

2. Select Add/Remove Windows Components. This launches the Windows Component Wizard.

3. In the Components list, select Networking Services and then click Details. The Networking Services dialog box appears, as shown in Figure 5-1.

4. Select Universal Plug and Play and then click OK.

5. Click Next to complete the wizard.

After the UPnP service is installed, you can configure any UPnP device on your own network by using Network Components. Each device presents its own UI. Most of the UPnP residential gateways I've seen recently have used Web-based UIs.

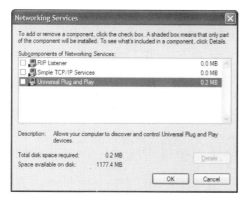

Figure 5-1: UPnP devices work with Windows XP automatically, but if you want to configure them, you need to install the UPnP service.

Network Setup Wizard — XP versus Manual Configuration

Realizing that setting up a home network was one of the most desirable yet difficult tasks that would face Windows XP users, Microsoft created a new wizard, the Network Setup Wizard, to handle this task. The Network Setup Wizard replaces two wizards from previous Windows versions, the Internet Connection Wizard and the Home Networking Wizard, which first appeared in Windows Me. As a result, you can handle numerous tasks, including:

◆ Configuring a shared Internet connection

◆ Setting up your Internet Connection Firewall (ICF)

◆ Sharing files, folders, and printers

The idea, as always, is simplification. Microsoft figured that a single all-purpose wizard could do the job because, after all, home networks and the Internet are both basically just networks.

Generally speaking, Microsoft had the right idea. But the Network Setup Wizard that ships in the initial version of Windows XP is pretty badly broken, with some components providing unexpected results and no way to back out of a change. So in this particular case, the Network Setup Wizard is largely unreliable, and I don't cover it in this book. I do not recommend that you use this tool to configure your home network.

Fortunately, configuring a home network is relatively easy, even if some of your machines are not running XP. Microsoft is working on an update to the home networking components in XP, which should ship after this book is available. I'll have more information about this update on the Web site for the book at www.xphomenetworking.com.

The other tasks offered by the Network Setup Wizard are also easy to set up and configure. You find out about sharing an Internet connection and ICF in Chapter 6, and sharing files, folders, and printers in Chapter 8.

Working with Workgroups

Microsoft's scheme for logically arranging computers on a small network is called a *workgroup*. It's an implementation of the classic peer-to-peer networking type, where each system on the network has equal billing and no central server exists. Typically, in a home network, you have just one workgroup — I call mine *thurrott* for obvious reasons. If you installed Windows XP Professional yourself, you were asked to specify your workgroup. XP Home Edition users don't have this option during setup; instead, Microsoft provides a default workgroup name of *mshome*. But you can change the workgroup name on a per-machine basis, regardless of which XP version you're using, so you'll probably want to make each machine in your home network part of the same workgroup. Here's how:

1. Open the Start menu, right-click My Computer, and choose Properties. This displays the System Properties dialog box.

2. Select the Computer Name tab, which should resemble Figure 5-2. This tab lists the following information:

   ■ The computer description, which can be a full sentence of English text

   ■ The full computer name, which is the machine name

   ■ The workgroup name

3. Enter a description for the computer if you want (for example, *Paul's PC*).

4. Click the Change button. The Computer Name Changes dialog box appears, as shown in Figure 5-3.

5. If necessary, enter a new computer name.

6. Select Workgroup and then enter the name of your workgroup.

7. Click OK, and you're welcomed to the new workgroup and then informed that you have to reboot the computer before the change takes effect. This is one of the few configuration changes in XP that requires a reboot.

8. Close the System Properties dialog box and reboot.

Figure 5-2: The System Properties dialog box lets you configure your network identification.

Figure 5-3: Changing the workgroup requires a reboot.

Thinking About Security

In January 2002, Microsoft announced a sweeping new security initiative called Trustworthy Computing, signaling a change in the way the company develops software. Previously, Microsoft had been driven by ease of use and features, offering consumers the most bang for their buck. But this emphasis caused a vast number of security exploits in various Microsoft products, and with complaints rising, the company finally did something about it.

As the most popular operating system in the world for both desktop and server systems, Windows is under constant attack from the outside world, and vulnerabilities are discovered almost weekly and then taken advantage of by enterprising hackers eager to embarrass the company.

As part of its Trustworthy Computing initiative, Microsoft's 9,000 software developers took at least a month off in early 2002 – some as long as three months – in order to be trained in the latest security development techniques. Then they tackled the company's core products, such as Windows and Office, and examined the code line by line, looking for vulnerabilities and bad coding practices. The results of this extensive code review will still be happening when you read these words, but the fruits of this effort began to appear in early 2002.

The first major update to Windows XP, Windows XP Service Pack 1 (SP1), will include all the fixes that came about as a result of the security code review. This update will ship in September or October 2002. For more information, please visit the Web site for this book at www.xphomenetworking.com.

While waiting for SP1 to be completed, you can do a number of things to keep your system up-to-date and as secure as possible.

Automatically Updating Windows XP

After you've booted into XP a couple of times, the system will prompt you with a feature called Automatic Updates. What this does is poll the Microsoft Windows Update Web site (see the next section) regularly in the background, looking for critical updates, such as security fixes and certain hardware driver updates that fix flaws that could compromise the reliability of your system.

Do *not* turn this feature off. Auto Update is your front line of defense against hackers and crackers, and best of all, it's fully automatic. Auto Update works in the background and pauses itself automatically if it detects that you need the download bandwidth. It's unlikely that you'll ever notice it's even running.

If you declined the original offer to use this feature, you can enable or reconfigure it later. Here's how:

1. Open the Start menu, right-click My Computer, and choose Properties. The System Properties window appears.

2. Select the Automatic Updates tab. Your display resembles Figure 5-4.

3. Under Notification Settings, select the setting you prefer. I recommend selecting the first option, Download the Updates Automatically and Notify Me When They Are Ready to Be Installed.

4. Click OK to close the dialog box.

If you enable this feature, Windows occasionally prompts you to install critical updates; these often require a reboot.

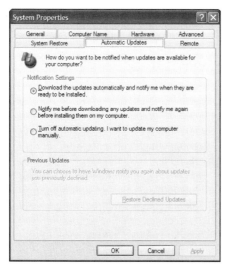

Figure 5-4: If you decide to reconfigure Automatic Updates, you can do so through the System Properties dialog box.

Using Windows Update

In addition to the critical updates provided by Automatic Updates, Microsoft hosts a special Windows Update Web site that provides XP users with regularly scheduled updates from a variety of categories, including security fixes/critical updates, Help file updates, compatibility fix updates, driver updates that are specific to your hardware, and more. You can visit Windows Update whenever you want; I usually check the site at least once a month.

To launch Windows Update (shown in Figure 5-5), open Internet Explorer and choose Tools→Windows Update. Alternatively, you can open Help and Support and choose the Keep Your Computer Up-to-Date with Windows Update option under Pick a Task.

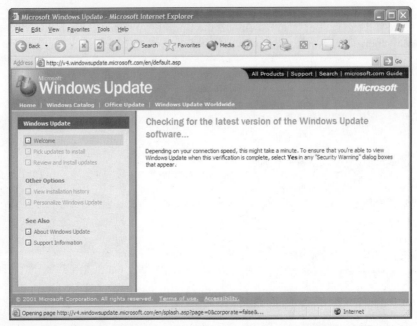

Figure 5-5: Windows Update is a central location for important Windows XP updates.

Using the Microsoft Baseline Security Analyzer

In late March 2002, Microsoft released an important security tool that all Windows XP users should download and run immediately. Dubbed the Microsoft Baseline Security Analyzer (MBSA), this tool looks for common security misconfigurations and presents a security report card with pass/fail grades, best-practice checks, and instructions for fixing any security issues discovered. MBSA also checks for security problems regarding Internet Information Services (IIS), SQL Server 7.0 and 2000, Internet Explorer (IE), and Office 2000 and XP. You can download the MBSA at the Web site for this book: www.xphomenetworking.com.

Chapter 6

Sharing an Internet Connection

YOUR INTERNET CONNECTIONS AND home network facilitate all of the wonderful things you can do with home networking technology. After the connections are in place, it's time to begin taking advantage of those connections, primarily in the form of resource sharing. And the most important resource you can share is your Internet connection.

With a shared Internet connection, all the machines on your home network can access the Web, instant messaging, e-mail, and all the other services that are available online. Internet-based gaming is also possible, with a few caveats.

In this chapter, you find out how to share your Internet connection through a Windows XP box and with hardware solutions. You also find out about the security concerns that should be addressed with such setups.

Looking at Connection Sharing

The concept of sharing an Internet connection dates back a few years to a low-level technology called *Network Address Translation* (NAT). This technology was designed to overcome the limitations of IP addressing, in that it became apparent by the mid-1990s that the number of free IP addresses would soon be depleted by the Internet. As a result, certain ranges of IP addresses were put aside solely for internal use at corporations and homes. These private, internal IP addresses can't see the outside world – the Internet – without being somehow translated into a more typical external IP address.

Enter NAT, a network service that sits on the edge machine of a network and translates private, internal IP addresses into a single external IP address, and vice versa. First used in servers, and then later in desktop machines for home networking use, the NAT service typically presents a single IP address to the outside world, obscuring the number of machines located internally. And it routes external and internal requests properly, ensuring that machines on the home network can interact seamlessly with Internet services.

There are disadvantages to NAT, however. Because each machine on a home network is not seen as a unique Internet host, some Internet services will not work properly through a NAT connection. However, many NAT devices, including home gateways and even PC operating systems such as Windows XP, can forward certain requests to certain local machines if you want. So, for example, if you have a Web server on a particular machine on your home network, you can configure your NAT device to forward Web server requests to the proper machine. But other services cannot be fooled so easily.

Most online games, such as Quake and Half-Life, require that clients have unique IP addresses. In such cases, only one machine on a home network can typically participate in any given online game at one time.

Introducing Internet Connection Sharing (ICS)

Microsoft first added simple NAT capabilities to its desktop operating systems as *Internet Connection Sharing (ICS)*. ICS was introduced with Windows 98 Second Edition (SE), and also appeared in Windows 2000 Professional, in Windows Millennium Edition (Me), and now, in Windows XP.

ICS is basically a super-simple front end to NAT. In fact, it's so simple that one check box in the user interface can enable it. After ICS is enabled, you can share an Internet connection from your XP machine among all the other machines on your home network.

For ICS to work, you need at least two network connections.

◆ A modem connection or network interface card (NIC), which is physically connected to your phone line or broadband connection. This connection manages the internet connection component.

◆ A connection to your internal network, typically through a hub or switch. This connection manages the connection between the different computers. So, each computer on the network uses this connection to get to the computer which is managing the internet through the first network connection listed above.

This ICS configuration is shown in Figure 6-1.

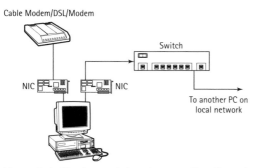

Figure 6-1: Sharing an Internet connection through
a Windows XP PC.

To set up and configure Internet Connection Sharing, you must first ensure that
your physical connections are correct. Then open up Network Connections by clicking Start and then right-clicking My Network Places and selecting Properties. The
Network Connections window shows you all the connections that are present in
your system, including any modem connections, NICs (wired or wireless), or
FireWire/IEEE-1394 adapters, as shown in Figure 6-2.

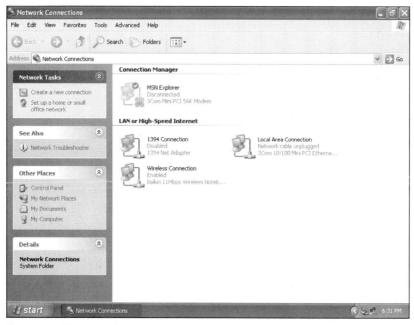

Figure 6-2: Networks Connections includes any connections, including modem, LAN,
broadband, and even FireWire/IEEE-1394.

By default, Windows XP provides simple names to each of the network connections. If you have two NICs, for example, they will be named Local Area Connection and Local Area Connection 2, which aren't very descriptive. So you should rename these, as discussed in Chapter 5. I recommend names such as Cable Modem Connection for your external Internet connection.

Chapter 5 also discusses the specific configuration for each connection, but that bears a short recap. The Internet connection will be configured according to the dictates of the connection.

◆ If it's a modem, then it's probably all set and doesn't need much further configuration beyond the initial setup (which is covered in Chapter 2).

◆ If it's a broadband account, then the connection could be set up via DHCP for dynamic addressing or with a static IP address, depending on your Internet service provider (ISP); check with your ISP for details.

Internal connections are typically configured for dynamic addressing. If you're using a Windows XP PC as your edge device, your XP-based PCs will be able to supply their own IP addresses. If you have other client machines, their capabilities will depend on which operating system they're running. Typically, Windows 9x/Me versions require static IP addresses; I discuss this configuration in Chapter 5.

Windows XP adds one cool ICS feature that wasn't present in previous Windows versions. Using XP, it's possible to let other XP boxes (or other clients that are compatible with a technology called *Universal Plug and Play,* or UPnP) configure a shared Internet connection remotely. Other XP users see an Internet Connection icon in their Network Connections window that optionally allows them to configure the connection as if there PC was directly connected to the Internet, instead of using a shared connection by the network. This is shown in Figure 6-3.

Why would you want to allow such a thing? Well, say you've got a broadband connection and you don't want to leave it on at night when no one should be using it. If you're upstairs in bed accessing the connection remotely from a wireless-enabled laptop, and you're ready to go to sleep, you have to get out of bed, walk to the Internet-connected machine and disable the connection. Using XP, you can do this from the laptop, without getting up. Good stuff.

After the connections are properly configured, you can enable Internet Connection Sharing by following these steps:

1. Open Network Connections if it's not open.

2. Right-click the connection you want to share, which will be a modem or broadband connection, and select Properties.

3. Click the Advanced tab. As shown in Figure 6-4, you see options for Internet Connection Sharing.

4. Select the option titled Allow Other Network Users to Connect through This Computer's Internet Connection.

5. If you'd like other users to be able to configure the connection remotely, select the option titled Allow Other Network Users to Control or Disable the Shared Internet Connection.

6. Click OK to close the dialog box.

After you've made this simple configuration change, the connection is shared. You don't need to reboot and neither do the client machines. To test the shared connection, try to access the Internet from your edge machine and any other PCs on the home network.

 If the connection doesn't work, you've got a configuration problem, probably on the client machines. When you enable ICS on a Windows XP box, it automatically configures the other NIC as the local gateway, so there's little you could do to fudge the sharing. Check the TCP/IP settings on the client machines to make sure they're configured properly. And when in doubt, try a reboot: It shouldn't be required, but we're talking about Windows here.

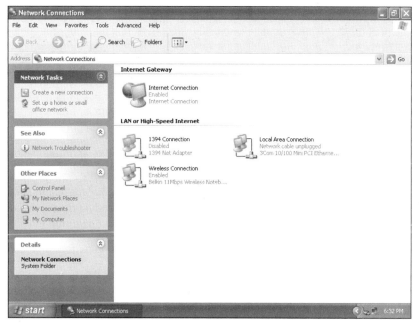

Figure 6-3: If you choose to let other users see and configure a shared Internet Connection, it appears in their Network Connections as an Internet Gateway.

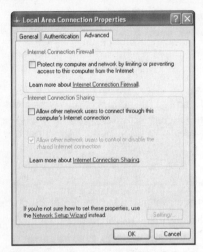

Figure 6-4: The Advanced tab of a network connection contains options for configuring Internet Connection Sharing.

Hardware Sharing Solutions

For some people, using a Windows XP–based PC as the edge machine isn't practical. There are many reasons why you wouldn't want a PC on the edge of your network. There are security concerns, and the whole network loses its Internet connection if the edge PC isn't running. In these instances, a hardware solution, such as a home gateway or broadband router, can be used to shield the home network from the outside world and provide NAT/Internet Connection Sharing capabilities.

There are some issues you should know about before you choose a home gateway for an XP system.

◆ XP includes support for a new generation of services that require technologies called *Universal Plug and Play* (UPnP) and *Session Initiation Protocol* (SIP). Most of the gateways sold before 2002 are incompatible with these crucial technologies, though a few of them can be upgraded to add such support.

TIP

For a hardware sharing solution that uses XP to its fullest, you need a gateway or router that is UPnP capable. Otherwise, you can't use such features as file sharing, Remote Desktop, Remote Assistance, and application sharing. Chapter 5 covers UPnP and SIP in detail.

◆ UPnP-compatible gateways and routers can be controlled by XP boxes in the manner discussed in the previous section. So if you want to enable the ability to turn off a broadband Internet connection remotely, for example, you need an UPnP-compatible hardware sharing solution.

Assuming you use a UPnP capable device, configuration is generally pretty simple. The hardware device will have at least two Ethernet *ports,* or connections (one for the broadband adapter and one for the internal network). More advanced units support four or more network connections so that you don't need a separate hub or switch, and some units even include integrated wireless capabilities, supplying three crucial services all in one device.

For more information about UPnP devices, check out the Web site for this book (www.xphomenetworking.com) and Connected Home Magazine (www.connected homemag.com), a magazine I write for that examines home networking issues regularly.

Working with Firewalls

Large corporations use a hardware device called a *firewall* to protect internal networks from outside problems, including unwanted network traffic and other more targeted Internet-based attacks. But with the proliferation of broadband Internet connections, home users also need protection from Internet-borne attacks. So the hardware firewalls of the past have been downsized into software applications that are now available on PCs.

Like its namesake, the firewall is your first line of defense against a problem. Hackers and "script-kiddies" have proliferated on the Internet, and they're targeting unprotected PCs and home networks that are connected via broadband accounts. A firewall keeps unwanted network traffic out of your home network, while allowing the users behind the firewall to get their work done and access network services. Like NAT, a firewall sits on the edge box. And like NAT, a firewall can run on either a Windows XP-based PC or a hardware sharing solution (like a broadband router).

If you're using XP as your edge box, a firewall will conceptually resemble Figure 6-5.

Because many XP users will connect to the Internet with a broadband connection, Microsoft built a simple firewall into XP. Dubbed *Internet Connection Firewall (ICF),* the XP firewall provides basic security for any XP machine, even if it's not the edge machine. I recommend enabling it, at the very least, on the edge machine.

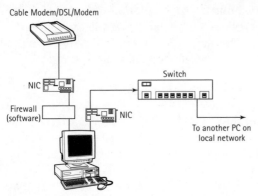

Figure 6-5: A software firewall prevents attackers from getting at your internal network.

 ICF is better than nothing. But ICF offers only *one-way* protection against remote attacks, because it monitors only incoming traffic. Your PC can be attacked through other means, such as an e-mail- or instant messaging-delivered virus, and then used as a "zombie" to attack remote servers. To better protect your PC and home network, look into third-party firewall products (which are discussed in the next section) and antivirus software (such as Norton AntiVirus or McAfee VirusScan).

Using and Configuring the Internet Connection Firewall (ICF)

Like Internet Connection Sharing, Internet Connection Firewall is enabled with a single check box; set it and forget it. To enable ICF, perform the following tasks:

1. Open Network Connections.

2. Right-click the connection that you'd like to protect and select Properties.

3. Click the Advanced tab.

4. Check the option under Internet Connection Firewall, as shown in Figure 6-6, then click OK.

Third-Party XP Firewalls

If you're looking for a bit more firewall security, consider a third-party firewall, such as Zone Alarm (www.zonealarm.com) or BlackICE Defender (www.iss.net). XP's Internet Connection Firewall feature is extensible. If you're using XP as the edge device on your home network, consider a software solution that integrates with the operating system at this deep level. Zone Alarm is one such product.

Firewall software is not for the casual user, though the companies plying this trade have certainly made ease-of-use headway over the years. I recommend checking trial versions of these applications before committing your hard-earned dollars.

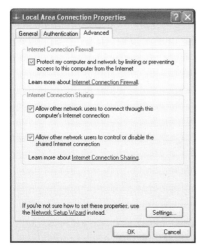

Figure 6-6: Like ICS, Internet Connection Firewall is a configure-free option.

 Firewall products often block traffic that you want, such as instant messages and shared files. You might need to perform some serious configuration before they're running exactly the way you want.

ZONE ALARM

Free for personal use, Zone Alarm can stop certain e-mail viruses and provide PC protection through its firewall feature. A version of Zone Alarm, called Zone Alarm Pro, adds dozens of other features, including better e-mail protection, Internet ad blocking, browser cookie protection, hacker intrusion tracking, and more. Zone Alarm Pro is not a free product. One particularly nifty feature, called Blocked Zone, allows you to block individual IP addresses or IP ranges from your local network. This can prevent nuisance Web sites and known hackers from getting to you.

BLACKICE DEFENDER

Aimed at consumers and small offices, Internet Security Systems' BlackICE Defender line provides intrusion detection, protection, and monitoring features. BlackICE monitors all network traffic, providing superior firewall capabilities and a hacker sleuth feature that tracks hackers back to the source. Unlike Zone Alarm, ISS doesn't offer a free BlackICE version, but you can download evaluation software to test before purchasing.

Playing Multiplayer Games Online

One problem you may face with multiplayer games such as Quake III Arena and Half-Life Counter-Strike is that they require each player to have a unique IP address. If you're hitting a game server from behind a NAT device, such as a Windows XP PC, only one such connection is allowed. Other users on your home network can't play the same online game using an Internet-based game server. If a second user connects to the same game server, the first user is disconnected.

For most people, this isn't particularly limiting. You can still host internal game servers and have LAN gaming parties. And local network users could access different online game servers at the same time (one on Quake III Arena and another on Half-Life, for example).

If more than one user must use the same server at the same time, contact your ISP about getting additional IP addresses. Most cable Internet suppliers will allow you to configure other IP addresses at a cost of less than $10 a month. Some DSL providers actually give out packages of up to 5 IPs per connection. If you go this route, you will probably need to manually configure individual NICs with static IP addresses. Contact your ISP for details.

Chapter 7

Working with Users and Passwords

IN THIS CHAPTER

- ◆ Understanding how XP handles multiple users

- ◆ Learn how to manage and configure users

- ◆ Logging on and off with users as well as using the new Fast User switching feature

WHEN MICROSOFT FIRST STARTED designing Windows XP, its plan was to move its consumer-oriented products to the NT code base. With Windows NT/2000 products commonplace in corporations around the world, Microsoft's business customers were familiar with concepts like users, logons, and passwords. But in the home, where Windows 9*x* products dominated, these concepts were considerably less widespread.

The goal was simple: Windows XP had to retain the security features of previous NT versions while making it easy for home users to get into the operating system and get work done. The *granular* security subsystem in NT/2000 was far too complicated for home users, so it was considerably cut back in XP Home Edition. XP Professional, on the other hand, retains the previous, more powerful security model.

Because most people will be using Home Edition, this chapter focuses on that version. However, I point out where Professional differs from Home Edition in its handling of users, passwords, user groups, and related topics. Whichever edition you use, understanding these topics will keep your PCs and the vital data they house safe from others.

XP Is a Multiuser Environment

Unlike previous consumer-oriented Windows versions, Windows XP supports multiple users. In days past, Windows 9x was designed to handle only a single user, where one user used one PC. If family members wanted used the same PC, they had to share the same desktop, the same color and graphical settings, and the same installed applications.

Multiuser in Windows 9x/Me

By default, Windows 9x operating systems, such as Windows 95, 98, 98 SE, and Millennium Edition (Me), operate in single-user mode. The desktop folder is located in C:\Windows\Desktop by default, and user customization features are stored in various locations under the C:\Windows directory structure. This setup works fine for single users or multiple users who don't mind sharing a system.

For Windows 9x users who want something more sophisticated, Microsoft offers a relatively hidden feature called Multiple User Profiles. Enabling this feature adds multiple user features to Windows 9x and provides users with their own desktops, Start menus, documents lists, and other personalized features. Third-party programs that are savvy to this feature — and there aren't many, to be honest, though Microsoft's Office suite does work this way — can save different settings for different users. When you enable this feature, users are asked to log on to use the PC. Multiple User Profiles has flaws:

◆ It was retrofitted to an operating system that has no underlying concept of security. Anyone can walk up to a Windows 9x machine, press Esc when it asks for a password, and gain access to a desktop and any of the features of the underlying system.

◆ It's almost impossible to find. Unless you really know what you're doing, you'd be hard pressed to stumble on to this feature in the Windows 9x UI.

But Multiple User Profiles was at least based on a good idea: the user logon system provided by Windows NT/2000. Under these operating systems, there is no default desktop, and users can't log on without a valid username. Instead, NT 4 provides a Profiles directory structure (C:\WINNT/Profiles by default) that maintains personalized folders for each user. In Windows 2000, this directory structure was moved to the more logical C:\Documents and Settings location. Under Documents and Settings, you find a folder for each user that's been set up on the system (Paul, Steph, and so on). And under these folders, you will find locations such as Desktop, Favorites, My Documents, and the like.

Today, multiple user support is all the more relevant because of the emergence of home networks, which bring with them concepts such as *authentication* and *access privileges*. With a single-user system, a logon and related password aren't necessary because users don't need to be authenticated to establish their credentials. However, on a network — home-based or otherwise — authentication is key. So a multiuser operating system such as Windows XP becomes all the more important.

XP's multiuser features are derived from those in Windows NT and 2000. Each user is granted a personalized environment.

New Multiuser Features in XP

Windows XP continues the multiuser functionality found in Windows 2000. It segregates individual user folders into the C:\Documents and Settings folder structure by default. XP also includes a number of user-based improvements. Most of these improvements are aimed at home users. These improvements include

◆ **Password Recovery:** When you first set up your password in Windows XP, you are prompted to optionally enter a password hint, which can help you later if you forget your password and need help. Also, XP lets you create a Password Reset Disk that helps you get into a locked account and change the password. You should obviously store such a disk in a secure location. The Password Recovery feature is covered in "Recovering a Lost Password," later in this chapter.

◆ **Simple Sharing:** Windows XP features a new dumbed-down file sharing scheme called *Simple File Sharing.* By default, it replaces the more powerful (but potentially difficult) file sharing feature used by Windows 2000. You can turn off this feature, thankfully.

◆ **Fast User Switching:** In previous Windows versions, you had to log off before another user could log on and access his or her customized environment. XP bypasses this need with a new feature called *Fast User Switching* that allows two or more XP users to be logged on simultaneously. Only one user is visible at a time, but the other users remain active in the background. For more on this feature, check out "Using Fast User Switching," later in this chapter.

◆ **.NET Passport integration:** If you're interested in an automated integration with Microsoft's .NET services, you can optionally configure your logon to simultaneously log you on to a .NET Passport account when you first start using your PC each day. This somewhat-useful feature is covered in Chapter 11.

◆ **Stored User Names and Passwords:** Many Web sites require you to log on before you can access protected content. In previous Windows versions, you would store your logon and password for these sites through Internet Explorer, which wasn't exactly the most secure method. In Windows XP, this is no longer allowed, although you can add sites you trust to IE's Trusted Sites list, as explained in Chapter 12. But XP also offers a *Stored User Names and Passwords* feature that lets you manage network passwords from a central, if well-hidden, location.

Compared to Windows 9.x, the multiuser features in Windows XP might come as a bit of a shock to users. You must set up at least one user account before you can use XP. Curiously, this account can be (and is) set up without a password. I think this is a huge mistake, so I cover the process of setting up passwords later in this chapter. If you configure XP with just one user account and no password, your XP system boots directly into your desktop, without requiring you to enter a password. However, until you enter a password, you won't be able to access network shares and other resources without some serious convolution that's barely worth discussing.

 Don't even *think* about using XP without a password. You need to create at least one user account, with an associated password, before you can use XP to its fullest. User accounts are the basis for security authentication in Windows XP. if you set up an account without a password, you're denying yourself access to certain services and opening up your system to possible attack.

Understanding Users and Security

Windows XP's user accounts are the starting point for protecting your PC and protecting your personal data. Here a few reasons why you should set up a user account:

◆ **To protect your vital personal files from your children.** Kids usually mean well, but they're often unwittingly destructive. By providing them with their own limited logon accounts, you can be sure that they will not be able to access (or destroy) your private data.

◆ **To protect personal data from other users.** Trusting your personal data to a family member is one thing, but the last thing you want is an outside – a hacker, perhaps – from accessing your data and deleting it, either inadvertently or purposefully. XP's user accounts are the basis for preventing this from happening.

Adding and Configuring Users

In Windows XP Home Edition (and Professional Edition in a home setting), you configure users through the User Accounts control panel, a new Web-style application, or task-based activity center, which supersedes the ugly old Local Users and Groups control panel from Windows 2000. To access User Accounts, shown in Figure 7-1, choose Start→Control Panel→User Accounts.

 If you're a former NT/2000 user and prefer to access user account settings the old-fashioned way, you can do so through the Computer Management console. Right-click My Computer and choose Manage. Then locate user information by clicking System Tools and then Local Users and Groups. This tip only applies to Windows XP Professional.

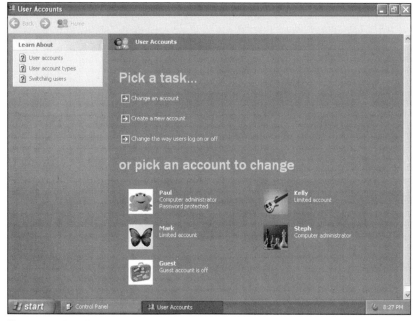

Figure 7-1: In Windows XP, you manage users and passwords from the User Accounts control panel.

The User Accounts control panel lets you add new users, configure existing users, and change the way users log on and off. What you see here depends on

- ◆ Which users you created when you first installed Windows XP
- ◆ Which users were created when you installed certain applications (developer-oriented applications such as Visual Studio .NET and SQL Server 2000 create user accounts automatically).
- ◆ Which type of user account you have. Limited users only see options for their own accounts and not options for other accounts.

    In this book, I assume that you have a non-limited account type.

You will also see a Guest account, which is a built-in account that is disabled by default. For more on this account, see "Using the Guest account," later in this chapter.

Adding a New User

To add a new user after Windows XP is installed, follow these steps:

1. Launch User Accounts by choosing Start→Control Panel→User Accounts.

2. Select Create a New Account. This opens the screen shown in Figure 7-2.

3. Enter a user account name and then click Next. You now see the screen shown in Figure 7-3.

4. Select an account type. Your choices are Computer Administrator or Limited:

   ■ A computer administrator can do just about anything on the machine, including installing applications and hardware, making changes to the system that affect all users, accessing and changing all non-private files, creating and deleting other user accounts, changing other user accounts, changing account names or types, changing account pictures, or creating, changing, or removing passwords.

   ■ Limited users, as you might expect, are more limited. They can change their own account picture and password. But they cannot change their account name or type, install applications or hardware, make changes to the system that affect all users, access and change all non-private files, create and delete other user accounts, or change other user accounts.

5. Click Next to create the account. The account then shows up on the main User Accounts window with a random account picture.

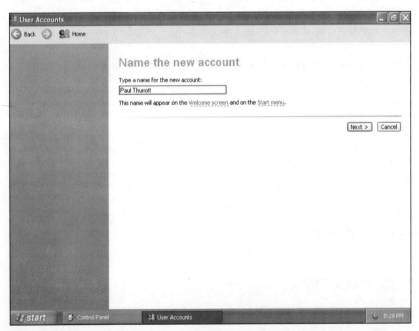

Figure 7-2: When creating a new user account, you must first enter a name for the account.

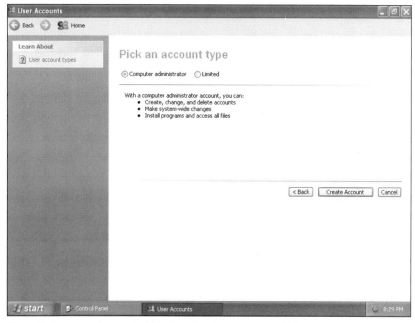

Figure 7-3: . . . and then decide what the account type will be.

Windows XP Professional supports other account types, which are generally only of interest to users in corporate settings or to users upgrading from Windows 2000 Professional Edition. If you must access the Computer Management console in XP Pro (right-click My Computer and choose Manage), you can change a user account to one of these account types:

◆ Administrators

◆ Backup Operators

◆ Guests

◆ HelpServicesGroup

◆ Network Configuration Operators

◆ Power Users

◆ Remote Desktop Users

◆ Replicators

◆ Users

Users with Computer Administrator access are given rights from the Administrators and Users account types once they log in. Limited users are members only of the Users account type.

Managing Users

To manage an existing user account, select that user account from the User Accounts application. You're presented with the list of choices shown in Figure 7-4.

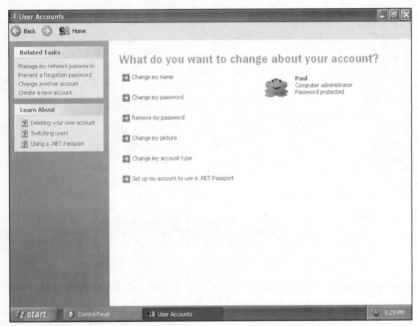

Figure 7-4: Computer administrators can change various attributes for any account, whereas Limited users can only change certain attributes for their own account.

Here, you can perform the following tasks:

♦ **Change your name:** The username you chose when you first set up your account is set in stone, but you can change the *display name,* which is used on the top of the Start menu and on the Welcome screen. So if you chose fairly boring account names like *paul1* or *steph2,* you can rename them after the fact and make them more friendly (*Paul Thurrott* or *Poopie*). To do this, select Change My Name and then enter a new name, as shown in Figure 7-5.

♦ **Set up or change your password:** To set up or change your password, select the Change My Password option on this screen. Passwords are discussed in more detail in the next section.

♦ **Remove your password:** I strongly recommend that you do not remove a password from your account. However, if you want to remove your password, select Remove My Password and then enter your current password. You then see the screen shown in Figure 7-6.

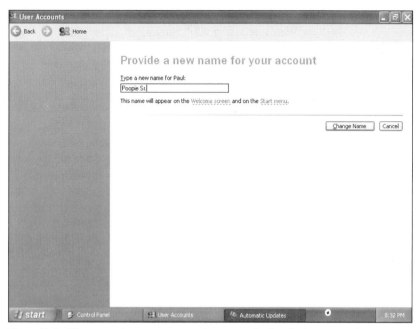

Figure 7-5: When you change an account name, only the display name changes; the actual account name remains the same.

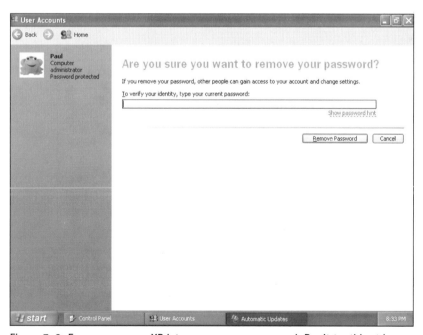

Figure 7-6: For some reason, XP lets you remove a password. Don't try this at home.

◆ **Change your picture:** To change the picture that appears next to your account name on the Welcome screen and Start menu, select Change My Picture. You then see the screen shown in Figure 7-7. You can select from the stock images supplied by Microsoft or find a photo of yourself or some other image you prefer.

I use photographs to differentiate users, as shown in Figure 7-8. This personalizes the system and makes the Welcome screen look cool.

◆ **Change your account type:** If your user account is a Computer Administrator, you can choose Change My Account Type and change the account to a Limited account type if you want. Note that Limited users cannot change their account to the Computer Administrator account type. However, any user with Computer Administrator privileges can change the account type for any other user.

There's one caveat with account types: You must always have one user with Computer Administrator privileges. Windows XP won't let you remove this account type if there is only one account using it.

◆ **Set up or change your .NET Passport:** You can tie your Windows logon to a .NET Passport account, which is convenient if you think you'll use the feature. See Chapter 11 for the details.

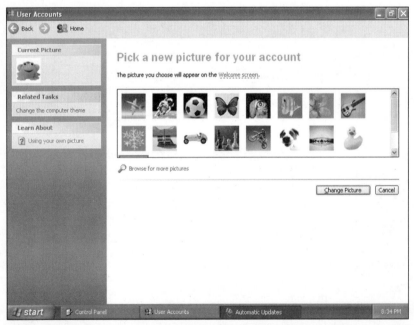

Figure 7-7: When you select a new picture, you can choose one supplied by Microsoft or one of your own.

Figure 7-8: Have your way with the Welcome screen. This stuff is supposed to be fun.

Using Passwords

I've said it before, and I'll say it again: Your Windows XP system is virtually unprotected if you do not use passwords. Furthermore, you cannot access many of XP's connection features, including the ability to use shared network resources, unless you set up a password for your account.

Curiously, XP doesn't require you to create a password when you first create users during XP Setup. Nor does it do so if you add users later through the User Accounts control panel. I have a huge problem with this, and though I've broached the topic with the Microsoft folks, the response I've gotten back is that some of their customers cannot have passwords, so they can't enforce this kind of rule. However, they could at least make it more difficult for users to create a password-less account rather than make it hard to add a password to an account, which is the current situation.

You can add a password to your own account – or other accounts, if you have Computer Administrator privileges – through the User Accounts control panel. Here's how to add and change passwords:

1. In User Accounts, select the user for which you'd like to add a password.

2. On the next page, select Create a Password. (This option is called Change the Password if you've created a password previously and you want to change it now).

3. On the next page, shown in Figure 7-9, enter your new password. You must enter it twice to confirm that you entered it correctly. Otherwise, you might not be able to log on to the system later.

4. If you want, enter a password hint, which can be any line of text that will help you remember your password in the event that you forget it. When you enter a password hint, an extra question mark button appears next to your name in the Welcome screen. When you click this button, your password hint appears in a little balloon help window, as shown in Figure 7-10.

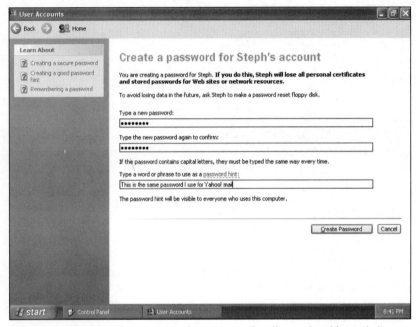

Figure 7-9: When creating a password, you can optionally supply a hint to help you remember it later.

Figure 7-10: When you set up a password hint, it's accessible from the Welcome screen.

RECOVERING A LOST PASSWORD

Windows XP gives you the option of creating a password reset disk for your account. You can't do this for other accounts, even if you're a Computer Administrator. (Limited account users cannot create password reset disks.) This incredibly insecure feature is a nod toward the consumer crowd, which could be left for a loop given the otherwise secure nature of Windows XP. The password reset disk lets you boot your XP system normally and then use a specially made floppy disk to delete your password. You can then log on without a password and create a new one that you (hopefully) won't forget.

If you choose to create such a disk, be sure to store it in a safe place. Otherwise, anyone can boot your system, reset your password, and gain access to your private data.

CREATING A PASSWORD RESET DISK   If you still think the password reset feature is a good one, here's how to enable it:

1. From User Accounts, select your user account.

2. From the Related Tasks section in the left side of the window, choose Prevent a Forgotten Password. This launches the Forgotten Password Wizard, shown in Figure 7-11.

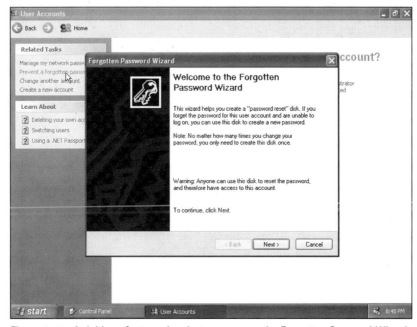

Figure 7-11: A dubious feature aimed at consumers, the Forgotten Password Wizard is best left alone.

3. Click Next and then choose which drive will be used to create the password reset disk. Normally, you use a floppy disk, but some removable disks work as well. CD-type disks, including recordable CDs, don't work, however.

4. Enter the password for the current account and click Next. The wizard then creates the disk.

5. Store the disk in a safe place.

USING THE PASSWORD RESET DISK   If you forget your password, you can use the password reset disk to get into XP. Here's how:

1. Turn on your PC.

2. On the Welcome screen, select your user account and click the green arrow next to the password input box. You then see an option to use your password reset disk, as shown in Figure 7-12. This option appears only if you have created such a disk.

3. Click this password reset disk option, and the Password Reset Wizard appears, as shown in Figure 7-13. This wizard guides you through the process of resetting your password.

4. When prompted, enter a new password and, optionally, a new password hint, as shown in Figure 7-14.

5. The wizard then changes your XP password, as well as the information on the password reset disk so that you don't have to make a new copy later.

6. Log on to Windows XP by using your new password.

7. Store the password reset disk in a safe location.

Figure 7-12: If you created a password reset disk, you can access it from the Welcome screen if you forget your password.

Figure 7-13: The Password Reset Wizard guides you through the process of creating a new password.

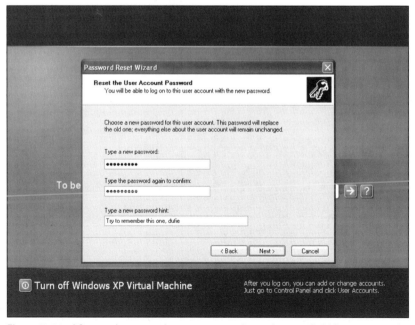

Figure 7-14: After you've created a new password — or, heaven forbid, no password — you can log on to Windows again.

PASSWORDS AND NETWORK CONNECTIONS

One of the most potentially confusing "features" in XP is actually designed to save you from yourself. Unlike previous Windows versions, Windows XP doesn't automatically save passwords you enter for network resources or Internet Web sites by default. (Authenticated network resources – those resources that accept your XP logon and password – do not need to be saved.) However, you can use a feature called Stored User Names and Passwords to store any logon/password combinations that you consider safe.

In previous Windows versions, you could just check a Please Remember This Password check box, and Windows would actually remember it. In Windows XP, this doesn't work, but a lot of software (such as Internet Explorer and FrontPage 2002, for example) hasn't caught on yet. The net effect is that you might believe the application when it says it's going to remember your username and password. It won't.

But you can make it remember such things, if you have a Computer Administrator account. Here's how:

1. In User Accounts, select your account.

2. In the Related Tasks pane on the left, select the Manage My Network Passwords option. This launches the Stored User Names and Passwords application, shown in Figure 7-15. Here, you see any network or Internet-related sites that previously required you to authenticate with a user account/password combination that differs from what you use to log on to your XP machine (such as your .NET Passport account). You can also add and remove locations if you'd like.

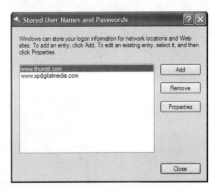

Figure 7-15: The Stored User Names and Passwords application lets you save authentication information for network and Internet resources.

Here are your options in this dialog box:

- **Add a stored username and password:** Click the Add button to display the Logon Information Properties dialog box, shown in Figure 7-16. This is where you enter the name of the server (a local machine name, such as *goldeneye,* or an Internet address such as *http://yourserver.com*), and the username and password you use to access that resource.

- **Remove a stored username and password:** Click the Remove button.

- **Modify an existing stored username and password:** Select the location and then click the Properties button. On this dialog box, you can change your stored username or password.

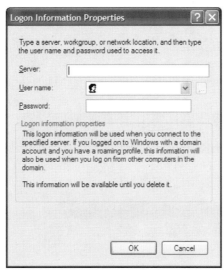

Figure 7-16: When you add a new location to store, XP asks for its location and your username and password information.

Configuring a User Picture

One fun thing you can do with user accounts in Windows XP is assign personalized images to each account. XP ships with a number of images, and one is assigned randomly to each user account. You can change this image to any image, including a photograph. I've created customized logon images for each member of my family, which makes for a cool-looking Welcome screen. Here's how you do it:

1. In User Accounts, select the account for which you'd like to change the account picture. (Limited account users can only change their own picture.)

2. On the User Options page, select Change My Picture or Change the Picture. You then see the default account pictures that ship in XP, as shown in Figure 7-17.

3. Select an image from the gallery, or if you'd like to select another image, click Browse for More Pictures. The Browse button launches a standard Open dialog box, which you can use to navigate to your picture or photo files. Find something fun and experiment a bit.

4. If you find a picture from the gallery that you like, select Change Picture. After you choose pictures for all your users, you'll have a fun, customized Welcome screen, like the one shown in Figure 7-18.

Figure 7-17: The images in the default account picture gallery aren't bad, but you can do better.

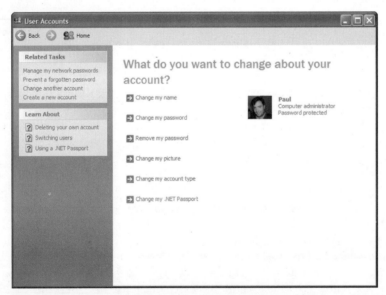

Figure 7-18: Customized photos personalize your system and logon.

Using the Guest Account

Windows XP ships with a special user account named Guest, which is enabled by default. You can use this account to grant users temporary access to your system so they can browse the Web and check their e-mail. The Guest account is quite limited, so users can't access your private data files or settings.

To enable the Guest account, open User Accounts, select Guest, and then select Turn On the Guest Account. After your visitors have left, repeat these steps to disable the Guest account.

Using the Welcome Screen

The friendly Windows XP Welcome screen is a radical departure from previous Windows versions, which offered only a stark Log On to Windows dialog box when the system first booted up. The Windows XP Welcome screen is a bit less secure than the Log On to Windows dialog box because it displays the names of most users. In a family setting, this doesn't really matter. The Welcome screen also facilitates a cool new XP feature, *Fast User Switching*. In this section, you find out about XP's Welcome screen–related features.

LOGGING ON TO WINDOWS XP
The Welcome screen provides a launching pad for users to log on to XP. When you log on, you're presented with your custom desktop and other personalized settings. More importantly, you are authenticated, and the system passes your credentials along when you attempt to access network resources.

LOGGING OFF
When you're done using XP, you can log off the system and return to the Welcome screen. There are two log off methods in XP:

- ◆ A normal logoff, in which all your applications are closed and the memory used by your session is returned to the system

- ◆ Fast User Switching, which is described in the next section

Only one user account can interactively use Windows XP at a time, so you must log off before another user can log on and access his or her personalized settings.

USING FAST USER SWITCHING
With Windows XP, you can use a new feature called Fast User Switching to switch users, rather than log off and log on as before. This returns XP to the Welcome screen; in the background, your previous account is still logged on and active. This means that all the applications you have launched are still running (and consuming memory, though XP is pretty good about doling out this resource effectively).

To see how Fast User Switching works, try the following (which requires two Computer Administrator user accounts):

1. Log on to one account, launch Windows Media Player, and play a CD.

2. Choose Start→Log Off. The Log Off Windows dialog box appears, as shown in Figure 7-19.

3. Select Switch User, and the Welcome screen appears. The music is still playing, and your user account notes that one application is still running, as shown in Figure 7-20.

4. Log on to another user account. Now, Windows Media Player stops playing the song, though Windows Media Player is still running in the background. To verify this, right-click a blank area of the taskbar and select Task Manager.

5. Select the Users tab in the Task Manager, as shown in Figure 7-21. You should see two active users.

6. Select the Processes tab and click the Show Processes from All Users option. You will see an entry for wmplayer.exe, even though the currently active user is not running Windows Media Player.

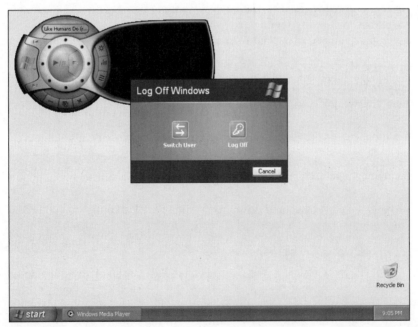

Figure 7-19. Windows XP introduces Fast User Switching, an alternative to logging off.

Figure 7-20: When a user is still logged on but not active, the Welcome screen notes that programs are running.

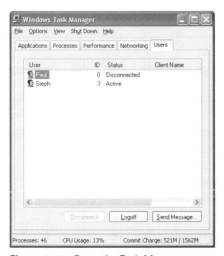

Figure 7-21: From the Task Manager, you can observe tasks running under your user account, or other user accounts.

CONFIGURING THE WELCOME SCREEN

You can configure various aspects of the Welcome screen from User Accounts. To do so, select Change The Way Users Log On and Off from the main User Accounts page. You then see two options, as shown in Figure 7-22: Use the Welcome Screen and Use Fast User Switching.

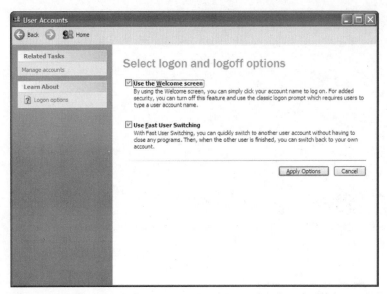

Figure 7-22: You can configure two main options related to the Welcome screen.

USE THE WELCOME SCREEN   When this option is selected, you use the Welcome screen to log on to Windows. If you deselect this option, the Welcome screen and the Fast User Switching feature are disabled.

When the Welcome screen is disabled, you use the old Log On to Windows dialog box to log on to Windows. This dialog box isn't as friendly as the Welcome screen; it only remembers the last used username, not the entire list of available users, for example. But it is a bit more secure because it doesn't list all the user accounts that are available on the system. However, this isn't normally a concern in a home setting.

USE FAST USER SWITCHING   You can selectively choose to enable Fast User Switching with the second option, which is available only when the Welcome screen is enabled. If you'd rather have people log off before another account can be accessed – perhaps on a system with less than 256MB of RAM (Fast User Switching often requires more memory) – then you can disable this feature here.

USING THE HIDDEN ADMINISTRATOR ACCOUNT

In addition to Guest, Windows XP Professional creates another special account, called Administrator, which is hidden by default.

The Administrator account is only in XP Pro systems. XP Home users don't have it.

When you set up Windows XP, you created a password for the Administrator account (you *did* create a password for this account, right?), and though the Administrator account doesn't appear in the Welcome screen, you can access it.

By default, Windows XP uses the friendly Welcome screen as a front end for user logon activities. But it's still possible to access the old logon dialog box, which was used with previous Windows versions. Or you can selectively disable the Welcome screen to access the Administrator account, which doesn't appear on the Welcome screen. Here's how:

1. From the Welcome screen, press Ctrl+Alt+Del twice. The Welcome screen then disappears and is replaced by the Log On to Windows dialog box.

2. In the User Name box, enter **Administrator**. Then enter the Administrator password and click OK to log on.

Chapter 8

Securely Sharing Network Resources

IN THIS CHAPTER

◆ Learn how to securely access resources on other computers attached to your network

◆ Browsing around the network with My Network Places

◆ Sharing resources and utilizing shared resources

◆ Accessing and using printers on the network

◆ Understanding how security in XP Home Edition differs from Windows 9x/Me and Windows NT/2000

AFTER YOUR USERS AND PASSWORDS are set up correctly on each machine on your home network, you can begin sharing resources. This is the beauty of a home network, of course: A PC is no longer an island of functionality.

The types of resources you might share depend on your needs. You might want to use a particular PC as a file or media server, or even a backup server, for example. Oftentimes, a particular printer is attached to a single PC, but you might need to print a document that was created on another system.

Whatever your needs, home networking makes it possible. This chapter examines the issues that arise when you want to share resources over a network, the types of resources you can share, and how you go about setting it all up.

Understanding Home Network Authentication

Users and passwords are crucial concepts to understanding network resource sharing. Your username and password determine what resources you can access.

Chapter 7 covers users and passwords.

XP supports two ways to authenticate your credentials on a home network:

◆ **Pass-through authentication:** Your Windows username and password are used to authorize access.

◆ **A more manual approach:** You can access network resources under the authorization of another username/password combination.

You find out about both approaches in the next few sections.

Using Pass-Through Authentication

In the default network authentication mode, you transparently use your Windows logon and password to access network resources. For this to work, you need to create an identical username/password combination on every machine on your home network in order to access those shares. That is, if you log on as paul with a password of abc123 on your own machine, you need to create such an identical account on every machine in your local workgroup.

When you configure your network this way, network access is very simple: No logon dialog boxes, no questions, no muss, no fuss.

In most home networking scenarios, pass-through authentication is the way to go.

Hand-Crafting Network Authentication

Automated pass-through is sometimes unwelcome, especially if you want to give your kids access to a PC with a shared printer, but not to a computer that has all of your digital music files. In this case, (and others like it) you can hard-code authentication on a *per-machine* basis by using the cunningly hidden Stored User Names and Passwords feature discussed in Chapter 7.

Here's how to use Stored User Names and Passwords to provide specific users with access only to specific network resources. Repeat these steps for each user for which you'd like to add some sort of network access:

1. On each PC, log on as the user for which you want to provide access (the user can be either a Computer Administrator or Limited user).

2. Open User Accounts, navigate to that user's profile, and select Manage My Network Passwords. The Stored User Names and Passwords application then launches.

3. Click Add to display the Logon Information Properties dialog box. Now, enter the name of the network resource for which you'd like to provide access. This can be a machine name (such as *goldeneye*) or even a specific resource on a machine (such as *goldeneye\documents*).

4. Now, add the username and password of a user that is set up on that machine. The username must take the form of *machine_name\user_name*, so if the username is *paul* and the machine name is *goldeneye*, you would use *goldeneye\paul*.

5. Click OK to close the dialog box and then add any other shared resources.

As mentioned previously, most home networks will be set up much more simply than this. In this chapter, I will assume that you have created a user account for yourself on every machine on the network that matches the user account you use on your main machine.

Using My Network Places

You can browse the local network using My Network Places, a Windows feature that debuted in Windows 95 as Network Neighborhood. Whatever you call it, this special shell folder is just like My Computer except that it's for your network, not your local system. It is populated by shared network resources and other network and Internet-related shortcuts you might create. Not surprising, these shortcuts are now called *network places*.

Some network places are created for you automatically.

◆ When a system on your local network shares a resource such as a folder, and you have been authenticated to access that resource, it appears in your My Networks Folder.

◆ My Network Places automatically includes

  ■ Web sites that you access from Microsoft FrontPage

  ■ MSN Communities, and other WebDAV-compatible Web properties you use

  ■ UPnP-compatible broadband routers on your local network

You can add other network places manually. For example, if you want to access a specific FTP site through the Windows shell, you can add it to My Network Places by using a handy wizard.

Browsing the Network

To browse your local network, choose Start→My Network Places, which displays
the My Networks Places window, shown in Figure 8-1.

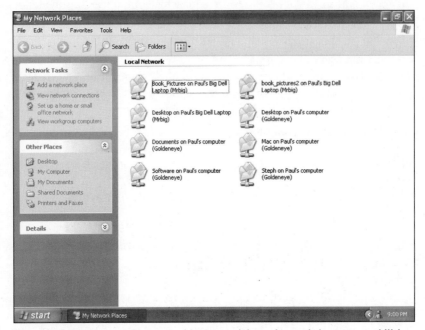

Figure 8-1: My Network Places provides network browsing and shortcut capabilities.

What you see here, of course, depends on your setup.

◆ If you have access to shared network resources, they show up under the
  Local Network heading.

◆ Internet-related network places show up under The Internet. These include

  ▪ Web sites

  ▪ FTP sites

  ▪ MSN Communities

What's hiding under the hood is your local workgroup, which used to be the
default My Network Places view in Windows 2000. To view the machines in your
workgroup, select View Workgroup Computers under Network Tasks. What you see
next resembles Figure 8-2, where the PCs in the Thurrott workgroup are shown.

Click Back to return to the main My Network Places display, or double-click any
of the available networked computers to view their shared resources. The Goldeneye
machine, shown in Figure 8-3, is sharing several file folders and an HP LaserJet
printer.

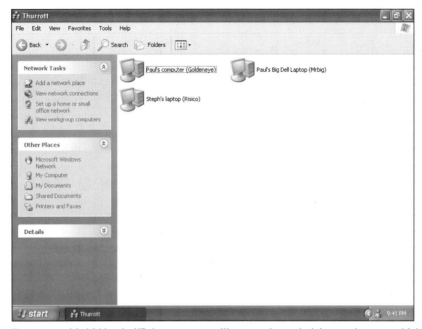

Figure 8-2: It's hidden in XP, but you can still access the underlying workgroup, which represents your home network.

Figure 8-3: XP machines can share folders, printers, and other resources.

Adding Network Places

To manually add a network place, navigate to My Network Places and select Add a Network Place from the Networks Tasks list. This launches the Add Network Place Wizard, which can create shortcuts to network or Internet locations. But this interface lets you access such a site as if it were on your local hard drive, albeit more slowly.

Here's how you can use this wizard to create a shortcut to Microsoft's FTP site:

1. Click Next to advance the wizard.

2. In the next page (shown in Figure 8-4), select Choose Another Network Location and then click Next. (**Note:** MSN Communities are covered in Chapter 12.)

3. In the next page, shown in Figure 8-5, enter the URL site (`ftp://ftp.microsoft.com` for the Microsoft FTP site), and then click Next.

4. In the next page, you can enter a username and password, if required. In this example, Microsoft FTP site is a public site, so you can leave it as its default setting, which is to log on anonymously. Click Next.

5. In the next page, give the network place a simple English name like *Microsoft FTP site* and then click Next.

6. Click Finish to create the shortcut (see Figure 8-6) and connect to the site.

Figure 8-4: When adding a network place, you must choose between Microsoft marketing and the task at hand.

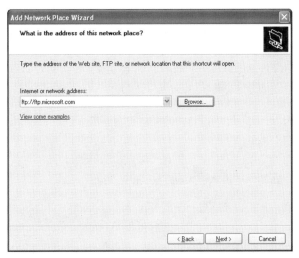

Figure 8-5: You can create shortcuts to local resources or
Internet-based servers.

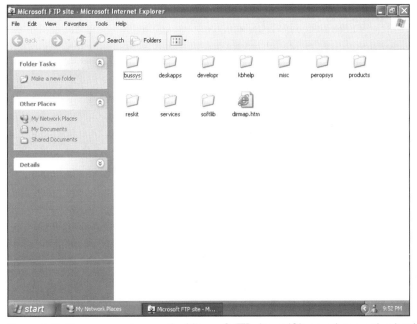

Figure 8-6: Now you can browse the Microsoft FTP site as if it were just another hard
drive on your system. A very slow hard drive.

Mapping Drives

In addition to creating network places, a network shortcut called *mapped network drive* (which debuted in Windows NT) is available in XP. A mapped network drive lets you assign a drive letter to a shared network folder that you need to access frequently. You can treat the mapped network drive just like the hard drive in your own PC.

Here's how to map a network drive:

1. Open My Computer and then choose Tools→Map Network Drive. This launches the Map Network Drive dialog box, shown in Figure 8-7.

2. Select an available drive letter from the Drive drop-down list box. I'll choose *N* for this example. You may choose any available drive letter.

3. Click the Browse button to locate the network resource you'd like to access. Alternatively, you might type in the fully qualified network address, such as \\goldeneye\software.

4. If needed, select Different User Name and enter your credentials for the network resource you're trying to access.

5. Click Finish, and the new virtual drive is added to My Computer under the new Network Drives section, as shown in Figure 8-8. XP also opens a new Explorer window pointing to your new virtual drive.

To remove a mapped drive, right-click it in My Computer and choose Disconnect.

Figure 8-7: The Map Network Drive dialog box lets you create a virtual drive that points to a shared network resource.

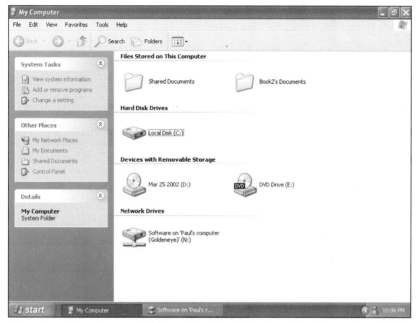

Figure 8-8: Mapped network drives appear in My Computer just like any drive.

Sharing an Internet Connection

Because sharing is the topic at hand, it makes sense to at least mention that you can share your Internet connection. But you knew that because you already read Chapter 6, which is dedicated to this very topic.

Sharing File Folders

Now that you've seen how shared network resources work, it's time to share some of your own. The most common shared network resources are file folders. As you might hope, Windows XP makes it really easy to share this sort of resource.

Working with Shared Documents

If you just want to share files between users on the same PC, the easiest way is to use the Shared Documents, Shared Pictures, and Shared Music folders, which are available from any user account. You can access these special shell folders in any My Computer window: Shared Folders is universally available, Shared Pictures shows up while you're viewing My Pictures, and a link to Shared Music is available from My Music.

The Shared Documents folder is public domain, meaning that any user on the system can view, modify, or delete files stored in this location. But if you want to share documents, music files, or pictures on a single PC, this is a great way to go.

Security and Sharing on the Network

When you want to share files and folders across the network, security enters the picture.

To prevent users from bungling the sharing process, Microsoft has created a Network Setup Wizard that can set up folder shares. Despite such lofty goals, the Network Setup Wizard is somewhat broken, though it will likely be fixed by the time Windows XP Service Pack 1 (SP1) ships in late 2002 (see the Web site for this book for more details: www.xphomenetworking.com). For this reason, a more manual approach is in order.

Here's the best way to securely share folders in Windows XP (I'll use the Shared Documents folder as an example):

1. Open My Computer, right-click Shared Documents, and select Sharing and Security. The Sharing tab of the Properties window for Shared Documents appears, as shown in Figure 8-9.

2. Click the hyperlink text that reads If You Understand the Security Risks but Want to Share Files without Running the Wizard, Click Here. This displays the Enable File Sharing dialog box, shown in Figure 8-10, which does its darnedest to get you to use that wizard.

3. Select Just Enable File Sharing and then click OK. The Sharing tab of the Properties window now changes to resemble Figure 8-11.

4. Select Share This Folder on the Network and enter a share name (choose something creative like *Shared Documents*). Notice that the Allow Network Users to Change My Files option is checked. If you uncheck this option, users accessing the resource over the network can browse your shares and view the files in this particular share, but not modify them or delete them.

5. Click OK. If you entered a share name that is longer than 12 characters, you see the dialog box shown in Figure 8-12. If your network is all XP and Windows 2000, then you can just click Yes to continue.

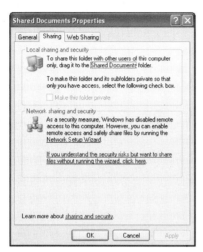

Figure 8-9: By default, Windows XP tries to hide sharing from you.

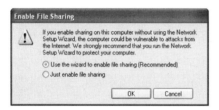

Figure 8-10: Seriously, I just want to enable file sharing.

 Older Windows versions, such as Windows 95, 98, Me, and NT 4.0, cannot access network shares with names like Shared Documents. If you have such a system on your local network, you need to choose a shorter name.

When you return to My Computer, you'll see that the Shared Documents folder now has a small icon modifier, in the shape of a hand holding up the folder, that indicates that it's now shared (see Figure 8-13).

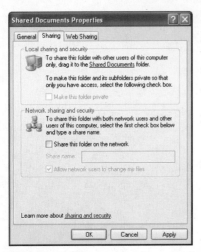

Figure 8-11: After you've gotten past the security checkpoint, you will see the simple file- sharing UI shown here.

Figure 8-12: You must keep share names short if you plan on integrating older versions of Windows into your network.

Figure 8-13: Shared resources feature this "handy" icon modifier.

Turning Off Simple File Sharing

The file sharing method discussed in the preceding section is new to Windows XP, and it's called Simple File Sharing because it attempts to obscure all the folder sharing complexities that existed in previous Windows NT and Windows 2000 versions.

Simple File Sharing requires Windows XP Professional. XP Home users are outta luck.

If you're using Windows XP Professional Edition, you can revert to the old file sharing method if you'd like. Here's how:

1. Open My Computer and choose Tools→Folder Options. This displays the Folder Options dialog box.

2. Navigate to the View tab, shown in Figure 8-14.

3. Scroll the Advanced settings list to the bottom and find the Use Simple File Sharing (Recommended) option. Uncheck this item and click OK to close the dialog box.

4. Now, right-click Shared Documents in the My Computer window and select Sharing and Security. As shown in Figure 8-15, things have changed considerably (compare this with Figure 8-11). You can add a comment field to the share, which displays in My Network Places; limit the number of users that can access the share simultaneously; and set advanced options for permissions and caching.

5. When you click the Permissions button, you see the dialog box shown in Figure 8-16. By default, every user that's authenticated to access your machine has full access to the files and folders contained by your share. However, you can use this dialog box to remove the Everyone group and fine-tune which users and user groups can access this share. So if you want to give specific access only to a particular user or group of users, you can do so. And if you want to *deny* specific access only to a particular user or group of users, you can do that as well. It's highly granular.

So if you're running Windows XP Professional, it's possible to wield far greater control over your folder shares than is possible with XP Home Edition. Depending on your needs, however, this might not be an issue; most home users will be well served by simple file sharing, regardless of whether they're using Home Edition or Pro.

The core difference between the two schemes may seem subtle, but think of it this way: Simple file sharing configures permissions at the folder level, whereas XP Pro's more advanced file sharing capabilities let you perform per-user permissions. XP Pro is more powerful, but it's also more complicated.

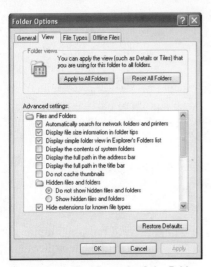

Figure 8-14: The View tab of the Folder Options dialog box includes a number of bizarre settings, including one for simple file sharing, if you're running Professional Edition.

Figure 8-15: After you turn off simple file sharing, you are presented with a more granular set of sharing permissions.

Figure 8-16: In XP Pro, you can set file share permissions on a per-user basis.

Sharing a Printer

You might have numerous computers in your home network, but chances are that you have only one or two printers. Thankfully, you don't need to move files around in order to print them on a printer that's attached to a different PC. Instead, you can simply share your printers so that every user on your home network can print, regardless of which machine they're using. Here's how:

1. Move to a PC to which there is a printer attached and choose Start→Printers and Faxes. This displays the Printers and Faxes window, which should contain one or more printer icons.

2. Right-click the printer you'd like to share and select Sharing. This displays the Sharing tab of the Properties dialog box for the printer, as shown in Figure 8-17.

3. Select Share This Printer and provide a plain English share name, such as HP LaserJet 5P or whatever. Then click OK to close the dialog box. Like the folder share you created earlier, the icon for the printer now includes a graphic hand icon modifier to indicate that it is shared.

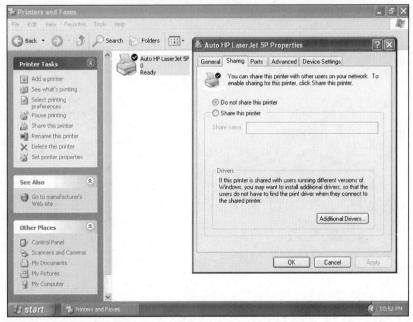

Figure 8-17: Sharing a printer in XP is extremely simple.

Connecting to a Remote Printer

To connect to a remote printer on your local network, use the following steps:

1. Choose Start→Printers and Faxes. The Printers and Faxes window displays.

2. Click Add a Printer from the Printers Tasks list. This launches the Add Printer Wizard. Click Next to continue.

3. In the next phase of the wizard, shown in Figure 8-18, select the A Network Printer or a Printer Attached to Another Computer option and then click Next.

4. In the next phase, leave the default choice, Browse for a Printer, selected and click Next.

5. In the next phase, the wizard searches for printers on the local network and displays the results in hierarchical view, as shown in Figure 8-19.

6. Select the printer and click Next, and then click Finish to close the wizard. You can now use the network printer as if it were attached directly to your PC.

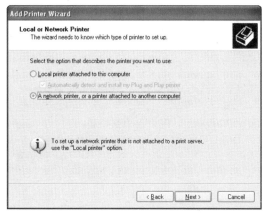

Figure 8-18: To access a network printer, just launch the Add Printer Wizard and have it search for network-attached printers.

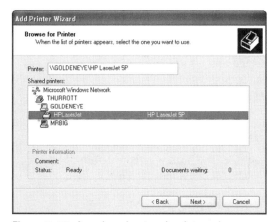

Figure 8-19: Any shared network printers show up automatically. Select one, and you're done.

Working with Older Versions of Windows

Most people who upgrade to Windows XP are Windows 9.x users, and many of these users choose to keep their old Windows 9.x machines and use them as nodes on their burgeoning home networks. This is perfectly acceptable – Windows 9.x and XP interoperate quite well – but you need to understand some ground rules first. This is because Windows 9.x and Windows XP were designed with very different technologies and goals. And if you want to make them work together, you're going to have to tighten up your 9.x systems a bit.

As discussed in Chapter 7, Windows XP is inherently multiuser, and you cannot install or use this operating system without creating at least one user account. This contrasts sharply with Windows 95, 98, 98 SE, and Millennium Edition (Me), which operate by default under the assumption that there is one user and, more often than not, this user doesn't need a username or password.

Security concerns aside, the Windows 9x model is fairly primitive, though it does offer a tack-on multiuser feature called Multiple User Profiles that is roughly analogous to the multiuser aspects of Windows XP. So before you can integrate Windows XP and 9x, you need to make sure that your 9x boxes require a logon that includes a username and password. This is a base requirement for letting users sitting at 9x box access network resources such as file folders and printers. And on the flipside, if your XP box isn't set up with a user account that matches the username and password of the current user on your 9x box, you can't access 9x-based shares either. It's a two-way street.

Working with Windows 9x/Me

Windows 9x is less stable, reliable, and scalable than Windows XP. For this reason, you should only use Windows 9x machines as clients on your network. Don't share any resources from a 9x box, aside perhaps from printers, and don't use a 9x machine as the gateway, or edge device, on your home network unless you want to spend the rest of your life troubleshooting and rebooting.

Instead, use XP for crucial network services wherever possible. Connect printers and large hard drives to XP machines so that they can share these resources with other machines.

And after everything is physically connected, you can set up identical users with the same logon and password on each machine – XP, 9x, whatever – so that these resources are available from every machine. The hard part is just setting up the 9x machines with a username/password that you can duplicate on XP.

Working with Windows NT/2000

Good news, Windows fans: The security model in Windows NT 4.0 and 2000 is identical to that in Windows XP, so you don't have any extra configuration to worry about. Just ensure that you create identical user accounts on each NT, 2000, and XP box, and you'll be fine.

Chapter 9

Lose the Tether: Wireless Networking

IN THIS CHAPTER

- ◆ Learn the different types of wireless technologies available

- ◆ Create and work with a wireless network

- ◆ Understanding how to use security in a wireless world

WIRELESS NETWORKING is one of the most exciting network technologies to appear in recent years and has set the industry on its ear, offering consumers fun new ways to access the Internet and other network resources. Since the mid-1990s, pervasive wireless was inevitable but always on the verge of happening. But as the industry finally rallied around high-speed standards such as Wi-Fi (802.11b), wireless took off.

Today you can choose from a wide range of cheap but powerful wireless devices, from network interface cards for your portable PC to wireless-ready printers.

Wireless is about freedom, the freedom to browse the Web and answer e-mail from your bed, deck, or backyard. It's about opening up a new era of relaxed computing that doesn't necessarily have to occur at a desk in your home office. Most importantly, wireless is about removing the tether of wired networking and giving users choices.

In this chapter, you find out about wireless networking technologies, how they're implemented in Windows XP, and the ways in which this exciting capability can change the way you use computers.

Going Wireless

I began my first experiments with wireless networking in mid-2000, when high-speed wireless technologies, such as Wi-Fi (802.11b), were still too expensive to be used outside of large companies. Back then, the only viable alternative was a pokey, 1.6 Mbps connection called *HomeRF*, which was conceived solely as a consumer-level technology. This plan was never realized, because the prices of faster technologies came down rather quickly later that year. But for a short time, I worked wirelessly on what I took to be the cutting edge.

It was more like the waiting edge. At 1.6 Mbps, wireless access was too slow. Simple Web pages and e-mail seemed to work okay, but accessing the local network through this connection was positively painful, with numerous timeouts and sleep-inducing waits.

But even at these speeds, wireless was able to deliver on its most exciting promise: freedom. I was able to get work done from the TV room in the cellar, from bed, or from the deck on warm summer days, using a laptop and a wireless networking card. Instinctively, I felt that wireless was the wave of the future, but that the speed would have to be improved dramatically before consumers latched on to it.

This speed increase happened shortly after my first experiments, as the prices of Wi-Fi components—which run at a relatively speedy 11 Mbps—finally hit consumer price points in late 2000. The age of wireless had begun.

Types of Wireless Networking

Today, the most common and popular forms of wireless networking are based around standard technology. These include the current volume leader, 802.11b, as well as a few follow-ups that bring increased speeds.

802.11B WI-FI

In a home scenario, the most common type of wireless network today is based around a technology called 802.11b, an awkward title that's often referred to as Wi-Fi. 802.11b is an Institute of Electrical and Electronics Engineers (IEEE) standard, meaning that Wi-Fi-compatible products from competing companies should be able to interoperate seamlessly. And this is pretty much the case, in my experience.

802.11b operates at a peak speed of 11 Mbps, though you'll typically experience speeds closer to 4 to 8 Mbps, unless you're physically adjacent to the wireless access point (discussed in "Working with a Wireless Network," later in this chapter). However, even at these speeds, Wi-Fi is a winner: All forms of Internet services run at acceptable speeds, save perhaps online games, and local networking is speedy enough for even large file transfers.

Where Wi-Fi starts to fall apart a bit is in security, which can be addressed, and scalability, because each wirelessly connected device has to share the 11 Mbps of total bandwidth, further lowering speeds if two or more users are connected simultaneously.

Still, for the home, 802.11b is hard to beat at the time of this writing. Prices are cheap, and the technology is stable and full-featured.

802.11A, 802.11G, AND THE FUTURE

To address the limitations of Wi-Fi, the IEEE has approved two newer wireless standards, both of which offer peak speeds of 54 Mbps, about five times the speed of Wi-Fi. Unfortunately, both of these standards offer different levels of compatibility with Wi-Fi, making the upgrade choice a difficult one.

The first of these new standards is called 802.11a. This technology runs on a different frequency band than 802.11b, meaning that it has more headroom for expansion and less chance of interference from electronics devices in the home, a problem facing Wi-Fi users. But because it runs on a different frequency band, it is also incompatible with Wi-Fi, meaning that Wi-Fi and 802.11a hardware cannot interoperate; you can use both technologies simultaneously on the same home network, but you cannot connect to an 802.11a wireless network using a Wi-Fi network card.

A second emerging standard, 802.11g, addresses the compatibility issues by running on the same frequency band as Wi-Fi. But 802.11g brings with it the same problems that face Wi-Fi: Because the 2.4 GHz frequency band used by these technologies is so crowded, the chance of interference is higher. And 802.11g isn't expected to ramp up to its peak speed of 54 Mbps as quickly as 802.11a as a result.

Choosing a next-generation wireless solution is therefore dicey. I expect 802.11b to remain the most popular solution through at least 2003, but by the time this book is published, you will probably have numerous 802.11a and 802.11g choices to look over as well. However you choose, remember that faster is almost always better.

Regardless of the technology you choose, setup and configuration will be similar. For the remainder of this chapter, I assume that you're working with Wi-Fi (802.11b)–based technology. However, you shouldn't have a problem following along if you choose a speedier solution.

Understanding Wireless Terminology

Like any good computer technology, wireless brings with it a new suite of technical terms that you must understand in order to even read product documentation. Here is a rundown of a few of these terms:

- **Network interface card (NIC):** A wireless NIC is often referred to as a wireless adapter because many of these devices aren't cards at all.

- **Access point:** Wireless connectivity is generally added to an existing wired network using a wireless *access point,* which is either a dedicated hardware device, a combination hardware device that offers other services, or even a wireless adapter, which can be used in ad hoc mode (described in the next section, "Setting Up a Wireless Network").

- **SSID (Service Set Identifier):** Wireless networks are given names, or *SSIDs,* which makes identifying them easy.

- **Wired Equivalent Privacy (WEP):** Wireless networks are secured using wireless network key (WEP) settings, an almost completely useless technology that is discussed in detail later in the chapter. Fortunately, there are workarounds to the limitations of WEP.

Don't be dazzled or depressed by all the terminology, however. As it turns out, setting up a wireless network is generally pretty simple. And when you're using XP, it's even easier than usual.

Setting Up a Wireless Network

Before you can set up your wireless network, you need to consider your needs, the hardware you'll use, and the cost. The simplest possible wireless network requires just two wireless network interface cards (NICs): You place one in a PC connected to your previously established wired network, and the other in the PC – typically a laptop – that will connect wirelessly. Such a network is called an *ad-hoc wireless network,* and it can only exist between two PCs.

But if you think you'll ever want to use more than one PC wirelessly – and I think I can assume this is the case – you have to add a *wireless access point* or a *wireless-enabled broadband router.*

Using an Access Point

A wireless access point is a piece of hardware that plugs into your existing network with a standard Ethernet cable, and it can supply wireless networking access to several PCs. Access points are much cheaper than they used to be, and many companies, including Linksys, D-Link, and Belkin, offer devices that don't cost much more than a wireless NIC. In fact, given the low price of these devices and the ease with which you can add one to your existing network, I don't recommend an ad hoc wireless network to any but the thriftiest user.

An access point is the logical starting point for anyone looking to add wireless support to an existing network. If you're using a switch, hub, or broadband router that offers multiple Ethernet ports, you simply plug in the access point's power cord and then connect it to the wired network using a standard 10 or 100 Mbps Ethernet cable.

Initial configuration is zilch, though you'll want to do a bit of work to secure the wireless connection, which I cover later in the chapter. In addition to the access point, such a setup requires one wireless network card for each PC that will access the network wirelessly.

Incidentally, this is the type of setup I'm currently using, and I went this route because I already had a properly configured home network and simply wanted to add wireless capabilities as cheaply and efficiently as possible.

Using a Wireless-Enabled Broadband Router

If you don't already use a hardware-based broadband router or similar device as your edge device, or are considering upgrading your current model, you can purchase a wireless-enabled broadband router. This type of device typically offers several services:

◆ Connects your home network to a broadband account, such as cable or DSL, providing firewall protection and DHCP and NAT services; it's like a home network in a box.

◆ Provides one to eight 100 Mbps Ethernet ports, so you can add PCs to a speedy, wired internal network.

◆ Offers wireless access (similar to that provided by a separate access point, without the need for a separate hardware device), either through built-in antennas or via a PC card expansion slot, which can accept a PC card–based wireless networking card, just like you'd normally use in a laptop. Note that if you have to add a PC card NIC, that's an additional cost, so this type of device is generally aimed at users who don't want wireless now but would like to add it cheaply later.

Like the access point setup mentioned previously, configuration of a wireless-enabled broadband router is minimal. And if you're using XP-compliant wireless NICs, you should be able to get online immediately.

Adding Wireless to XP Desktops

After the wireless-connection-sharing hardware is added to your network, you can enable wireless connectivity on your Windows XP clients, which can be laptops or desktop PCs. You generally upgrade laptops to wireless using a PC card–based or USB-based wireless NIC, though newer portable machines include integrated wireless, which is the preferred method if you can get it. (Integrated wireless NICs don't take up precious USB and PC card space, leaving these expansion options open for other uses; they also tend to drain less battery power.)

For a desktop PC, you can add wireless connectivity through an internal PC card, which requires you to open up your PC, or via an external USB connection, which is much simpler but saps USB bandwidth and can generally be a bit more expensive.

Whichever type of wireless hardware you choose, be sure to purchase an adapter that is specifically Windows XP–compatible. This is because XP-compatible wireless NICs integrate very nicely into the XP user interface and are therefore easier to configure and use. However, if you can't find one that is specifically XP-compliant, you can use any NIC that says it will work with Windows 2000. These cards require you to manually install drivers using a CD-based setup application.

XP-compliant wireless adapters, however, are literally plug and play. When you connect such a device, XP notes its discovery by using a small balloon help window like the one shown in Figure 9-1. Then the balloon help changes to note the exact name of the device, and you're alerted that the hardware is ready for use.

By default, wireless connections display an icon in the system tray, indicating its online status. If the adapter is not able to detect a wireless network, it displays a red cross through its tray icon. Otherwise, the icon appears normally and resembles a small computer monitor.

Figure 9-1: You gotta love the way Windows XP detects, installs, and configures compliant wireless networking adapters.

Working with a Wireless Network

One of the most exciting Windows XP features is its native support for wireless connectivity based on the Wi-Fi standard. But this feature is far more powerful than simple device detection. Instead, XP clients also automatically detect any nearby wireless networks, and you can access this list through a simple UI element I'll discuss shortly. But XP also automatically connects to the fastest possible network connection on the fly, a feature that has many positive ramifications.

Say you've got a wirelessly enabled laptop that also features a standard 100 Mbps Ethernet port for wired network connectivity. If both connections are active — that is, the wired network is plugged in, and the wireless network connection has detected a wireless network to which it has access rights — XP automatically uses the faster, wired network. Likewise, if you have a choice of wireless networks — more typical in an office situation, naturally — then XP picks the wireless network with the best connectivity. And best of all, it constantly polls the available networks, looking for the best connection, and switches if necessary.

At home, XP won't generally have multiple wireless networks from which to choose. However, XP will be sure to use whatever bandwidth is currently available. And because wireless connectivity ebbs and flows based on physical proximity to the wireless access point and other factors, it continually adjusts to the available bandwidth. Likewise, multiple wirelessly enabled XP boxes will duke it out for wireless bandwidth, based on the needs at the time. A machine streaming video from the Web, for example, needs more bandwidth than one simply polling for e-mail every ten minutes. XP always handles these situations automatically.

Depending on the type of network card you've installed and whether you were required to reboot — generally not the case, and definitely not the case for XP-compliant NICs — your wireless network connection may or may not have automatically connected to your wireless connection. If it did not connect, you can force XP to look for available wireless networks.

To do so, locate the wireless network connection icon in the system tray and double-click it (or right-click it and choose View Available Wireless Networks). This displays the Connect to Wireless Network dialog box, shown in Figure 9-2.

Figure 9-2: The Connect to Wireless Network dialog box lets you quickly access any available wireless networks.

What you see here depends largely on your setup, but you should see at least one wireless network listed under Available Networks, and it should match the wireless network you recently set up (hopefully you changed the default name of the network so that it isn't listed as *default, linksys,* or similar).

If you don't see any wireless networks, you haven't set up your wireless access point correctly. Unfortunately, in this case, you don't have much recourse beyond checking the physical connections and then consulting the documentation for your particular hardware. The good news, however, is that this stuff generally "just works," to borrow a Microsoft marketing phrase. Every once in a while, things really do work as advertised.

If you see other wireless networks — that is, wireless networks that you didn't set up and configure — it's possible that they belong to neighbors or others nearby. Be a good neighbor and don't use your neighbors' bandwidth and let them know that their network is open to the world, if it is (see "Implementing Wireless Security," later in this chapter, for details). And be sure to protect yourself so that they're not using your bandwidth as well (again, see the security section).

Normally, you will see just one wireless network, however, and it will be your network. If this is the case, then life is simple: Just select the network and click Connect. This network is then placed at the top of the list of networks to which the adapter will attempt to connect in the future, and you should never have to think about it again.

Configuring Wireless Connectivity

If you click the Advanced button in the Connect to Wireless Network dialog box, you're presented with the Wireless Networks tab of the Properties dialog box for the wireless connection, as shown in Figure 9-3. You can also display this dialog box by visiting Network Connections and double-clicking the wireless connection. This is where you configure the client's wireless connectivity.

Figure 9-3: Using the Wireless Networks tab, you can manage wireless connections past, present, and future.

At the top of this tab is the Use Windows to Configure My Wireless Network Settings check box. If your wireless NIC is XP-compliant, this option should be checked. If, however, you had to run a CD-based Setup application to configure a Windows 2000–compatible wireless card, leave this option unchecked and use your card's software, rather than XP's built-in capabilities, to connect wirelessly.

In the Available Networks section, you see a list of available wireless networks, similar to the list displayed by the Connect to Wireless Network dialog box. And like that list, this list is live, in that it represents the currently available wireless networks only and not networks you may have connected with at one time in the past. You can click the Refresh button to prompt XP to manually poll for wireless networks, though the system generally does a good job of detecting such networks on its own. You can also select an available network and then click Configure to configure that network. By doing so, you see a dialog box similar to the one in Figure 9-4, which is discussed in the next section, "Implementing Wireless Security".

At the bottom of the Wireless Networks tab of the connection's Properties dialog box is a section listing preferred wireless networks. The order of this list is based on XP's experience with wireless network connections it has used in the past. So if you've only used one wireless connection, then that's all you see in the list, and you don't need to configure anything.

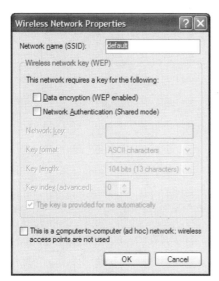

Figure 9-4: You can configure a wireless connection automatically or manually, your choice.

However, if you travel a lot and come into contact with multiple wireless networks, or work in an environment in which there are multiple wireless networks and you have a need to manually configure which network you should be using, you can use this section of the dialog box to override XP's built-in detection abilities and specify a preference list for wireless networks. You can move wireless networks up and down in the list, add or remove wireless networks from the preferred list, or view configuration information about each of the wireless connections you've visited in the past, even if they're not currently available.

If you click the Advanced button, you're presented with advanced wireless network access options, as shown in Figure 9-5. Here, you can choose whether to connect only to certain types of wireless networks (such as access point–based networks only) or whether to allow automatic connections to non-preferred networks. For the most part, these options are designed solely for corporations in which there are multiple network types, and you can safely ignore this dialog box.

Connecting and Disconnecting with Wireless Networks through the Start Menu

If you're using an XP-compliant wireless network adapter, you will have a special Start menu item, listed under the Connect To item. Similar to a connectoid you'd see for a dial-up networking connection, the Wireless Network Connection option enables you to quickly connect to a wireless connection from the Start menu, as shown in Figure 9-6.

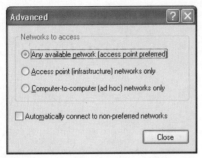

Figure 9-5: Generally of use only in corporate settings, this dialog box lets you configure which types of wireless connections you can access.

Figure 9-6: XP treats wireless connections like dial-up connections, making it easy to select one directly from the Start menu.

So why would you need such a thing? Frankly, you probably won't in a home setting because XP will automatically connect to whatever wireless connection it can find. But if you bring a laptop back and forth between home and work, and use two different wireless connections in each location because of configuration differences, this choice can be a handy shortcut. Just choose Start→Connect To and then the correct wireless connection, and you're in business.

Implementing Wireless Security

Even more so than with wired networks, wireless network security is paramount. Unless you're interested in other people stealing your wireless bandwidth or even your personal data, you must take steps to ensure that your wireless network is secure. Sadly, two facts are operating in concert to ensure that this process is somewhat more difficult than it should be.

The first is that the underlying technology behind Wi-Fi was not designed with security in mind and is therefore rather insecure. Security features were retroactively tacked onto Wi-Fi, but as with any such fixes, the end result is somewhat ineffective.

The second is that wireless hardware ships in a completely insecure mode that most users never think to correct: Instead, they set up their hardware, see that it works, and never read the instruction booklet. Don't be a statistic: Use the following instructions to secure your wireless network.

The bad news is that some of these instructions will bypass some of the cool wireless auto-detection features in XP. But think about it: You only have to configure wireless networking once, and then it should just work going forward.

The other bad news is that all of these security configuration options are hardware dependent, so the exact steps differ depending on whether you bought a Linksys, D-Link, or whatever wireless access point. Each wireless connectivity device includes some sort of management console, generally Web-based, that you can access to make configuration changes. The first step, then, is to locate this console and secure it by supplying it with a logon password. Read your documentation and discover the ins and outs of your hardware's management interface. And then secure your wireless network. Here's how.

Don't Broadcast Your Wireless Network

By default, wireless access points broadcast the name, or SSID, of your wireless network so that wireless clients can discover and access it more easily. However, this broadcast capability is simply a homing beacon for anyone who wants to steal your bandwidth or access your private data. So the first thing you should do is change the name of your wireless network (and give it a complicated name, rather than something simple like default or linksys) so that hackers can't guess what name to use. Then stop the access point from broadcasting the name.

When you make this change, you have to manually configure your XP-based wireless adapters so that they know to look for the right wireless network. Here's how you configure XP for a broadcast-less wireless network:

1. Open Network Connections, right-click the wireless network connection, and choose Properties. This displays the Properties dialog box for the wireless connection.

2. Navigate to the Wireless Networks tab if necessary and click Add. This displays the Wireless Network Properties dialog box, shown in Figure 9-7, in which you can add the name of a wireless network.

3. Enter the name of your wireless network in the Network Name (SSID) text box and check the Data Encryption (WEP Enabled) check box. This second option is discussed in the next section.

4. Click OK to close the dialog box and return to the Wireless Network Connection Properties dialog box.

5. Under the Preferred Networks section, delete any network names other than the one you just entered.

6. Click OK to finish.

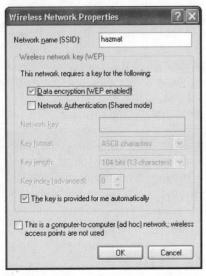

Figure 9–7: When securing your network against broadcasting, you can use the Wireless Network Properties dialog box to manually configure the network.

Implement WEP

To counter the inherent insecurity of wireless connections, which broadcast information through the air in a manner than can be easily intercepted by people with the right tools, the Wi-Fi architects grafted a technology called Wired Equivalent Privacy, or WEP. WEP is a set of key-based technologies that enables wireless authentication and encryption capabilities. The authentication service adds a key, like a password, that is required for clients to access the wireless network, in the same way that your logon and password are required before you can access your home network. Likewise, the encryption service encrypts wirelessly transmitted data, using either 40-bit or 128-bit encryption, in an effort to prevent eavesdroppers from intercepting your data.

Taken on its own, WEP doesn't actually work, though it's better than nothing, and will of course stop all but the most technically proficient hackers. And in combination with the other security techniques outlined in this section, WEP is actually quite effective.

After you've configured your wireless access point to use WEP, you need to configure your clients for this technology as well. This process is outlined in the steps in the preceding section.

Require Specific MAC Addresses

The final task you can perform requires configuration only at the access point. Most access points can be configured to accept connections only from specific network adapters. This effectively shuts out other users from accessing your network wirelessly.

Network adapters are identified by their MAC (Media Access Control) address, a series of alphanumeric characters that is guaranteed to be unique to each adapter. In fact, MAC addresses are so unique that Microsoft has tied its Windows Product Activation (WPA) technology to those retail Windows systems that include network adapters (new PCs tie WPA to the BIOS, which is likewise guaranteed to be unique).

Your access point management console will likely let you specify which network adapters (MAC addresses) are allowed to access the wireless network, so you need to find this information, which will require a visit to each PC.

In Windows XP, you can discover the MAC address of your wireless network adapter various ways, though curiously none of them are easy to get to through the GUI. So the simplest way is to use the command line and follow these steps:

1. Open a command line window (choose Start→All Programs→Accessories→Command Prompt).

2. Type `ipconfig /all` and then press Enter.

The output will resemble the following:

```
Windows IP Configuration

        Host Name . . . . . . . . . . . : A31
        Primary Dns Suffix  . . . . . . . :
        Node Type . . . . . . . . . . . : Unknown
        IP Routing Enabled. . . . . . . . : No
        WINS Proxy Enabled. . . . . . . . : No


Ethernet adapter Wireless Network Connection:

        Connection-specific DNS Suffix  . : ne.client2.attbi.com
        Description . . . . . . . . . . . : High Rate Wireless LAN MiniPCI Combo
Card
```

```
Physical Address. . . . . . . . . : 00-20-E0-8A-89-9A
Dhcp Enabled. . . . . . . . . . . : Yes
Autoconfiguration Enabled . . . . : Yes
IP Address. . . . . . . . . . . . : 192.168.1.101
Subnet Mask . . . . . . . . . . . : 255.255.255.0
Default Gateway . . . . . . . . . : 192.168.1.1
DHCP Server . . . . . . . . . . . : 192.168.1.1
DNS Servers . . . . . . . . . . . : 24.218.0.228
                                    24.218.0.229
                                    24.147.1.58
Lease Obtained. . . . . . . . . . : Monday, March 18, 2002 4:58:10 PM
Lease Expires . . . . . . . . . . : Tuesday, March 19, 2002 4:58:10 PM
```

The MAC address is listed next to *Physical Address.* If you have more than one network adapter, be sure you get the correct one.

After you have this information for each wirelessly connected device, you can enter it into the wireless access point and ensure that only PCs using your own network adapters can access your wireless network.

Feel safer? Good! Now, enjoy your wireless connection. And don't let me catch you in the bathroom with that laptop.

Chapter 10

Advanced Home Networking

IN THIS CHAPTER

◆ Understanding complex networks; including routing and bridging to bring disparate networks together

◆ Learn how to monitor your network and to repair network problems

◆ Using Windows XP with Windows 9x/Me, Windows NT/2000, Linux and Macs

IN THE PREVIOUS few chapters, you find out some of the ways in which you can set up your home network, using wired and wireless technologies, and configuring user accounts and network resource sharing. Windows XP makes it really easy to perform these tasks because Microsoft felt that home networking was an emerging market that needed to be addressed. As such, the company got the basics down and made some previously indecipherable NT/2000 networking concepts pretty approachable, even by so-called normal people.

But XP can also perform a number of more complex networking tasks, and some of these tasks didn't exactly get the same treatment by the XP networking folks or, in one particularly glaring case, were actually broken somewhat when Microsoft attempted to add a pretty front end.

In this chapter, I examine some of these more complex home networking topics, including combining and bridging networks, network monitoring, and the ways in which Windows XP machines can coexist in a heterogeneous environment with other Windows versions, the Macintosh, and Linux.

Combining Networks

Anytime you combine two or more network types into your home network, you create a mixed networking environment, where individual networks may or may not interoperate, depending on how you've set up your home network. By default, most networking components assume that they're part of the only available network, and this works fine in those cases when there is indeed only one network. But if you want to combine two or more networks, you have to do a little planning.

149

These days, the most common mixed network is created when you add wireless capabilities to a previously installed wired network. Wired networks – usually 10 or 100 Mbps Ethernet – are great for connecting desktop PCs, especially when they're in the same room. But when you want to work with laptops or PCs that are in a physically distant room, wired networks aren't always the obvious choice. Furthermore, not everyone has the know-how or wherewithal to wire their homes with Ethernet. In such a case, it's time to look at alternatives, and that might require augmenting an in-office wired Ethernet network with some other networking type.

In my own home, I have a variety of network types, and though my case might be atypical, it's a good example of the ways in which you can combine different network types to achieve certain goals. Within my home office, I have a number of PC desktops and laptops that are connected via a 100 Mbps wired Ethernet network. This approach makes sense because all the equipment is in the same room and I want the fastest speeds combined with reasonable pricing. However, because I have several laptops and a Pocket PC and want to network them from anywhere in the house, I've also set up wireless networking. This allows me to check e-mail and browse the Web from the bedroom, the back deck, or the TV room.

I've also purchased a Digital Audio Receiver (DAR), which allows you to access your PC-based digital music collection from anywhere in the house and output it to your best stereo (in my case, the one in the TV room) or to self-powered speakers. The DAR can network via wired Ethernet or home phone-line networking. I chose the latter, because I didn't want to wire the home for Ethernet and extra phone jacks were readily available (using the DAR doesn't disrupt phone conversations at all). And because the data traffic generated by the DAR is so small, using Ethernet wouldn't have provided any benefit.

So I have three different network types running simultaneously at home, and each serves a very specific purpose. They all share the same Internet connection, and it's possible to access shares on any of the machines – laptop or desktop – from any of the other machines, regardless of how they're connected to the network. Additionally, some of my machines aren't even PCs. As of this writing, I have one machine dedicated to testing Linux, and this machine is connected to the network via a wired Ethernet card. An Apple iBook running Mac OS X connects wirelessly through its 802.11b/Wi-Fi compatible Airport card. So it's a big, happy family in some ways, with various levels of interoperability between each system, a topic discussed towards the end of this chapter.

Network Routing and Bridging

If each of your PCs has only one network adapter installed, you will typically ensure that each adapter is part of the same network subnet, ensuring interoperability. And, really, regardless of what type of network each PC uses – wireless or wired – you can pretty much use the default settings, and it should all just work, especially if your machines are all running Windows XP.

Why You Might Want Two or More Network Subnets

When at least one PC includes two or more network adapters, however, things can get interesting, because each of these adapters is likely part of a different subnet. Here are a couple of obvious scenarios where this might be the case:

♦ **You're sharing a broadband Internet connection from your XP-based PC.** When you connect any XP-based machine directly to a cable modem or DSL modem, and then want to share that connection with other machines on your internal network, you need two network adapters. In this case, the two networks shouldn't interoperate in any way; you don't want anyone on the outside to gain access to your internal network shares, right? But fortunately, the very act of sharing the connection sets up this protection. Your internal network will be configured to work with the `192.168.x.x` range of protected IP addresses that are reserved for this purpose, and XP will install its firewall component to protect against inbound hack attacks.

♦ **You need to connect to two different internal networks that don't need to interoperate.** Earlier in the chapter, I discuss my DAR, a network-connected digital audio device that loads playlists and digital audio from a PC on my home network. In this scenario, I'm using phone wire-based networking, called Home PNA, to connect the PC with the DAR. So the PC with all my digital music on it has two network adapters, one for the internal wired Ethernet network and one for the Home PNA network that interoperates with the DAR. I don't care if these two networks interoperate because the DAR doesn't need to access other machines on the Ethernet network. As with the previous scenario, the default setup works just fine: Plug it all in, and it just works.

♦ **You need to connect to two different internal networks that do need to interoperate.** Now things get interesting. If, for some reason, you need or want to create two separate home networks with different subnets, and then connect them some way so that the machines on each network "see" and interoperate with each other and share the same Internet connection, the configuration is a bit more advanced. That's what the first section of this chapter is all about.

Historically, you used a networking technology called *routing* to make two or more networks (or, to be more technically correct, two *network segments*) interoperate. A machine that bridged the two networks — that is, the machine with two network adapters — acted like a hardware router, intercepting network traffic and routing it to the correct machine on either network as needed. This routing happens every day on the Internet and in large corporate networks all around the world. As a home networking solution, however, it's a bit complex and requires a server operating system such as Windows 2000 Server or Windows .NET Server.

Networking Bridging

To make such a thing possible on home networks, however, Microsoft added a feature called *networking bridging* to Windows XP. Network bridging works just like routing, except that it has been prettied up and simplified for the masses. At least that's the theory; depending on how you set up network bridging, XP could hose the whole thing, requiring you to go back and fix the whole mess.

But I'll get to that in a moment. For now, I want to concentrate on the theory of network bridging. You have two networks, say a wired Ethernet network that's connected in some way to a broadband Internet connection, and a wired network. But the wireless network connects to the wired network through an XP-based PC that includes both wired and wireless adapters, instead of the simpler wireless access point approach (see Chapter 9 for details on the easy way to set up wireless networking).

When you create a network bridge — that is, you bridge, or connect, two different networks — XP creates a single subnet for the whole virtual network, configures the whole mess behind the scenes, and handles ugly details such as IP addressing, dynamic IP address allocation, and the like. It's like an enterprise network in a box, if you will. The end result is a single IP address for all the bridged network connections. (Remember, there can be two or *more* adapters involved in a bridge; you can add and remove adapters from the bridge network whenever you want.) It all sounds really nice, doesn't it? Well, it would be, if it worked. The problem is that XP's default method for enabling network bridging is quite broken. That's right, it often doesn't work at all.

WHEN GOOD NETWORKS DO BAD BRIDGING

Think back a minute to the design goals for Windows XP, which is the first NT-based operating system Microsoft has unleashed on the clueless masses used to the hand-holding found in what a colleague calls the "Wintendo" operating systems (for example, Windows 98 and Windows Me). Windows XP is supposed to be just as easy to use while offering consumers the wealth of stability and reliability that could only come from the complex underpinnings of NT. And if there's anything complicated about computing, it's gotta be networking. And if there's anything complicated about networking, it's just gotta be network routing and bridging.

So how does one make such a thing simpler and accessible to mere mortals? Well, in Microsoft's case, as always, it made a wizard. If Microsoft needs to step a user through a multistep process, you just know a wizard's going to be involved. And in this case, that wizard is the Network Setup Wizard. But unlike most of the company's excellent wizards, this thing is seriously broken.

Interestingly, Microsoft admits that the wizard is broken, and the company beta-tested an XP update in mid-2002 aimed at improving, among other things, the Network Setup Wizard. These changes weren't ready in time to cover them in this book, but I'll provide more information about this update on the Web site for this book (www.xphomenetworking.com). But Microsoft addresses key complaints about the wizard: That it doesn't document the changes that it's making, it often doesn't do what the user expects it to do, and that most crucial problem of all, it often just doesn't work.

In the meantime, my advice regarding network bridging in XP is very simple: Skip the wizard and configure bridging manually if you really need to do such a thing. The manual approach actually does work, and it's really not any harder than the wizard. Best of all, there's no doubt what's happening.

CREATING A NETWORK BRIDGE

Creating a network bridge the hard way is actually pretty easy. Here's how:

1. Open Network Connections. (The quickest way is to right-click My Network Places and choose Properties.)

2. Simultaneously select the two network connections you'd like to bridge, right-click, and choose Bridge Connections, as shown in Figure 10-1.

Figure 10-1: We don't need no stinkin' wizard: It's easy to bridge connections directly from the shell.

A Network Bridge dialog box appears, and the connections are bridged. When the process is completed, Network Connections resemble Figure 10-2, with a new Network Bridge section that includes icons for the two bridged network connections and one for the logical bridge itself. You configure network bridging from the logical bridge.

Figure 10-2: Bridged network connections act and work as a single entity.

Like most networking configurations, network bridging affects every user that logs on to that machine, so any bridge you create will be global in scope.

ADDING AND REMOVING CONNECTIONS FROM A NETWORK BRIDGE

Adding a network connection to a preestablished network bridge is simplicity itself: Simply right-click the appropriate connectoid in Network Connections and select Add to Bridge. XP will churn and bubble a bit, and the deed will be done.

The steps to remove a particular network connection from the bridge are equally simple: Right-click the connection you want removed and select Remove from Bridge. No fuss, no muss.

You can only have one network bridge on an XP machine, but that bridge can contain as many network connections as you'd like to throw at it. In my experience, wired Ethernet, wireless, and Home PNA network connections can all be bridged, but IEEE-1394 (FireWire) connections cannot.

ENABLING AND DISABLING BRIDGES

Because a network bridge functions like a single network connection, you can choose to enable and disable it just as you would with any network connection. When you do so, all the connections in the bridge are enabled or disabled along with the bridge.

To disable a network bridge, right-click the bridge icon and choose Disable, as shown in Figure 10-3.

Figure 10-3: Disabling a bridge disables all the connections associated with it.

To enable a network bridge, right-click the bridge icon and choose Enable.

 You can still selectively enable and disable connections that are part of a bridge.

REMOVING A NETWORK BRIDGE

If you create a network bridge and it's not all that you hoped and dreamed for, I've got news: It's really easy to remove and return to your previous setup. To do this, you must first remove each of the network connections that are part of the bridge. Then right-click the network bridge icon and choose Delete. Select Yes when XP asks you whether you're sure.

Monitoring and Fixing Home Network Connections

NT old-timers are a crusty bunch, secure in the knowledge that they've chosen an operating system that's better than UNIX, the other networking operating system mainstay, and more secure and powerful than the children's toy that was Windows 9.x/Me. But as NT was morphed into Windows 2000 and now Windows XP, NT administrators and other power users have had to deal with a bewildering move toward user-friendliness that replaced the familiar, but arcane, command line tools of yore with a suite of simple GUIs that anyone can use. For these people, the inevitable is kind of hard to stomach.

For the rest of us, however, the move toward simpler networking has simply opened up opportunities. For example, it was possible to manually configure Windows NT 4.0 for network address translation, thus sharing a single Internet connection between several machines on a local network. To make this work, however, you really had to know what you were doing, and it wasn't exactly documented clearly anywhere. But when Windows 2000 shipped, this functionality was simply exposed through a feature called Internet Connection Sharing (ICS). And to further grate on the nerves of NT command line commandos, ICS requires the user to simply check one check box in the UI to enable it. What could be simpler?

In XP, virtually all the things you want to accomplish with networking are this easy. This time around, Microsoft has ensured that virtually any networking task you would previously perform with the command line or some bizarre hidden administration console can now be done through a simple UI that virtually anyone can find and master. It's called progress, people.

Quick: Is Your Network Connection Up or Down?

One good example is network monitoring. In the old days, if networking was on the fritz, you'd crack open your trusty command line window and see what was going on. For example, you could use the `ipconfig.exe` command line application to view your network connections and see how they were configured. The output looks something like this:

```
Windows IP Configuration

        Host Name . . . . . . . . . . . . : goldeneye
        Primary Dns Suffix  . . . . . . . :
        Node Type . . . . . . . . . . . . : Unknown
        IP Routing Enabled. . . . . . . . : No
        WINS Proxy Enabled. . . . . . . . : No

Ethernet adapter Local Area Connection:
        Connection-specific DNS Suffix  . : ne.client2.attbi.com
        Description . . . . . . . . . . . : CNet PRO200WL PCI Fast Ethernet Adapter
```

```
Physical Address. . . . . . . . . : 00-08-A1-10-E8-FF
Dhcp Enabled. . . . . . . . . . : Yes
Autoconfiguration Enabled . . . . : Yes
IP Address. . . . . . . . . . . : 192.168.1.100
Subnet Mask . . . . . . . . . . : 255.255.255.0
Default Gateway . . . . . . . . : 192.168.1.1
DHCP Server . . . . . . . . . . : 192.168.1.1
DNS Servers . . . . . . . . . . : 24.218.0.228
                                   24.218.0.229
                                   24.147.1.58
Lease Obtained. . . . . . . . . : Saturday, March 30, 2002 1:07:07 PM
Lease Expires . . . . . . . . . : Sunday, March 31, 2002 1:07:07 PM
```

Networking experts can look at this information and tell at glance whether the connection is online and configured correctly. For the rest of us, of course, this is just a bunch of numbers. Fortunately, XP makes getting such information – and making heads or tails of it – much, much easier.

Here's how. Say you want to know whether your network connection is available, how long it's been online, and whether its IP address is assigned properly by a DHCP server. In NT 4.0 or Windows 2000, you might use ipconfig.exe or another heinous command line tool. In XP, you just have to open Network Connections, right-click the connectoid, and select Status. This displays the dialog box shown in Figure 10-4 (note that the Signal Strength entry appears only on wireless connections).

Here, you can see whether the connection is connected, how long it's been connected, the speed of the connection, and, if it's a wireless connection, the signal strength. If you click the Support tab, you see a display like that in Figure 10-5, with information about the IP address, including how it was obtained.

Figure 10-4: In XP, networking information doesn't require a command line.

Figure 10-5: For more connection information, select the Support tab.

If you want to see which DNS servers are configured for the connection, or other information, click the Details button.

Repairing a Connection

One other common problem involves stopping and restarting a connection. Say you want to lease a new IP from the DHCP server for some reason, or a particular connection just isn't working, but you know the network is up and running. In the NT 4.0/2000 days, you'd bring up the command line window and perform the following steps, which would release your DHCP lease and then renew it:

```
C:\Documents and Settings\Paul>ipconfig /release
Windows IP Configuration
Ethernet adapter Local Area Connection:
        Connection-specific DNS Suffix  . :
        IP Address. . . . . . . . . . . : 0.0.0.0
        Subnet Mask . . . . . . . . . . : 0.0.0.0
        Default Gateway . . . . . . . . :
C:\Documents and Settings\Paul>ipconfig /renew
Windows IP Configuration
Ethernet adapter Local Area Connection:
        Connection-specific DNS Suffix  . : ne.client2.attbi.com
        IP Address. . . . . . . . . . . : 192.168.1.100
        Subnet Mask . . . . . . . . . . : 255.255.255.0
        Default Gateway . . . . . . . . : 192.168.1.1
C:\Documents and Settings\Paul>
```

Good stuff, huh? You might recall that XP provides a much simpler way to do this, using the Disable and Enable options that are available with each network connection. But there's an even easier way, if you can believe that. That's because XP offers a one-step repair option that releases and renews your DHCP lease with only one mouse click.

To perform this action – which has the same effect as the two ipconfig commands shown earlier – just select a network connection and choose Repair This Connection from the Network Tasks list on the left. *Voilà!*

 If you're an NT old-timer and you can't stand all the froufrou GUI stuff in XP, I've got good news: All that old command line stuff still works. So *ipconfig* away to your heart's content.

Using Windows XP in a Mixed Network

While Microsoft would like you to upgrade every one of your PCs to Windows XP, the reality is that most people aren't going to do that right away, and maybe not ever. There are several reasons for this. Despite the obvious superiority that Windows XP has over previous Windows versions and other operating systems, it's fairly expensive ($100 to $200 for an upgrade, depending on whether you choose XP Home Edition or Professional) and requires fairly modern hardware and lots of RAM. Chances are, if you've got an older PC lying around, it's not up to snuff for XP and is therefore better off running an older Windows version or even something like Linux. And if you've got a Macintosh, of course, your options are limited to Apple's OS offerings unless you want to run Windows inside of a virtual machine, which isn't viable for day-to-day work.

So what's the alternative? Actually, it's simple: Just keep on keeping on. Windows XP will integrate quite nicely with previous Windows versions on a home network and can even interoperate with Linux and the Mac given the right push. I take a look at these issues in this final section of the chapter.

Working with Legacy Windows

If you're running Windows for Workgroups or newer (this list includes Windows 95, Windows 98, Windows 98 Second Edition, Windows Me, Windows NT – any version – or Windows 2000), you can network your version of Windows with XP. The trick is to configure each of the machines with TCP/IP and set up user accounts and passwords as described in Chapter 8. Older Windows versions tended to use a legacy networking protocol called NetBEUI that is only sort-of supported on Windows XP. But NetBEUI isn't routable, so it's barely worth discussing: Just switch everything over to TCP/IP, and all will be right with your world.

An additional issue comes up if you follow Microsoft's prescribed method for creating an XP-based home network. Using the Network Setup Wizard, you can actually create client setup diskettes that you can then bring to Windows 9.x/Me systems and use them to automatically set up networking on these machines. Don't do this. Actually performing the necessary steps isn't hard, and it will build experience and confidence with TCP/IP, the native networking protocol used by all modern operating systems.

For more information about integrating legacy Windows versions into your home network, check out Chapter 8.

Upgrading to XP

If you're running an older Windows version on a Pentium III 500 or newer (that is, a 500 MHz Pentium III or equivalent, or better) that has at least 256MB of RAM, you might consider upgrading that machine to Windows XP. Here are a couple of caveats:

◆ XP isn't as compatible with hardware and software as is Windows 9.x/Me. Before plunking down your hard-earned cash and committing to the upgrade, be sure that everything you want to use will actually work with XP. You can do this with the XP Upgrade Advisor, a free software download available from the Microsoft Web site (www.microsoft.com/ windowsxp/pro/howtobuy/upgrading/advisor.asp).

◆ If you're running Windows NT/2000, XP is actually *more* compatible with modern hardware and software than NT/2000, so this could be a no-brainer. However, you cannot uninstall XP if you upgrade from NT/2000, something you can do if you upgrade from Windows 9.x/Me.

◆ Think about file systems. If you upgrade a Windows 9.x/Me system to XP, Setup will ask you if you'd like to upgrade the file system to NTFS, which is more secure than the FAT or FAT32 file system your current operating system is running. Think carefully here, because an upgraded file system is far more inefficient than a freshly formatted disk, so you'll be losing disk space in the process.

◆ A Windows 9.x/Me upgrade is actually a clean install of the operating system with a lot of work going on behind the scenes. But an NT/2000 upgrade is an in-place upgrade, which won't clean up any of the software deadwood you might have collected over the years. Again, choose wisely.

I've written about the XP upgrade extensively on my SuperSite for Windows. For more information, please visit my Windows XP Installation and Upgrade Overview on the SuperSite: www.winsupersite.com/showcase/windowsxp_sg.asp.

Working with the Macintosh

Despite its steadily declining market share, Apple's Macintosh has undergone a technical renaissance in recent years thanks to the return of Steve Jobs and his

NeXTStep-based operating system, which has recently been updated and released as Mac OS X ("ten"). Mac OS X features a reliable UNIX-like core, the stable Mach microkernel, and Apple's legendary user interface ease-of-use goodness. And because it's a modern operating system developed in a Windows world, it even features some interoperability functionality.

The problem is that most Mac users will be running Mac OS 9 or older for the foreseeable future. That's because Mac OS X, like Windows XP, requires a modern system with tons of RAM, and it's a poor performer on older boxes (it's actually much worse than XP in this regard). Furthermore, Mac OS X achieves backwards compatibility only through a bizarre "Classic" environment, which must be loaded before you can run older applications.

Regardless of which Mac version you're using, however, you will be able to use your shared Internet connection from the Mac. But performing other network tasks — like sharing files and printers — is a different story.

MAKING MAC OS 9.X AND OLDER WORK ON A WINDOWS NETWORK

Legacy versions of the Mac do not include any native compatibility with Windows, so you'll have to purchase a third-party solution that makes a Mac box look and act like a Windows box on your home network. I recommend Thursby Software's excellent DAVE application, which installs on the Mac and makes it look like just another Windows machine from My Network Places. And from the Mac, Windows shares appear as normal mounted volumes like you'd see on an AppleTalk network.

DAVE also lets you share PostScript and inkjet printers between the Mac and Windows. For more information, please visit the Thursby Software Web site (www.thursby.com).

For file compatibility between Windows and Mac OS 9.x, you can run Microsoft Office:mac 98 or 2001.

MAC OS X AND WINDOWS

Mac OS X offers a little more native Windows compatibility out of the box than its predecessors. First, you can access — but not browse for — Windows shares using Mac OS X's Connect To Server feature. Unfortunately, Apple doesn't offer a workgroup browser like the My Network Places feature in XP, but if you know the exact path to a Windows-based network share, you can get there from the Mac OS X Finder. Here's how:

1. From the Finder, select Go and then Connect to Server. This launches the Connect to Server window, shown in Figure 10-6.

2. In the Address text box, enter a fully qualified network share path, preceded by *smb://*. For example, to access the *mac* share on the machine *goldeneye*, use

   ```
   smb://goldeneye/mac
   ```

3. Click Connect, and the SMB/CIFS Filesystem Authentication dialog box appears, as shown in Figure 10-7.

4. Enter your workgroup name, username, and password, and then click OK. If your credentials are accepted, a new network volume appears on your desktop (in this example, it's named *mac,* which is the name of the shared resource I connected to).

5. Double-click the network volume to browse the share, as shown in Figure 10-8. You can drag and drop files between the share and your Mac OS X desktop normally, as you would if you were accessing your local hard drive.

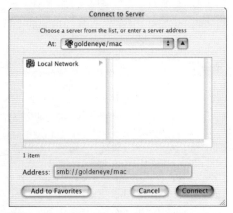

Figure 10-6: If you know where you're going, Mac OS X includes everything you need to connect to Windows file shares.

Figure 10-7: Here, you enter your workgroup logon information.

Aside from the fact that you can't browse for, or discover, Windows shares from Mac OS X, there's another little problem that crops up when you network Macs and

PCs in this way. Because of differences in the way that Macs and Windows PCs interact with the underlying file system, the Mac leaves behind bizarre files called xxxxx and xxxxx in every single shared Windows folder the Mac accesses remotely. So as you move around the file system on a network share, the Mac is leaving these files behind.

The first time I saw these files, I assumed that my system had contracted a virus, and I spent a considerable amount of time removing them and inoculating my system. Finally, I discovered what they were and that they're harmless, but I still don't like the fact that Mac OS X leaves behind such file detritus. To counter this activity, I create a share called *mac* on my main file storage machine and place all Mac-oriented downloads, files, and documents in that share. So if I want to copy anything over to the Mac, it goes in the mac folder share. And if that folder has a few weird Macisms in it, no problem: That's what it's for, anyway.

I contacted Apple about this problem, and the company said that it plans to update its Windows networking features in the future to include My Network Places–like browsing functionality and, perhaps, to remove the need for these extra files (or, at the very least, hide them so users won't be confused).

If you want to browse Windows network shares from Mac OS X, there's an OS X–native version of DAVE available. Also, a company called Objective Development makes a similar product called Sharity, which I use and recommend (www.obdev.at/).

FILE COMPATIBILITY

In late 2001, Microsoft released a Mac OS X–compatible version of Office called Office v. X. This suite offers file compatibility with Windows Office versions and is really cool looking to boot (see Figure 10-8).

Working with Linux

Few events in the past several years can rival the emergence of open-source solution Linux, a free UNIX-like solution that has risen from its roots as a hobbyist toy to seize major market share in the small server market. Linux proponents hope to see it achieve similar success on the desktop as well, and though it's unlikely that Linux will ever rival Windows as a desktop solution, it's already surpassed the Macintosh in many markets.

The appeal of Linux comes from its adaptability and, yes, from the fact that it's free. You can download one of many free Linux distributions, burn an installation CD, and get going in the world of open-source software. Most Linux solutions ship with a wide range of software – some might say *too* wide a range of software – giving you everything you need to get started.

And compared to just a few years ago, Linux is much easier to install and use than ever before, in some ways even rivaling the user interface niceties seen in Windows XP and Mac OS X.

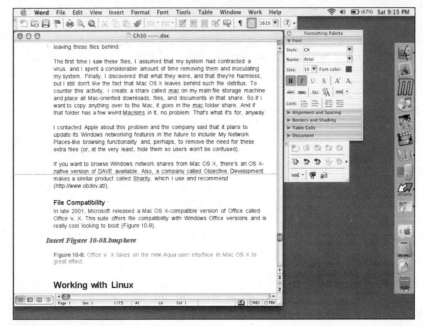

Figure 10–8: Office v. X takes on the new Aqua user interface in Mac OS X to great effect.

To interoperate with Windows, you need to install software called SAMBA, which is included with every Linux distribution. SAMBA allows a Linux machine to browse Windows workgroups and access Windows file shares. But it also makes your Linux box appear as a Windows box on Windows workgroups, spoofing XP and other Windows versions into thinking that they're dealing with one of their brothers. If only they knew!

Linux is a great solution when you've got an older machine that can't run modern versions of Windows, because it's possible to install a bare-bones Linux setup that doesn't task the underlying hardware. For this reason, Linux makes an excellent file server if you have such a need.

Linux is also a lot of fun to play with, if you're into hand-tuning your configuration. Because of the sheer number of possible user interfaces and applications that are available in Linux, you can really customize the system exactly the way you want it. By comparison, Windows (and the Mac) are relatively rigid.

But Linux is also less refined than its mainstream rivals. So you'll be putting up with weird issues we stopped worrying about in Windows years ago. It's computing on the frontier. For many people, that's where it's at.

Part III

Internet

Chapter 11

Windows XP/.NET Integration

IN THIS CHAPTER

- ◆ Understand and using .NET in XP

- ◆ Integrating the new .NET Passport into WIndows XP and Windows Messenger

- ◆ Handling errors from .NET

MICROSOFT DESIGNED WINDOWS XP to be a bridge to the future — a future called .NET (pronounced "dot net"). The goal of Microsoft's Web services platform is to take consumers and businesses alike to a budding nerdvana that will free us from the shackles of desktop computing and make us all more productive, happier, and healthier. Well, maybe not healthier.

There's just one problem. This technology isn't even close to being ready for primetime. Microsoft is proceeding with baby steps, phasing in .NET technology over time, converting existing technology to the .NET platform, and in some cases, even labeling non-.NET technology as .NET technology, no doubt in an effort to further confuse an already confusing topic.

Windows XP contains hooks to various fledgling .NET technologies. This chapter takes a quick look at .NET and examines the ways you can interact with it from Windows XP now and in the near future.

An Introduction to .NET

So what is .NET, you ask? Primarily it's a marketing term for products and technologies that Microsoft is creating to move personal and enterprise computing beyond the desktop and into a distributed Internet-based environment. .NET — which was originally called Next Generation Windows Services (NGWS) — is also a *platform*, one that Microsoft sees as the successor to Windows. This platform is based on *Web services,* which are, in turn, defined by a language called *XML*. These services will sometimes be free and sometimes require monthly or yearly paid subscriptions.

You probably noticed that I used lots of technical terms in that .NET description. And that, really, is the problem with .NET: There are a lot of new terminology and technologies to explain about .NET before you can get people up to speed. But if .NET is successful, we'll just take it for granted in the same way that we take common PC technology, like the desktop GUI or the mouse, for granted.

To understand .NET, you have to remember that PCs are no longer islands of activity and functionality, and that thanks to the global Internet and pervasive home networking technologies, we're moving to an ever increasingly connected world. So why not take advantage of this fact and actually use this interconnectivity?

Before networking, the Internet, and .NET, you could only utilize services that originated from your PC, typically from applications such as Word or Excel. With a network, it's possible for local applications – such as Word or Excel – to take advantage of services on other networked PCs or servers. For example, a company might use a central dictionary list that all networked Word users can access. And with the Internet and a special application called a Web browser, you can search for information across the globe and access services from machines in distant locations.

.NET to the Future

.NET is the next logical step to continue to enhance the interconnectivity between computers using the Internet. Using the existing Internet infrastructure and emerging standards-based technologies, you will be able to use a .NET-compatible client to access services from around the world. So, for example, a future .NET version of Word might have hooks to integrate with dictionaries in, say, London, Bangladesh, and Brasilia. And you will be able to print documents to online printing services anywhere in the world.

.NET will see its biggest gains in new types of applications and services, rather than legacy applications such as Word. You'll be able to track stock prices, airline fares, local traffic and weather conditions, and any other important information through a system of .NET-based alerts and notifications. You will be able to store your private information in an online database and authorize online stores to bill certain credit card or other accounts, without those stores having access to your account information. And this stuff will interoperate with a wide range of devices, not just Windows PCs. You will be able to get notifications and alerts on next-generation cell phones, for example, or Pocket PC devices, or even televisions.

But Before That Can Happen. . . .

Of course, the full realization of these .NET technologies is years away from happening. In the meantime, Microsoft is taking some interim steps with the following technologies:

◆ **.NET Passport:** Microsoft's first real-world, available .NET technology is Passport – recently renamed .NET Passport – an online service that enables you to set up a single password to sign in, securely, to any participating Web site or service. And in addition to the single sign-in feature, compatible .NET e-commerce sites can offer Passport customers an express purchase option that makes online shopping easier and more convenient. Few sites actually use this feature at this time, and no users that I know personally have taken advantage of it.

♦ **.NET Enterprise Servers:** Microsoft has a slew of products that fall under the .NET Enterprise Servers moniker. However, none of these products actually expose .NET services in any way. A future generation of .NET Enterprise Servers — beginning with the next-generation Windows Server, Windows .NET Server, which is due in late 2002 — will finally realize this goal.

♦ **Visual Studio .NET:** For developers, Microsoft released an amazing suite of tools called Visual Studio .NET in early 2002. This suite provides multiple ways in which to program for .NET environments. The release of Visual Studio .NET is expected to kick off a new generation of .NET software from third parties.

♦ **.NET Alerts:** For consumers, Microsoft launched .NET Alerts in late 2001. These alerts integrate with Windows Messenger and provide notifications for new e-mail messages, traffic conditions, Expedia flight updates, and the like. Over the coming months, the number and scope of .NET Alerts are expected to grow dramatically.

♦ **.NET My Services:** By the time this book is available, Microsoft should have released a beta version of its upcoming .NET My Services, a free .NET-based consumer service that will form the basis for other Microsoft and third-party services.

Read on to find out ways in which Windows XP can integrate with the .NET services that are available now and in the near future.

Using .NET Passport

.NET Passport provides Web-based, single sign-in capabilities and e-commerce express purchase functionality. The goal is to make it easier for you to use those parts of the Web that require you to log on and identify yourself. For example, today, you must maintain separate accounts at each e-commerce site you visit. So if you frequent, say, Amazon.com, Buy.com, and Yahoo!, you must maintain separate account profiles at each site, each with its own logon/password information and associated shipping address, credit card number, and preferred shipping type.

If .NET Passport is successful, you can maintain a single account with a central Passport server that provides authentication and express purchase services to those e-commerce sites. You sign in to the service just once, and any compatible site — that is, any site that uses the .NET Passport service — recognizes you and the information you choose to make available.

You'll notice that I used the phrase "if .NET Passport is successful." That's because the success of .NET Passport is not guaranteed. Prior to Microsoft's move to .NET, Passport had been in operation for a few years, and not that many sites had signed on, although a few big names did participate, including eBay, Starbucks, Hilton, Victoria's Secret, and, of course, all Microsoft's MSN Web properties.

Microsoft has made some changes to .NET Passport that are expected to eventually expand the service into something far bigger than it is at the time of this writing. And most of those changes occur within the context of Windows XP.

Windows XP and .NET Passport

Windows XP is the first Microsoft operating system to integrate the .NET Passport service, much in the same way that previous Windows versions integrated Web browsing through Internet Explorer. .NET Passport integration takes two forms in XP: one that's been available in previous Messenger versions (called MSN Messenger) and one that's brand new to XP.

MESSENGER INTEGRATION

Windows Messenger is an instant messaging (IM) application on steroids. In addition to the more typical text chatting functionality, it offers voice and video chat features, application sharing and whiteboarding, and more. (For more information on these features, check out Chapter 15.)

But Messenger offers more than just real-time communications. In addition to these features, Messenger integrates with the .NET Passport service through Web-based e-mail accounts at Hotmail.com or MSN. When you sign up for a free Hotmail account (see www.hotmail.com for details) or a Web-based MSN account (which requires a monthly fee), you are automatically signed up for .NET Passport as well, and that account and e-mail address are associated with the .NET Passport service.

What this means is that you can register your Hotmail or MSN account so that you receive notification in Messenger when you get new e-mail. You can also receive notification when friends and family members are online, which makes it easier to strike up a conversation. And if you allow this type of access, your contacts can be alerted when you're online as well.

LOGON INTEGRATION IN WINDOWS XP

Messenger integration is available to users of previous Windows versions because the feature is available in MSN Messenger, the Messenger version that works with Windows 9x, Me, NT, and 2000. Windows Messenger ships only with XP, so XP users get a higher level of .NET Passport integration.

Here's how it works: In XP, you can configure .NET Passport to automatically log you on to the service when you log on to your XP system. And because XP supports multiple users, each user can have his or her own .NET Passport integration as well. So say you have a Hotmail account. You can configure XP to automatically log you on to Messenger with that account, and thus to .NET Passport, every time you log on to Windows and load your desktop.

If you're interested in this feature, you can save yourself a step. If you're not interested in .NET Passport, Messenger, or a free Hotmail account, you might find this feature a little invasive. XP is a bit over the top when it comes to asking you to create a .NET Passport account, a criticism that many have leveled against Microsoft's all-too-obvious cross-selling in the operating system. You find out how you can remove this functionality in "Preventing Windows Messenger/.NET Passport from Starting," later in the chapter.

If you want to take advantage of .NET Passport — and frankly, I do and recommend it, even if you're not interested in IM-type chatting functionality — then XP makes it easy. The next section looks at that process.

Configuring Passport for Auto-Login

When you create a new XP account and log on for the second time, you're presented with the balloon help window, shown in Figure 11-1. When you click this window, the .NET Passport Wizards starts.

Figure 11-1: Microsoft isn't subtle about asking you to use Passport in Windows XP.

If you canceled the balloon help window in the past, you can still associate your XP logon with .NET Passport. Here's how:

1. Choose Start→Control Panel and then select User Accounts. This launches the User Accounts application, shown in Figure 11-2.

2. Select your account. You can only associate a .NET Passport account with the user currently logged on; you cannot associate a .NET Passport account with one of the other XP accounts.

3. The next screen, shown in Figure 11-3, displays configuration options for the account. Select the Set Up My Account to Use a .NET Passport option to launch the .NET Passport Wizard.

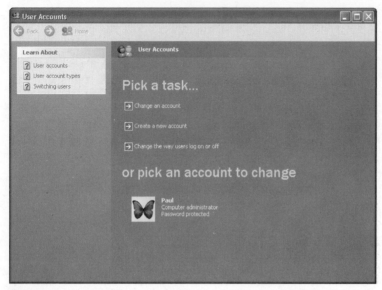

Figure 11-2: The User Accounts application allows you to configure the users that log on to the local system in XP.

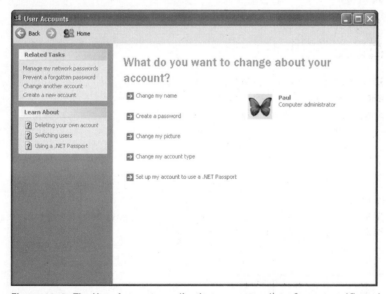

Figure 11-3: The User Accounts application presents a list of user-specific tasks.

After the wizard begins, you can associate your XP user account with a .NET Passport by following these steps:

1. Click Next to begin. The wizard connects to the Internet and downloads information from the .NET Passport servers.

2. In the next step, shown in Figure 11-4, you can associate an e-mail address with a .NET Passport. If you have one – typically a Hotmail account – select Yes and then click Next to continue. Otherwise, select No and set up a free Web-based MSN account. Follow the steps for creating your new MSN account and then continue.

3. In the next two steps, enter your Hotmail or MSN account (something like *my_account*@hotmail.com) and then a password for your .NET Password account. You can (and should) choose a password that's completely different than the one for your XP account.

   Also, you can optionally configure the .NET Passport to log on automatically using the password information you provide here. This option is enabled by default, and, frankly, you should leave it that way unless you want to enter your .NET Passport password every time you log on to Windows (thereby bypassing the point of this whole exercise). Click Next to continue.

4. When the wizard is completed, your XP account and .NET Passport are connected. You can change this option at any time by revisiting the User Accounts application and changing the settings for your .NET Passport account.

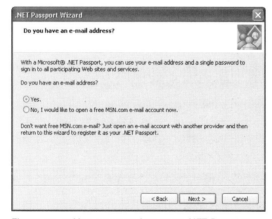

Figure 11-4: You can associate your .NET Passport account with an e-mail address to create a single sign-on for compatible Web sites.

Using Windows Messenger with Passport

After your accounts are synchronized, log off from XP and log on again. The Messenger icon appears in the lower-right corner of the screen and is animated as it logs you on to the Passport service. If you have any new e-mail, you see a notification window like the one shown in Figure 11-5. Click the window to launch your Web browser, which automatically navigates to your Web-based MSN or Hotmail inbox.

Figure 11-5: The Messenger service provides notifications for events such as new e-mail.

CONFIGURING MESSENGER

To configure Messenger, choose Tools→Options from the main Messenger window. This opens the Options dialog box. The following options are available:

◆ **Personal:** On this tab, you can do the following:

■ Choose what name you want to appear to your contacts and other users (*Paul,* for example). Unlike your .NET Passport account, the name does not have to be unique (there could be thousands of Pauls out there, for example).

■ Configure your Passport profile at the MSN Membership Directory. Properly configuring your Passport profile is important; I recommend checking this out immediately.

■ Choose the fonts and emoticons you see in Messenger conversations.

◆ **Phone:** The Phone tab lets you configure the phone numbers you use and set up an account for a mobile device. Be careful with the phone number options because anything you type here is visible to any of your contacts; I recommend leaving these options blank.

The Mobile Settings link takes you to the MSN Mobile Web site, where you can configure a compatible cell phone, alphanumeric pager, Pocket PC, or other device to interoperate with your Passport account. If you have a compatible device, you can configure it to receive text messages and alerts when you're away from your computer. For example, my

Motorola StarTAC 7868 cell phone is compatible with this feature, so when I'm away from my phone, I receive text messages that might otherwise be sent to Messenger.

◆ **Preferences:** This important tab lets you configure general preferences, such as

  ■ Whether Messenger should run when Windows starts

  ■ How Messenger alerts you when different actions occur

  ■ Where files received during a Messenger file transfer are delivered by default

◆ **Privacy:** On the Privacy tab, you determine who can see your online status and start conversations with you. By default, all .NET Passport users, including your contacts, can see whether you're online and start a conversation with you. My account is set up so that only my contacts can see my online status and start conversations with me.

  You can also view which users have added you to their contact lists and other contact-related options.

◆ **Accounts:** On this tab, you configure whether Messenger signs into a .NET Passport account (the norm) or another communications service, which is generally used in corporate settings. For example, some companies want to take advantage of the technologies behind Passport – such as instant messaging – but not actually use the global Passport service, perhaps to prevent their employees from spending the day chatting with the outside world. Home users can safely ignore this tab.

◆ **Connection:** The Connection tab determines whether Messenger uses the global system settings for using an Internet connection (the default) or a customized setting, where you can configure proxy server information. Again, home users can safely ignore this tab.

After you've configured Messenger to work with Passport, you can use Messenger's instant messaging and other real-time communications features, as described in Chapter 14.

CONFIGURING PASSPORT

You can also configure various Passport-related services, which are currently available only from the Passport Web site and not through a UI component in Windows. To configure .NET Passport, visit Passport Member Services on the Web (www. passport.com). Here, you can edit your .NET Passport profile (address, birth date, and the like), edit your password information, create and edit your .NET Passport wallet, and configure your mobile phone to access .NET Passport using a numeric PIN instead of a password.

Pay particular attention to the following areas:

◆ **.NET Passport profile:** By default, the e-mail address associated with your .NET Passport can be placed in an Internet White Pages directory, which could lead to heavier-than-usual amounts of spam. To prevent this, view your .NET Passport Profile and uncheck the three options related to sharing, as shown in Figure 11-6.

◆ **.NET Passport wallet:** Eventually, one of the primary benefits of .NET Passport will be its express checkout service, which will enable you to automatically sign on to compatible Web sites and purchase items without having to type in your credit card information every time. For this feature to work, you first need to set up a .NET Passport wallet (once called an *MSN e-wallet*), which is essentially a database entry on Microsoft's servers that contains your credit card information. How you feel about Microsoft and security will determine whether you decide to configure this information. My advice is simple: Wait. Even if you trust Microsoft, not enough Web sites are currently using Passport to justify the risk.

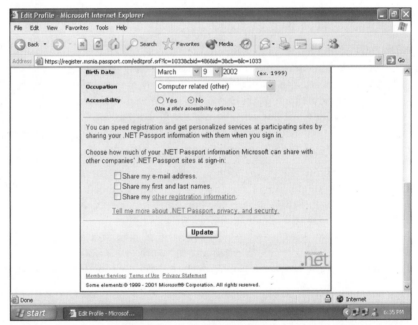

Figure 11-6: If you're concerned that other users might send spam to your account, be sure that you correctly configure your Passport profile.

◆ **Mobile phone number:** If you have a compatible Web-enabled cell phone, you can configure a numeric PIN (personal information number) that will let you log on to your .NET Passport by using numbers rather than your normal alphanumeric password. This feature is somewhat limited because few phones have this capability, and most of those that do have it offer small, text-only screens that are compatible with a small percentage of the wider Web. However, if you have such a phone, you may want to configure this feature.

Receiving .NET Alerts

One of the cool new features in Windows Messenger is .NET Alerts, online services that provide you with a wealth of timely information, including scheduling alerts through MSN Calendar, location-specific traffic alerts, weather updates, stock quotes, and more.

Technically speaking, the .NET Alerts service is just a delivery mechanism that has server- and client-side parts. Microsoft hosts the server stuff on its .NET Passport servers. The client-side parts are available in Windows Messenger and, increasingly, in other .NET Passport–compatible clients such as smart cell phones and other mobile devices. If you remember the *push* technology that appears in the version 4.0 Web browsers (Netscape Navigator 4.0 and Netcaster, and Internet Explorer 4.0 and Active Desktop/Channels), then you might think of this as the next logical extension of push technology. The difference is that this time the information being pushed to users is being channeled through a user interface that actually makes sense, rather than through a Web browser.

But just because Microsoft provides the servers and clients doesn't mean that .NET Alerts come only from the software giant. Microsoft has teamed with a variety of third parties — called *alerts providers* — to provide alerts to .NET Passport customers. Many alerts are free, and some are subscription based, and I think we can expect to see more and more of the latter going forward.

After the two pieces are in place, you can receive alerts, which are small notification messages that you configure to your liking. If you have XP, you're all set: Windows Messenger is built in, and it's already set up to work with .NET Alerts. The next three sections take a look at the types of alerts that are currently available, though this list should grow dramatically by the time you read this.

Microsoft Alerts

As you might expect, Microsoft offers a number of alerts through its MSN online service, all of which are currently free:

♦ **MSN Calendar:** Every .NET Passport user gets a free MSN Calendar account, which lets you store appointments and other scheduling information online. You can configure alerts to notify you of certain appointments and set times, and these alerts are individual to each appointment. This is a highly desirable and nicely implemented alert.

- ◆ **MSN Carpoint:** MSN Carpoint is a leading Web site for automobile users, and it provides traffic alerts for hundreds of metro areas. You can specify certain types of alerts, certain days and times of day, and particular car model information.

- ◆ **MSN Money/CNBC:** MSN Money/CNBC offers a number of alerts, including stock alerts, where you're notified if certain stocks or mutual funds move up or down a certain percentage, or at certain times of the day; account alerts, which provide you with important account balance information; or content alerts, which notify you when certain CNBC analysts write new articles.

- ◆ **MSN Music:** Microsoft's MSN Music Web site is an online resource for all things musical, including streaming Internet radio stations, music recommendations, and music-related news. You can configure MSN Music alerts to notify you when your favorite artists are appearing locally in concert or release new albums.

Third-Party Alerts

Third-party alerts are often free, but more subscription fee alerts are beginning to appear. Here are some of the currently available third-party alerts:

- ◆ **eBay:** eBay is the most popular online auction on the Internet, and if you've ever lost out on an important auction because of a last-minute bid, you'll appreciate this alert. It notifies you whenever an auction you've bid on has changed or ended.

- ◆ **FYE.com:** The online arm of a retail music store, FYE.com alerts provide you with information about top-selling albums, upcoming releases, and FYE recommended music.

- ◆ **McAfee.com:** One of the most popular antivirus vendors, McAfee offers free information about new virus outbreaks. If you subscribe to McAfee's one or two-year antivirus subscription programs, you can have the company send you an alert when your subscription is about to run out so you can renew it.

- ◆ **uBid Online Auctions:** Online auctioneer uBid provides alerts for auctions you've been outbid on, auctions you've won, and same-product auctions, which are auctions that feature a product you tried to win but were outbid on.

Configuring Alerts

You can sign up for and configure .NET Alerts directly through the main Messenger window. Here's how:

1. If you don't see an MSN Alerts tab on your main Messenger window, as shown in Figure 11-7, choose Tools→Show Tabs→Microsoft .NET Alerts.

2. Once the Microsoft .NET Alerts is in the main Messenger window, click on the yellow bell to see what, if any alerts you have and to sign up for alerts if you have never configured any a this point.

3. Click the Sign Up Now button, which launches a browser window, and navigate to the MSN Alerts sign-up page.

4. Click the Sign Up for Microsoft .NET Alerts link. This opens the general settings screen in Internet Explorer, as shown in Figure 11-8. Here, you decide how alerts will be delivered by default (though you can change this on a per-alert basis, which is nice). You can also open this page by visiting alerts.microsoft.com and choosing General Settings.

How you configure this delivery setting depends on how you want to receive alerts. If you're only using Messenger, then the default option, Always Deliver My Alerts to My Computer (Messenger), is sufficient. Otherwise, you can configure .NET Alerts to deliver alerts to various locations (Messenger, e-mail, or a mobile device) based on your online status.

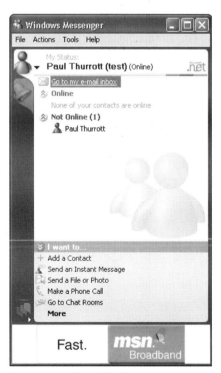

Figure 11-7: The MSN Alerts tab resembles a yellow bell.

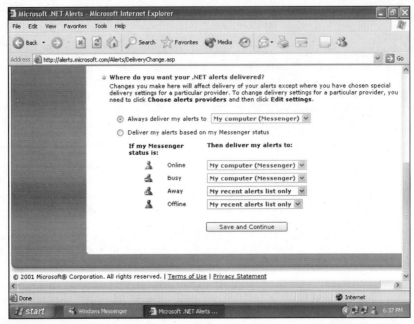

Figure 11-8: You can configure how you want .NET Alerts to be delivered, based on your online status.

5. After customizing your general settings, choose which alerts you'd like to use. A number of choices are available, as shown in Figure 11-9. Click any alert type to launch a new window and configure the alert.

After adding alerts, they appear on the Alerts tab of the main Messenger window. In this example, I've signed up for an MSN Money alert regarding Microsoft's stock price. To configure an alert, click the pencil graphic under Go to Alerts Site. You can also add more alerts by clicking Add Alert.

.NET Alerts arrive in the form of a notification window, just like that used by Hotmail e-mail.

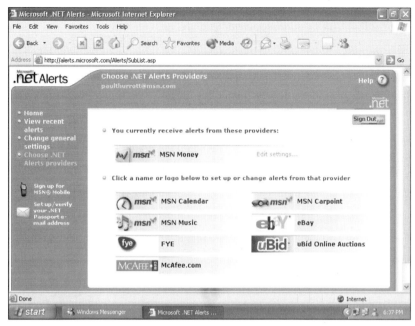

Figure 11-9: Several .NET Alerts are currently available, and more are on the way.

A .NET My Services Preview

Sometime in late 2002, Microsoft will unleash its first .NET-oriented Web services, called .NET My Services. These services build on .NET Passport and .NET Alerts and provide a base platform for consumer-oriented services that Microsoft and other companies can subsequently build on. The goal behind these services is to provide consumers with an online location to store their personal information and control the ways in which other entities can access that information. A version aimed at businesses will appear later as well.

For consumers, .NET My Services will be exposed as applications and services that run under Windows and, eventually, other platforms such as Mac OS X and even Linux. Microsoft .NET Passport will provide user-authentication capabilities, and Windows Messenger and other end-user applications will interact with various .NET services, which will include the following (some of which are available already):

- ◆ **.NET Profile:** Basic information about a user, including name, nickname, special dates, and photographs

- ◆ **.NET Contacts:** An electronic address book

- ◆ **.NET Locations:** Electronic and physical location and rendezvous information

- ◆ **.NET Alerts:** A list of notification subscriptions (now available)

- ◆ **.NET Presence:** Online status information and support mobile devices to use if offline (now available)

- ◆ **.NET Inbox:** E-mail and voice mail inbox, based on Hotmail, though it will work with other existing e-mail services as well (now available)

- ◆ **.NET Calendar:** Time and task management (now available as MSN Calendar and the MSN Calendar alerts service)

- ◆ **.NET Documents:** Online document storage

- ◆ **.NET ApplicationSettings:** Global application settings, such as font size and resolution

- ◆ **.NET FavoriteWebSites:** Favorite Web sites, à la Favorites in Internet Explorer, but server based and thus available from any connected device

- ◆ **.NET Wallet:** .NET Passport–based eWallet information, such as receipts, payment instruments, coupons, and other transaction records (now available)

- ◆ **.NET Devices:** A list of PC and non-PC devices used by an identity, with per-device settings and capabilities (now partially available through MSN Mobile services)

- ◆ **.NET Services:** A listing of the services that are provided for an individual identity

- ◆ **.NET Lists:** A server-based list capability

- ◆ **.NET Categories:** A way to group .NET Lists

Like most .NET technologies, .NET My Services will be exposed as XML-based Web services. For more information about this exciting technology, please check the Web site for this book at www.xphomenetworking.com.

Preventing Windows Messenger/.NET Passport from Starting

If you've read about the exciting ways in which .NET Passport and Windows Messenger can enhance your life and concluded that this admittedly invasive technology is not for you, I've got good news for you: You can prevent Windows Messenger from starting on your system.

Messenger isn't normally removable through the normal Add or Remove Programs applet in the Control Panel, but in XP Professional Edition, you can use a little-known application called the Local Group Policy Editor to prevent any user on your XP system from accessing Messenger. Or you can control whether Messenger starts on a user-by-user basis; this method works in XP Home Edition as well as Pro.

Preventing Windows Messenger Globally

To prevent every XP Professional user from accessing Messenger, follow these steps:

1. Choose Start→Run.

2. Type **gpedit.msc** and click OK to launch the Local Group Policy Editor, shown in Figure 11-10.

3. On the left side of the editor, expand Computer Configuration, expand Administrative Templates, then Windows Components and then Windows Messenger, as shown in Figure 11-11. You then see two items to configure: Do Not Allow Windows Messenger to Run and Do Not Automatically Start Windows Messenger Initially.

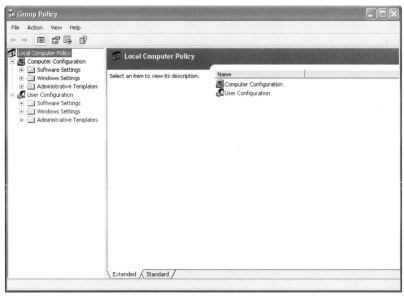

Figure 11-10: The Local Group Policy Editor, available only in XP Pro, allows you to configure features for the entire system, or per user.

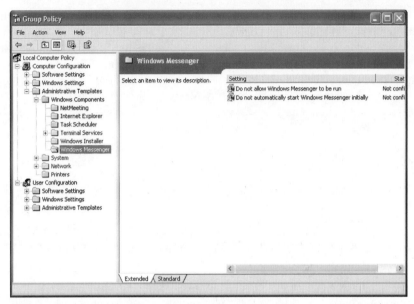

Figure 11-11: You can configure Windows Messenger not to run automatically when you start Windows, or you can disable it altogether.

4. Right-click the Do Not Automatically Start Windows Messenger Initially option and select Properties. The Settings dialog box appears, as shown in Figure 11-12.

5. Select Enabled and click OK. Then close the Local Group Policy Editor.

Figure 11-12: You configure individual settings from the Settings dialog box.

This setting only prevents Windows Messenger from loading initially. But that usually does the trick. You can also use the editor to prevent Messenger from ever running, using the fist option shown in the figure, "Do Not Allow Windows Messenger To Be Run.

Preventing Windows Messenger on a User-by-User Basis

To prevent Windows Messenger from loading on a user-by-user basis, log on to the specific client computer as the user that won't be using this feature and then perform the following steps (note that you have to repeat these steps for each user on the system):

1. Choose Start→Run.

2. Type **regedit** and click OK to launch the Registry Editor, as shown in Figure 11-13.

3. Expand the tree view on the left to HKEY_CURRENT_USER, then Software, then Microsoft, then Windows, then CurrentVersion, and then Run. You will see a number of Registry keys on the right, including one called MSMSGS, which is the Windows Messenger service.

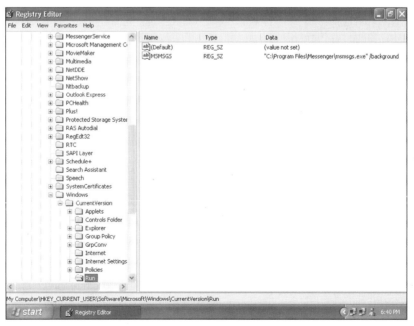

Figure 11-13: In XP Home, you have to turn off Messenger individually for each user; you do this with the Registry Editor.

4. Right-click the MSMSGS key and select Delete.

5. Close the Registry editor.

Chapter 12

Browsing and Searching the Web

IN THIS CHAPTER

◆ Using the new Internet Explorer 6.0 in Windows XP

◆ Exploring the enhancements to MSN Explorer

◆ Tightening down your browser using IE security zones, security Levels and privacy features

◆ Working with non-Microsoft browsers and using their features under XP

TODAY, WEB BROWSING IS as common as almost any other PC task. But Web browsing has changed a lot since the mid-1990s, when single-purpose applications such as Mosaic, Netscape Navigator, and the first versions of Microsoft's Internet Explorer (IE) burst on the scene. Since then, browsers have become full-featured suites that provide access to a variety of online services, including e-mail, File Transfer Protocol (FTP) capabilities, and various *push* technologies, which replace the sometimes mindless meandering we call browsing with individually targeted information.

Microsoft's reaction to the Web browser phenomenon was as controversial as it was prescient. Instead of simply bundling its IE browser application with the Windows operating system, Microsoft *integrated* the product, or *commingled* its code with that of Windows so that the two products became one. The similar tasks of browsing local resources (such as file folders on the hard drive and Windows Help files), network resources (network shares), and Web sites could be performed by the same code. It sort of makes sense, but that's not what a federal court found. Instead, in a landmark ruling that was upheld on appeal, Microsoft was found to have *illegally* bundled IE with Windows to harm competition.

Legal issues are a matter for another book, however. What we're dealing with here is a set of Web browsing products — IE and MSN Explorer — which are very much integrated into Windows today. Although it's possible to remove them, to varying degrees, from Windows XP, both IE and MSN Explorer offer best-of-breed Web browsing functionality for new and experienced users alike.

Using Internet Explorer

Windows XP ships with Internet Explorer 6, the latest version of IE at the time of this writing. IE 6 is a subtle improvement over the previous IE 5.*x* generation, which included IE 5.0, 5.01, and 5.5. Specifically, IE 6 includes improvements in three core areas, as described in the following sections.

Digital Media Enhancements

Internet Explorer 6 includes features aimed at making digital media experiences more enjoyable. For image lovers, IE 6 includes an integrated Image toolbar (see Figure 12-1) that lets you quickly access image-related tasks, such as copying, printing, e-mailing, and accessing the XP My Pictures folder.

IE 6.0 also features an interesting image resizing feature for those images that are too large to fit within the current browser window. With previous IE versions, the image would have scrolled off the visible area of the browser, but in IE 6.0, the image is resized on-screen so that it fits properly, as shown in Figure 12-2. A small button appears in the lower right of the image when you mouse-over that area so that you can easily resize it to its original dimensions by clicking on the image that appears in the corner.

For music lovers, IE 6 includes an integrated Media Bar, shown in Figure 12-3, which lets you access online music, videos, and other multimedia content without having to access another application. Of course, this being XP, you're given the choice, and you can decide to play such clips in Windows Media Player instead.

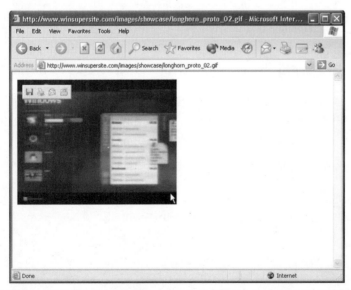

Figure 12-1: The Image toolbar lets you quickly access image-related tasks, directly from IE.

Figure 12-2: Images that are too large to display within the browser window can be automatically resized to fit.

Figure 12-3: The Media Bar lets you play multimedia content without requiring a second, separate application window.

IE 6.0 Is More Reliable

Aping a crucial new feature found in Office XP and Windows XP, IE 6 offers an error-reporting tool that kicks in whenever IE crashes. This tool lets you optionally report problems back to Microsoft so that it can fix bugs in future IE versions. I strongly recommend that all Windows XP users take advantage of this error-reporting tool whenever a problem occurs, ensuring that future Microsoft software is as reliable as possible.

As time goes on, common problems will cause a link to appear so that you can apply a fix. If you experience a known issue for which there is a fix, the IE error-reporting tool will direct you to download the fix so that you won't have this problem again. Good stuff.

IE 6.0 Provides Better Privacy Online

Sun Microsystems CEO Scott McNealy has said of privacy, "Get over it, you gave up your privacy a long time ago." But curt denunciation of privacy in this connected era notwithstanding, many entities are working to ensure that your personal information remains as private as possible. IE 6 includes some recent technologies that protect your privacy on the Web.

IE 6 gives you better control over *cookies*, small text files that are created on your system by Web sites that wish to provide customized browsing experiences to their users. Cookies are debated, but they're here to stay. So IE 6 lets you define preferences for cookies, including which cookies it will accept and which it will decline.

The technology behind this feature is called the Platform for Privacy Preferences (P3P). This topic is covered in more detail in "Privacy and the Web," later in the chapter.

Other IE Features

Like previous IE versions, Internet Explorer 6 provides a best-of-breed Web browsing experience. Here are some of the major IE features you might want to take advantage of:

◆ **New XP-style customizable user interface:** The version of IE 6 that's included with Windows XP adopts the new XP "Luna" look and feel, with colorful new toolbar icons and fully integrated dialog boxes, menus, scroll bars, list boxes, and other on-screen elements. Web form controls even take on the XP look and feel, as shown in Figure 12-4, making your overall Web experience all the more elegant.

◆ **Integrated Outlook Express:** IE 6 includes a new version of Outlook Express with e-mail and Usenet newsgroup functionality. This IE component is covered more closely in Chapter 13.

◆ **Windows Messenger integration:** Microsoft's real-time communications tool, Windows Messenger is also integrated directly into the IE user interface, making it easy to send a quick URL to one of your online contacts. Messenger is discussed in detail in Chapters 11 and 13.

◆ **Best Web site compatibility:** Of all the available Web browsers out there, IE is the most compatible with Web standards such as Hypertext Markup Language (HTML), eXtensible Markup Language (XML), and Cascading Style Sheets (CSS). More important, IE is (by far) the most compatible with existing, real-world Web sites. More Web sites render correctly (as their authors intended) on IE than any other browser.

◆ **Java compatibility:** Microsoft made the crucial decision to ship XP without support for Sun's popular Java programming language, but you can download support for Java from Windows Update or Sun's Web site. This gives IE users access to the 7 million Java-enabled Web sites.

◆ **Integration with the .NET platform:** As discussed in Chapter 11, Microsoft is moving to a future platform called .NET, and IE is ready. Microsoft expects that Web clients using IE 6 will be one of the most common ways for users to consume upcoming .NET Web services.

Searching the Web with IE

One of the most popular things you can do with Internet Explorer is search for online content. To facilitate this task, Internet Explorer 6 includes an integrated Search bar called the Search Companion and in-line searching capabilities in the Address bar. Here are some popular ways to find what you need with IE 6.

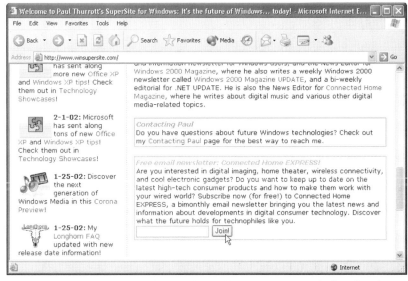

Figure 12-4: Under Windows XP, IE and even Web pages automatically take advantage of new-look UI widgets.

SEARCHING WITH THE SEARCH COMPANION

If you click the Search toolbar button in IE, the Search Companion opens in the left side of the IE window, as shown in Figure 12-5. By default, the Search Companion features an insipid little animated dog.

Figure 12-5: The Search Companion features a cute little dog by default.
I recommend killing it immediately.

If you don't find the dog annoying, you can type a question, phrase, or word into the text box, and IE will use the MSN Search engine to search. A typical set of search results is shown in Figure 12-6.

However, you can fine-tune IE's search functionality, which I recommend. First, get rid of the dumb dog. And then use a better search engine than the one provided by MSN.

To get rid of the animated character, click the Turn Off Animated Character option. Fido will walk (slowly) into the distance and disappear, leaving you with the dog-less search pane shown in Figure 12-7.

Now, you can customize the search engine preferences. Click Change Preferences to access the list of Search Companion options shown in Figure 12-8. Some of the options here are actually related to local system file searching, which gives you an idea of how IE and the underlying operating system are interconnected.

Click Change Internet Search Behavior to change the way IE performs searches, as shown in Figure 12-9. You have two options here: the default Search Companion, and Classic Internet search, which causes IE 6 to act like previous IE versions and access a single search engine.

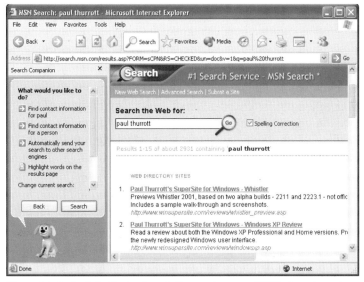

Figure 12-6: By default, the Search Companion uses MSN's Search engine.

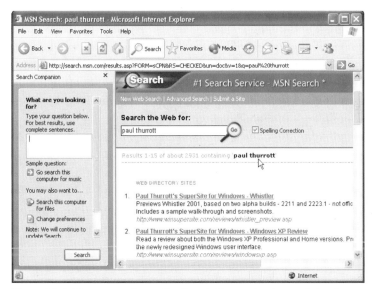

Figure 12-7: You can configure the Search Companion in a variety of ways, including removing the animated assistant.

Microsoft says that its search engine is aggregating searches from various search engines, but I've seen little to back up that claim, and it's pretty clear that MSN is getting a larger than usual share of the search duties if you use the Search Companion. To choose a rival search engine (I recommend Google), click With Classic Internet Search and select the search engine you'd like to use. Then click OK.

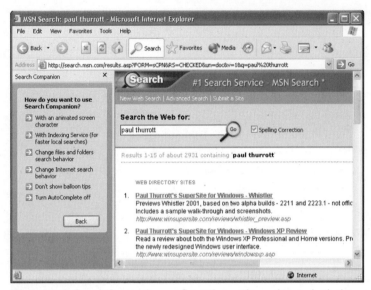

Figure 12-8: Search Companion configuration options relate to both the local computer and Internet searches.

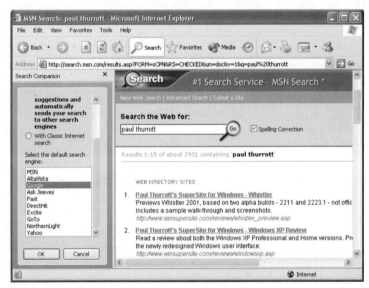

Figure 12-9: Choose the Web search engine you like.

If you chose another search engine, your search results now come up in that service's Web site, such as the Google results such in Figure 12-10.

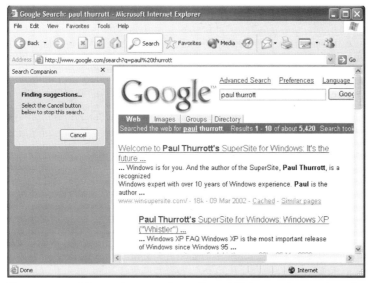

Figure 12-10: After you've properly configured IE, it uses the search engine of your choice.

SEARCHING FROM THE ADDRESS BAR

In addition to the integrated Search Companion, IE 6 also offers a shortcut for performing searches directly from the Address bar. This is nice for touch-typists, because you can easily access the Address bar by pressing Alt+D. However, it's a bit limited because MSN Search is always used.

To perform a search using the Address bar, follow these steps:

1. Select (highlight) all the text in the IE Address bar. (If the last click was in the browser window, pressing Alt+D will select all the text in the address bar.)

2. Type ? followed by the search phrase. For example, to search for information about Paul Thurrott, you could use:

   ```
   ? paul thurrott
   ```

3. Hit Enter or click the Go button. Your results are then displayed on the MSN Search page, as shown in Figure 12-11.

USING A SEARCH ENGINE

If you're not interested in using the integrated search functionality in Internet Explorer 6, simply navigate to a search engine directly and search from there. Again, I recommend Google, but other popular search engines include Excite, Netscape, and AltaVista.

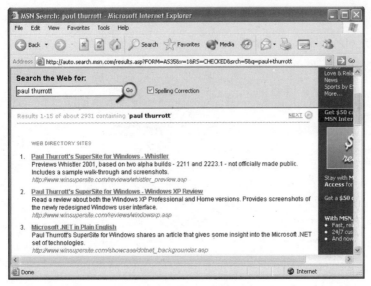

Figure 12-11: You cannot easily configure Address bar searches. Instead, they use the MSN Search page.

◆ **Google:** www.google.com

◆ **Excite:** www.excite.com

◆ **Netscape:** search.netscape.com

◆ **AltaVista:** www.altavista.com/

For Beginners Only: The MSN Explorer Experience

If Internet Explorer is a little too complex for you, or you use a Microsoft Web-based e-mail system such as Hotmail or MSN e-mail, consider the company's consumer-oriented browser environment, *MSN Explorer.* Actually, MSN Explorer – shown in Figure 12-12 – is more than just Web browsing and e-mail: It also integrates Windows Messenger instant messaging functionality and a other MSN Web services into a single attractive window that many people find quite appealing. MSN Explorer is positioned as the user interface for MSN dial-up customers; as such, it presents a decidedly uncluttered alternative to market leader America Online (AOL). But all Windows users can use it, regardless of whether they use MSN dial-up.

Figure 12-12: MSN Explorer is a consumer-oriented front end for Microsoft's
MSN Web properties.

MSN Explorer Features

MSN is designed for relatively unsophisticated users, but it actually offers a nicer
Web experience than IE in many cases, especially for Hotmail and Web-based MSN
e-mail, which looks much nicer in MSN Explorer than in IE or other Web browsers.
Thus, even more technical users might find MSN Explorer interesting. Here are the
major features offered by this all-in-one experience:

◆ **Integrated Hotmail/Web-based MSN e-mail:** MSN Explorer offers a fairly
elegant looking front end for Hotmail and Web-based MSN e-mail (see
Figure 12-13), easily besting any other Web-based e-mail system in the
world. If you use Hotmail and don't care to use Outlook Express or
Outlook, but would rather have a Web-based solution, you could do a lot
worse than MSN Explorer.

For more information about Hotmail, check out Chapter 13.

◆ **Integrated MSN Web services:** MSN Explorer integrates MSN Web services
(not to be confused with .NET Web services) such as MSN Money Central,
MSN Communities, MSN eShop, and MSN Music directly into its top-
mounted toolbar, making it easier to move among these sites. You can also
add links to other services, such as MSN File Cabinet, ESPN Sports, Expedia
Maps, Expedia Travel, MSN Entertainment, MSN CarPoint, and MSN Mobile.

Figure 12-13: Hotmail and MSN Web-based e-mail look better in MSN Explorer than in other Web browsers.

◆ **Integrated Media Player:** IE 6.0 includes a Media Bar, but MSN Explorer had an integrated Media Player first, and it works like IE's Media Bar. Users choose between a single application or multiple applications when playing back Web-based multimedia files. You can dock the integrated media player (shown in Figure 12-14) at the side of the window, or you can undock and resize it.

◆ **Automatic update delivery:** Like IE, Microsoft updates MSN Explorer with bug fixes and other updates on a regular basis. Unlike IE, MSN Explorer can be updated to new features automatically so you don't have to manually search for updates. This is a crucial and important feature, and it's curious why IE wouldn't offer similar functionality. On the other hand, IE updates are often available through Windows Update.

◆ **Easy conversion from Internet Explorer:** When you configure MSN Explorer for the first time, your IE Favorites and Outlook Express contacts are automatically ported over so you don't have to manually re-create that information.

◆ **Multiple user logon:** MSN Explorer supports multiple user accounts, so you can have multiple online personalities, or identities, all available from within the same XP user account. This feature is mainly for users of older Windows versions; they make it hard or impossible to work with multiple users.

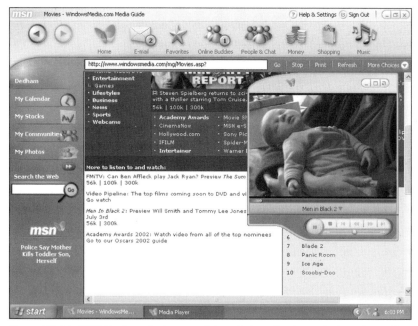

Figure 12-14: MSN Explorer features an integrated media player that can be easily undocked.

Searching the Web with MSN Explorer

Because of its charter as an MSN Web services front end, MSN Explorer's searching capabilities aren't as customizable as those in Internet Explorer. MSN Explorer features an integrated Search the Web bar, but it defaults to MSN Search, and there is no way to change that.

Likewise, the in-line Address bar searching capability in IE also works in MSN Explorer, but this cannot be configured to use anything but the MSN Search site.

Implementing Web Security

Whether you choose Internet Explorer or MSN Explorer, ensure that your online experience is as safe as possible. These days, there are numerous Internet-borne vulnerabilities. Most are aimed at your critical data or personal information. Don't be a statistic. Here are some steps to make your browsing experience as safe as possible.

To access the Internet Properties dialog box, right-click IE in the Start menu and choose Internet Properties. If IE isn't in the Start menu, choose Control Panel→Network and Internet Connections→Internet Options.

Using Security Zones and Security Levels

To implement security in Internet Explorer, Microsoft has established a concept called *security zones,* which are named locations that are applied to different Web addresses. You access security zones from the Security tab of the Internet Options dialog box, shown in Figure 12-15.

Figure 12-15: Internet Explorer provides default security zones, which simplify Internet security set up.

The following security zones exist in IE 6:

◆ **Internet:** This zone includes basically any public Web site address that you haven't specifically placed in another zone. So `www.microsoft.com`, `www.apple.com`, or whatever would be included in this zone.

◆ **Local Intranet:** If a Web site is located on your local network, it is included in this zone.

◆ **Trusted Sites:** You can manually place trusted Web sites in your Trusted Sites zone. This allows you to have IE automatically save logon/password combinations for secure sites, for example.

◆ **Restricted Sites:** This zone contains the addresses of Web sites that could potentially damage your computer or its data. If you do not trust a certain Web site, add it to this list. You won't be able to browse to that address and open yourself to problems.

WORKING WITH SECURITY LEVELS

Additionally, you can apply a security level to each of these zones. Microsoft includes High, Medium, Medium-Low, Low, and Custom security levels in IE. You can change various security levels by selecting a security zone and then clicking the Custom Level button. This displays the Security Settings dialog box, shown in Figure 12-16.

Figure 12-16: To fine-tune the configuration of your security zones, you can individually access various security settings.

IE 6 offers several stock security levels, which work fine for basic security levels, however, to really fine tune and get complete control over IE security, the Custom Level button is the key. This button is used quite a bit these days, given all the secuirty issues that have arisen and it gives you control over the following potential online elements:

◆ **Microsoft ActiveX Controls and Plug-ins:** When IE 3 debuted in 1996, it included a new component technology called *ActiveX*. It allowed developers to create visual controls and back-end code modules that would run over the Internet and add interactivity to Web pages. ActiveX went over like a lead balloon for much of the world, though it was actually a pretty decent technology. It's still supported, but the big complaint against it is that ActiveX controls and browser plug-ins could be used to deliver viruses and other vulnerability exploits. So IE 6 lets you configure whether signed (safe), unsigned (unsafe), or other (completely unsafe) ActiveX controls will run.

Previous IE versions supported a type of browser *plug-in* that some referred to as a *Netscape plug-in* (Netscape's browser was the first to use this). Like Netscape, Microsoft no longer supports this technology. IE 6 is the first IE version that does not support Netscape-style plug-ins.

◆ **Downloads:** You can configure whether IE automatically downloads files or fonts. For example, files that cannot be displayed in the browser typically initiate a dialog box that asks you what you'd like to do with that file; downloading it is usually the default action.

◆ **Microsoft Virtual Machine (VM):** Though Windows XP doesn't ship with a Java run-time environment, you can download one from Windows Update. If you do, you gain access to Java content on the Web. However, Java applets and other content could cause problems. So you can determine whether Java content is totally disabled, or enabled with various safety levels.

◆ **Miscellaneous:** A mixed bag of security-related features that don't have a home elsewhere. The Miscellaneous group lets you configure whether desktop items can be installed, whether the browser can access data sources on domains other than those used to display the current Web page, and whether the HTML META-REFRESH is allowed just to name a few items.

◆ **Scripting:** Like ActiveX controls and Java, the use of scripting languages such as JavaScript/ECMAScript/Jscript and VBScript is controversial. For this reason, you can choose to display scripting, disable Java-related scripting, and the like.

◆ **User Authentication:** This setting determines how Web-based logon dialogs are handled. For example, the Internet zone disables automatic logon by default — you have to repeatedly type in your password every time you access a public Web site that requires authentication (unless you place the URL of that site into your Trusted Sites zone). Intranet sites store your logon info, so you don't have to do this.

ADDING SITES TO THE TRUSTED SITES ZONE

If you find yourself having to re-logon to secure Web sites repeatedly, you might be put off by IE's default user-authentication setting — it requires you to type in your password every time you access such a site. But you don't have to reduce the security for the whole Internet zone to save yourself some time on a few sites. Instead, just add the URL for the secure site to your Trusted Sites zone. Here's how:

1. Open the Internet Options dialog box and navigate to the Security tab.

2. Click the Trusted Sites icon. This enables Trusted Sites configuration, as shown in Figure 12-17.

3. Click the Sites button. the Trusted Sites dialog box appears.

4. To add a site, type the name of the root server domain (that is, *https://www.server_name.com* and not the full URL to the page you generally access) under Add This Web Site to the Zone, and then click Add.

5. Click OK when you're done adding sites to your Trusted Sites list.

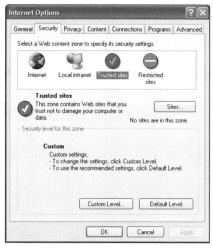

Figure 12-17: To add a site to your Trusted Sites list, choose Trusted Sites and then Sites.

Now, when you navigate to any destination under that address, you only have to enter your password once, and subsequent accesses will be automatically authenticated.

This change could present a security problem if anyone can access your system while it's logged on with your user credentials. Ensure that your system requires a logon and automatically returns to the Welcome screen after a short period of inactivity to be safe.

The preceding steps work for the Restricted Sites zone. Just start by accessing Restricted Sites instead of Trusted Sites.

Privacy and the Web

The IE 6 privacy features are based around two technologies. One is just emerging and the other has been around since the early days of the Web.

◆ The emerging technology is called the *Platform for Privacy Preferences* (P3P). It is a Web standard that establishes Web site privacy policies.

◆ The older technology has a cute name – *cookies* – and a somewhat undeserved sinister reputation.

The following sections look at the ways in which IE protects your privacy with these two features.

Configuring Privacy Features

To configure the privacy features in Internet Explorer 6, you open the Internet Options dialog box and navigate to the Privacy tab, shown in Figure 12-18.

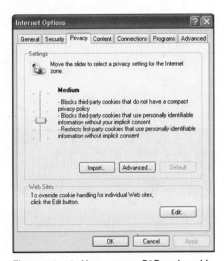

Figure 12-18: You manage P3P and cookie settings from the Privacy tab.

Here, you can determine the privacy setting IE uses when you're browsing *public* Web sites (sites that could be considered part of the Internet zone). Possible settings include:

◆ **Block All Cookies:** IE 6 doesn't accept any cookies, and existing cookies already found on your PC cannot be read by Web sites.

This keeps many Web sites from working. It's a draconian measure, unless you're not a big fan of the Web.

◆ **High:** Cookies without a P3P-compatible compact privacy policy are blocked. Likewise, cookies that use personal information without explicitly warning you are blocked.

◆ **Medium High:** *Third-party cookies* (cookies that do not originate on the site you're visiting — often online advertisements) without a P3P-compatible compact privacy policy are blocked. Third-party cookies that use personal information without explicitly warning you are also blocked. *First-party* cookies (cookies that originate on the site you're currently visiting) that use personal information without explicitly warning you are blocked.

◆ **Medium:** This is the default setting. There are two very subtle differences between this setting and Medium-High:

   ■ Whereas Medium-High blocks third-party cookies that use personal information without explicitly warning you, Medium blocks third-party cookies that use personal information without *implicitly* warning you.

   ■ First-party cookies that use personal information without *implicitly* warning you are restricted.

◆ **Low:** Third-party cookies without a P3P-compatible compact privacy policy are blocked, and first-party cookies that use personal information without implicitly warning you are restricted.

◆ **Accept All Cookies:** A fool's paradise where any and all cookies are allowed.

I cannot stress enough how foolish it would be to accept all cookies.

Additionally, you can override automatic cookie handling and simply define how first- and third-party cookies will be handled. Click the Advanced button, and you see the Advanced Privacy Settings dialog box, shown in Figure 12-19. You can set these two cookie types to be always accepted, always blocked, or always prompt you for acceptance (which sounds like a good idea until you try it: You'll be surprised by how often you need to okay cookies).

Figure 12-19: To override the default
cookie settings for the Internet Zone,
use the Advanced Privacy Settings
dialog box.

My recommendation regarding cookies is simple: First-party cookies are okay, but third-party cookies are *never* okay. So click Advanced, then click on the Override Automatic Cookie Handling check box, which then allows you to modify the First-Party Cookies and the Third-Party Cookies options. Set up first-party cookies to be accepted, and third-party cookies to be blocked. I like to enable session cookies as well, which is important on e-commerce sites such as Amazon.com. But that's up to you.

Other Web Browser Solutions

Though Microsoft will recoil in shock at this bit of advice, there are some other good Web browser choices with features that aren't yet available in IE. On the other hand, the browser alternatives tend to be less stable and compatible than IE, so proceed with caution. Here are my favorite two IE alternatives, along with some reasons why you might consider them over IE.

Mozilla/Netscape 6.x

Almost three years before Microsoft shipped Windows XP, browser company Netscape announced that it was opening up the source code to its upcoming Netscape 5 Web browser suite and starting the open-source *Mozilla* project, which would take advantage of the resources of the open-source community to develop a next-generation Web browser product. Mozilla is shown in Figure 12-20.

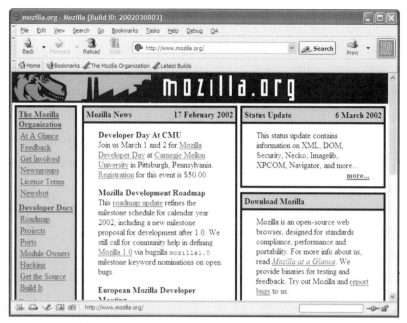

Figure 12-20: Mozilla is a full-featured, standards-based Web browser. It's free, too!

After numerous false starts, Mozilla is here, though it's still being improved almost daily. The underlying Mozilla technology is also being used as the basis for other Web browsers, including a good one from Netscape, eponymously titled Netscape 6. When compared to IE, Mozilla offers the following benefits:

◆ **Cross-platform:** Mozilla runs on Windows, Mac 9.*x* and OS X, various UNIX versions, Linux, and many other operating systems, and Web pages rendered in the browser appear virtually identical on all platforms.

◆ **Fast page rendering:** Mozilla's *Gecko* page renderer is quite fast, resulting in attractive, standards-compliant pages.

◆ **Skinnable user interface:** The Mozilla *shell* (the border around the Web page display) is customizable with a small selection of skins, some of which are of high quality. I expect this area to improve soon.

◆ **Optional tabbed user interface:** Mozilla can be configured to display new browser windows inside the same parent window using a tabbed design like that shown in Figure 12-21.

◆ **Automatic pop-up ad elimination:** One of the most annoying "features" of the Web are the many sites that pop up annoying advertisements in windows that appear either in front of or behind the window you're currently using. Mozilla will get rid of such ads automatically, if you want.

Figure 12-21: Mozilla's tabbed user interface lets you load multiple Web pages into the same window.

◆ **Sidebars:** Mozilla offers a configurable Sidebar that sort of resembles the various Explorer bars (Search, Favorites, Media, and History) that you can add to IE, with one crucial difference: You can completely configure which Sidebars you see and add new ones from the Web. Mozilla ships with What's Related, Search, Bookmarks, and History Sidebars displayed, but you can add many more (almost 200 at the time of this writing), including Sidebars for news, weather, sports, and numerous other topics. The What's Related Sidebar – shown in Figure 12-22 – is almost reason enough to use Mozilla; I use this feature a lot.

◆ **A simple Web page editor:** Mozilla includes a nice Composer application that makes short work of simple, static HTML Web pages. Microsoft used to ship an editor called *FrontPage Express* with IE 4.0, but the freebie Web page editor disappeared in subsequent versions.

Opera

A spunky little browser company from Norway provides a commercial IE alternative called Opera.

Figure 12-22: The Mozilla Sidebar offers a wide range of functionality, including the cool What's Related Sidebar.

The free version of Opera displays banner-style ads in the upper right of the application window. If you pay for Opera, the ads disappear. At the time of this writing, Opera cost about $40; the company offers discounts for students, upgraders, and volume purchasers.

Opera is shown in Figure 12-23. Here are some of the benefits of using Opera:

◆ **Completely customizable user interface:** Like Mozilla, Opera offers a fully customizable user interface. Unlike Mozilla, this feature is fully fleshed out, and numerous UI customizations are available, including the ability to make the browser look like Mozilla or IE if you want!

◆ **Browser detection avoidance:** Because so many sites are written specifically for IE or other browsers, you can configure Opera to identify itself as a different browser so it can render pages that might otherwise attempt to lock you out.

◆ **Different page-viewing modes:** You can choose whether browser windows open within a main Opera shell window or in their own windows, as they do in IE. If you use a single window, Opera uses a tabbed interface similar to that in Mozilla.

◆ **Keyboard navigation:** All browsers support keyboard controls, but Opera is the friendliest for keyboard commanders.

◆ **Zoom in/out functionality:** Other browsers let you adjust text size globally, but Opera includes a feature that lets you zoom in and out of Web pages, which magnifies all on-screen elements, including graphics. This is a great feature for the visually impaired.

◆ **Integrated dictionary, search, and language translation:** Double-click a word display in a Web page, and you receive a menu with options related to searching, an online dictionary and encyclopedia, and even a foreign language translation.

◆ **Cross-platform:** Opera runs on fewer platforms than Mozilla. Opera is available for Windows, Mac 9.*x* and OS X, Linux, Solaris, and a few other operating systems.

Figure 12-23: Opera offers a hugely customizable user interface, a tabbed user interface, and other compelling options.

Chapter 13

Collaborating with E-Mail and Newsgroups in XP

IN THIS CHAPTER

◆ Understand and use the latest Outlook Express to handle your emails

◆ Learn about Usenet newsgroups and how to access them through Outlook Express

◆ See how to create and use MSN's Hotmail as well as integrating it with Outlook Express

◆ Learn how to apply email filters and security settings to help manage all those unwanted emails

THE INTERNET HAS CHANGED a lot since its early academic incarnations, with more and more consumers jumping on board. Although some ancient Internet technologies (such as Gopher) have fallen by the wayside in favor of more impressive tools and services, some classic Internet functionality continues to this day, largely unchanged. I discuss two of these technologies, e-mail and Usenet newsgroups, in this chapter.

◆ E-mail, or *electronic mail,* is probably familiar to most people. An electronic version of the paper-based mail – or *snail mail* – we receive at home six days a week courtesy of the U.S. Postal Service, e-mail is delivered to electronic mailboxes and read with e-mail applications such as PINE, Pegasus, Netscape Mail, and Microsoft's offering, Outlook Express (OE). You can read e-mail messages, create and send new e-mail messages, and reply to existing messages with such an application.

◆ *Usenet newsgroups* allow groups of people to see and respond to the same messages. Usenet messages, or *posts,* are very similar to e-mail messages, except that they are posted to a public newsgroup, or electronic bulletin board, where anyone can read them, reply to them, and post their own messages. Popular newsgroup postings often develop into long *threads,* conversations that often veer wildly off topic and degenerate into unrelated territory.

TIP Because Windows XP includes Microsoft's Outlook Express to access e-mail and Usenet newsgroups, this chapter focuses on Outlook Express. However, Microsoft also offers a Web-based e-mail service called Hotmail. It's useful for people who often move from machine to machine and don't want to be tied to a PC-based application.

Introducing Outlook Express

Outlook Express (OE), ostensibly named after the commercial Outlook application found in various versions of Microsoft's expensive Office suite, is a free e-mail and newsgroup client that should satisfy the needs of even the most demanding user. Interestingly, Outlook Express is not a true subset of its Outlook cousin; it includes numerous features, such as newsgroup support, not found in Outlook. For Internet-based e-mail, Outlook Express and Outlook are roughly identical, however, and when it comes to the price, it's hard to beat *free*.

Windows XP ships with OE 6, a slightly modified version of the application that shipped with Internet Explorer (IE) 5.5 in Windows Me. OE began life as Internet Mail and News, two separate applications that appeared around the same time as IE 3 in 1996. Given the nearly identical user interfaces and underlying code, Microsoft decided to combine the two into Outlook Express in time for IE 4's release in 1997. Since then, the application hasn't changed dramatically, though it's been updated with support for Microsoft's Hotmail services and other features. In Windows XP, OE 6 uses the XP look and feel, as shown in Figure 13-1.

NOTE If Outlook Express ever crashes (hey, it's a Microsoft app) and you need to find its process name in the *Task Manager* (right-click an empty area of the taskbar and choose Task Manager) to put it out of its misery, the process name isn't oe.exe or something similar. Instead, the Outlook Express executable is named msimn.exe, for *Microsoft Internet Mail and News*. Go figure.

When you install XP, OE is the default e-mail application (unless you upgrade from a Windows version that configured a different application for e-mail). If OE isn't at the top of the Start menu, as shown in Figure 13-2, you can access the shortcut for this application from the All Programs menu at the bottom left of the Start menu.

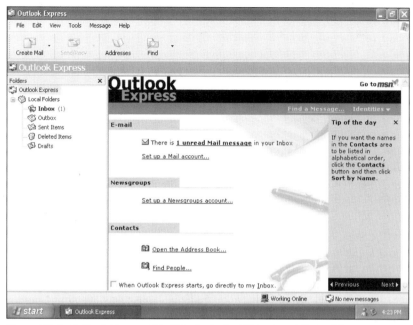

Figure 13-1: Outlook Express 6 in XP adopts the XP look and feel, with new high-resolution icons, XP-style UI widgets, and the XP color scheme.

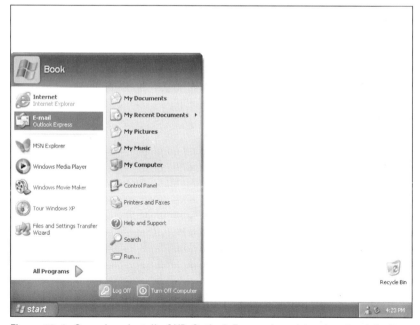

Figure 13-2: On a clean install of XP, Outlook Express is registered as the default e-mail application; if not, it's in the All Programs menu.

You can configure the default e-mail application in XP at least three ways:

◆ Right click on Start and choose Properties. Then click the Customize button to display the Customize Start Menu dialog box. Under the Show on Start Menu section, you will see choices labeled Internet and E-mail; the choice next to E-mail is the system's default e-mail application. Choose Outlook Express or your favorite e-mail application from the list if it isn't already selected.

◆ Display the Internet Properties dialog box (right-click the Internet Explorer icon in the Start menu and choose Internet Properties) and navigate to the Programs tab. On this tab, the E-mail choice is also set to the default e-mail app and provides you with a drop-down list of choices. The choices you get are based on the installed applications.

◆ Use OE's Options dialog box to make it the default e-mail (and newsgroup) application; this method is described in the section titled "Configuring OE Options," later in this chapter.

However you do it, when Outlook Express runs for the first time, the Internet Connection Wizard starts (as shown in Figure 13-3) and asks you whether you'd like to configure an e-mail account. The next section explains how that works.

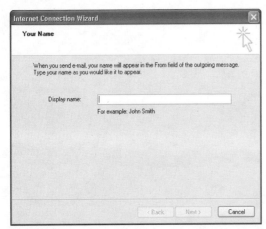

Figure 13-3: OE uses the Internet Connection Wizard to create a new e-mail account.

TIP If you don't see the Internet Connection Wizard window shown in Figure 13-3, you can manually launch this wizard by choosing Tools→Accounts from within OE. In the Internet Accounts dialog box, click the Add button and then click Mail.

Configuring Outlook Express for E-Mail

Like most Internet features, e-mail tries to hide a lot of the complexity of the underlying technology, which is nice for those of us who aren't fluent in Base 16 math. For example, on the Web, you might think of a Web site by its English name (Microsoft), its URL (www.microsoft.com), or its IP address (a four-part number like 192.168.0.1).

Like Web addresses, e-mail accounts have several names. So you might think of my address as my full name (Paul Thurrott), a shorter, more convenient nickname (paul), or my fully qualified e-mail address (paul@thurrott.com). As with the Web, the fully qualified address is the most important, but from an end-user standpoint, you generally work with the first two names the most often. However, when configuring an e-mail client such as OE, you're going to have to be fluent in a few technical details. Follow these steps to use the Internet Connection Wizard:

1. The first step of the Internet Connection Wizard asks you to create your display name, which is the name shown in the From field when others receive e-mail from you. This can be anything; your real name, a shorter nickname, or even a bizarre sequence of letters and numbers. I recommend that you use your real name. So in the first step, I'd type *Paul Thurrott*. Click Next to continue.

2. In the next step, you need to enter your fully qualified e-mail address (in the form *account_name@domain_name.extension*, where extension is typically com, net, org, gov, edu, or biz). In my case, this is paul@thurrott.com, and you should enter the appropriate address for your own account. Again, once you have done this, click Next to proceed.

 As you step through this wizard, you might run into configuration information you don't understand. Your ISP should be able to get you this information easily, so check the company's support Web site or call it if you get stuck.

3. Next, you need to choose the type of e-mail account and enter server information, as shown in Figure 13-4. There are three e-mail types:

   - *POP3* is an older Internet e-mail standard. Most ISPs use it.

   - *IMAP* is a newer Internet e-mail standard with more functionality. It's becoming increasingly common.

   - *HTTP* refers to Web-based e-mail, such as Hotmail. I cover Hotmail configuration later in this chapter, in the section titled, "Using MSN Hotmail".

4. If you choose POP3 or IMAP, you need to enter incoming and outgoing mail server names. (If you are configuring Outlook Express to use Hotmail, then I recommend you skip to the section titled "Using Hotmail with Outlook Express" later in this chapter to continue.) Once you have configured these settings, click Next to proceed.

   ■ The incoming server is the mail server at your ISP that collects mail sent to your e-mail address. In my case, this is `mail.thurrott.com`, but you should enter the appropriate server name for your account.

   ■ Outgoing mail, or SMTP, is used to send mail from your account. Because of the potential for abuse, outgoing mail servers are often secured in some way so that only appropriate users can send mail. So it's a good idea to get this one correct, or you won't be able to send mail. My outgoing mail server is also named `mail.thurrott.com`.

 It's entirely possible that the incoming and outgoing mail servers will have the same name. How is this, you ask? Well, mail servers use different ports to communicate with the Internet. Even though the names are the same, the mail will never get misdirected.

5. Next, enter your Internet mail logon information. This consists of an account name and password. Typically, the account name is that part of your fully qualified e-mail address that comes before the @ sign, though a different account name is possible.

 Many e-mail addresses can point to the same e-mail account. For example, you might have a `feedback@thurrott.com` account for feedback from people visiting your Web site and a `sales@thurrott.com` address for sales-related e-mail. All this mail travels to the same account in OE. You could use OE's Rules feature to direct mail to appropriate folders. I look at this and other OE features in this chapter.

6. Outlook Express lets you enter and save a password (by checking the Remember Password option), or you can enter your password manually each time you check the mail server for new messages. What you choose here will depend largely on your feelings of convenience versus security. Personally, I'd rather make sure that my PC was secure and then automate the e-mail logon process (that's crucial for me because I set OE to check

e-mail automatically every five minutes; and I don't want to re-enter my password every five minutes; that would be a real hassle). But what you choose here depends largely on your own situation.

This section of the wizard also allows you to check an option called *Log On Using Secure Password Authorization* (SPA). Your ISP will tell you if this is required. Otherwise, leave it unchecked and click Next to proceed. You are now all done and are shown a Congratulations screen. Click Finish to end the wizard.

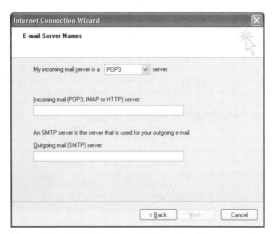

Figure 13-4: In this phase of the wizard, you must supply the server type and addresses.

After that, the wizard completes and you're dumped into the Outlook Express mail window. Click the Inbox link under the Local Folders node of the Folders list to display the Inbox, which is a folder used to contain e-mail that you receive. OE also includes other folders, as described in the following list:

◆ **Outbox:** This folder temporarily stores e-mail messages you've sent until they are forwarded to the outgoing mail server for delivery.

◆ **Sent Items:** After your sent e-mail has been delivered, a copy of that mail is moved, by default, from the Outbox to the Sent Items folder. So this folder contains a list of all the mail you've actually sent.

◆ **Deleted Items:** If you delete an incoming or sent e-mail, it is sent to this folder by default. Deleted Items acts like the Windows Recycle Bin, and you can configure it to auto-empty every time you close OE if you want.

◆ **Drafts:** If you begin typing a long e-mail and need to save it and continue later, it is sent to the Drafts folder by default. You can open any message in Drafts, continue typing, and then send it or save it again.

These folders are shown in Figure 13-5. In the next section, you find out what other steps you should complete to configure OE as your e-mail client.

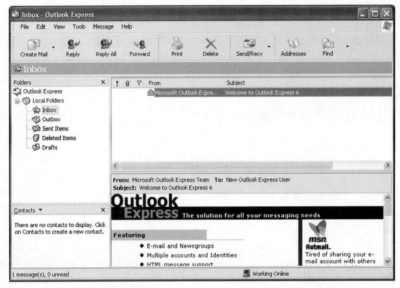

Figure 13-5: By default, Outlook Express supplies Inbox, Outbox, Sent Items, Deleted Items, and Drafts folders.

TIP One of the nice things about OE is that you can configure it for multiple e-mail accounts of different types (POP3, IMAP, HTTP). So if you have multiple accounts, you can set up each one, independently, in OE.

Further Outlook Express Configuration

After you've configured an e-mail account, you need to further configure OE so that you can send and receive e-mail through that account. There are two additional places in OE where you can go to configure Account preferences and Options for OE. Both of these are described next.

CONFIGURING ACCOUNT PREFERENCES

In the preceding section, you use the Internet Connection Wizard to configure an e-mail account. But the wizard only covers the basics. you might need to configure some additional items before you begin sending and receiving e-mail. Here are the steps you need to follow to completely configure your e-mail account:

1. Choose Tools→Accounts to display the Outlook Express Internet Accounts dialog box.

2. Click the Mail tab to display your configured e-mail accounts. By default, OE gives the accounts you've created names that are based on the incoming mail server name for some reason. So the account I created previously is listed as `mail.thurrott.com`, as shown in Figure 13-6.

 Previous versions of Outlook Express let you assign a friendly name with the wizard for each e-mail account you created. I'm not sure why this was dropped, but the steps that follow describe how to change this name to something friendlier.

3. Select the appropriate mail account and click Properties to further configure the account. This displays the Mail Properties dialog box, shown in Figure 13-7.

4. On the General tab, under the Mail Account section, give your account a friendly name if you want and fill in the Organization field if needed. You can also set up a different reply address here if you'd like, which would be a different e-mail address; people who reply to any e-mail you send from this account will automatically mail the account you specify here instead. Note that the Include This Account When Receiving Mail or Synchronizing option is enabled by default. If you don't want to automatically check mail from this address for some reason, deselect this option. Normally, however, you will want to leave it enabled.

5. On the Servers tab, you see many of the options that you set previously with the Internet Connection Wizard. There is one other option, however: My Server Requires Authentication. Only enable this option if your ISP specifically mentions that this is required. When enabled, you can click the Settings button to further configure the outgoing mail server. For example, you can use the same logon settings as your incoming mail server (the default) or log on with a unique account name and password. Again, your ISP will specify whether this is required.

6. The Connection tab determines whether the network traffic generated by OE uses a specific network or dial-up connection. By default, it's disabled, which means that OE will use whatever connection is available. For most people this is exactly what they want. However, if you want to force OE to use a specific connection or cause a dial-up connection to be launched to check mail, this is the place to be.

7. The Security tab can be ignored in most home and small office/home office (SOHO) situations. It allows a corporate administrator to assign digital certificates and encryption preferences, which isn't normally needed at home.

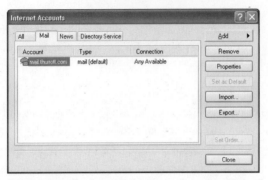

Figure 13-6: The Internet Accounts dialog box lists all
the mail and newsgroup accounts you've set up.

Figure 13-7: Each e-mail account has a
Properties dialog box through which you
can configure various options.

8. The Advanced tab configures, well, advanced e-mail account settings (go figure). Here you can configure incoming and outgoing mail server ports. By default, the outgoing mail server uses port 25, and the incoming mail server uses port 110; your ISP will notify you if these need to be changed.

   This tab also contains another important item: You can choose whether to leave a copy of your mail on the server when you receive it. Typically, this option applies only to POP3 and Web-based (HTTP) e-mail because IMAP leaves mail on the server by default. If you're not sure whether you're going to use OE or you will be checking mail from more than one PC or application, you might want to leave mail on the server. Otherwise, when you receive your mail, it is downloaded for good. Think about this one a bit before moving on.

9. When you're done, click OK to close the Mail Properties dialog box and then click Close to close the Internet Accounts dialog box.

CONFIGURING OE OPTIONS

After you complete the e-mail account settings, you need to perform some general Outlook Express configuration. As with most Microsoft applications, you do this with the Options dialog, which you open by choosing Tools→Options. The OE Options dialog box, shown in Figure 13-8, offers numerous tabs and configuration options.

Figure 13-8: The OE Options dialog box sports numerous tabs with dozens of available options, so you'll want to take some time and go through this carefully.

Each OE Options dialog box tab is described in the following list:

◆ **General:** As you might expect, this tab includes some general options. Mostly, you shouldn't change them, but you can consider a few changes:

■ If you have a broadband connection or a connection that is always on, you might want to change the Check for New Messages option to occur more frequently than every 30 minutes. I get tons of e-mail, so I check every 5 minutes.

■ You can configure OE to go directly to the Inbox folder when started, which I recommend.

■ You can determine whether OE is the default e-mail and Usenet newsgroup application.

- The last option under Send/Receive Messages determines whether the connection is dialed automatically when it's time to check for new e-mail. If you're using a dial-up connection, this is particularly useful. If you are using an always-on connection, like a broadband connection, this option should be left at Do Not Connect status. You wouldn't want a dialup connection box to appear every five minutes trying to dial your ISP.

◆ **Read:** This tab configures the look and feel of e-mail messages and newsgroup postings that you receive. The top section determines how e-mail is marked as "read."

I don't like some of the Read tab default settings, personally. Consider these changes:

- The first option marks messages as read when selected for at least five seconds. I recommend unchecking this option so mail is marked as read only when you actually open the message. Otherwise, you might inadvertently miss messages because they were selected, even if you didn't actually read them.

- If you click the Fonts button, you can choose the typeface and general size of fonts used to display rich text and HTML e-mail (called the *proportional font* by OE) and plain text (fixed-width font). Font sizes are not measured in point sizes, as is usually the case, but rather in newbie-friendly Smallest, Smaller, Medium, Larger, and Largest sizes instead.

◆ **Receipts:** This tab determines whether you receive a *read receipt* when your sent e-mail has been read. I strongly recommend not configuring this option, which is off by default anyway. Most modern e-mail programs filter out read-receipt messages anyway, and they're just an annoyance for most people. But if you absolutely, positively need to know whether and when someone reads your e-mail, this is where you look.

◆ **Send:** The Send tab configures the way in which you send and format mail. You can turn off OE's default behavior of saving sent mail in the Sent Mail folder, for example, and configure other settings. I recommend leaving most of these settings as is. However, the Mail Sending Format defaults to HTML format, which should almost always be changed to Plain Text. E-mail is too fleeting to waste time applying complicated colors, images, and styles to it, and it's also a waste of bandwidth. Stick with plain text and let your message do the talking, not some lame HTML template.

◆ **Compose:** The Compose tab specifies the look and feel of mail that's sent out from your accounts. You can specify the font to use (I recommend 11 point Verdana, not the abysmal 9 point Arial that's used by default), the

HTML stationary (again, stay away from this if you can help it), and whether a virtual Business Card (vCard format) is sent with each e-mail message or newsgroup posting. When you create a new Business Card entry in your Address Book, it is maintained in a vCard format. which This will be discuss briefly later in this chapter, under "Using the Address Book".

 TIP It's in poor taste to send a business card with each message. The card is essentially an attachment.

- ◆ **Signatures:** If you'd like a certain block of text to appear at the end of each e-mail message automatically, you can use a *signature*. This tab lets you add and manage these electronic signatures.

- ◆ **Spelling:** If you also install Microsoft Office, you will see a Spelling tab that lets you check spelling before sending any e-mail message. I recommend using this feature; misspelling a word can ruin the effect of an otherwise professional e-mail.

- ◆ **Security:** The Security tab lets you link the OE security to a Security Zone in Internet Explorer (see Chapter 14 for details). Given the variety of e-mail-based viruses that have appeared over the past few years, it's a good idea to spend a little time here. You can configure OE to reject potentially dangerous e-mail attachments, secure your mail through a digital ID, and encrypt e-mail messages. OE's security features are covered in more detail in "Understanding E-Mail Security," later in this chapter.

- ◆ **Connection:** By default, OE shares Internet Connection properties with IE, but this tab lets you change that if needed. If you use a dial-up connection, you can use this tab to determine whether OE lets the connection hang up after mail is delivered.

- ◆ **Maintenance:** This tab includes several useful options, including

  - ■ An option to empty deleted mail on exit (If you followed my advice in the New Connection Wizard, you're already using this).

  - ■ A Clean Up functionality to compress and shrink your mail files.

  - ■ A Store Folder button that determines where your e-mail messages are stored. This is helpful if you need to back up your e-mail or want to move it someplace, such as under My Documents.

TIP

Outlook Express stores your e-mail in a bizarre location by default: `C:\Documents and Settings\[your user name]\Local Settings\ Application Data\Identities\{A bizarre string of numbers}\ Microsoft\Outlook Express`. Worse, this location is hidden by default. For backup and sanity purposes, I recommend moving the store to a more logical location, such as a My E-Mail folder under My Documents. Use the Store Folder button on the Maintenance tab to change the location.

Sending and Receiving E-Mail with Outlook Express

After you've configured OE, you're ready to send and receive e-mail. Microsoft supplies a sample e-mail for you to read, but you can also send an e-mail to yourself to test that you configured everything correctly (don't worry, no one has to know you did this). To send an e-mail, click the Create Mail button (or press Ctrl+N) to display the New Message window, shown in Figure 13-9.

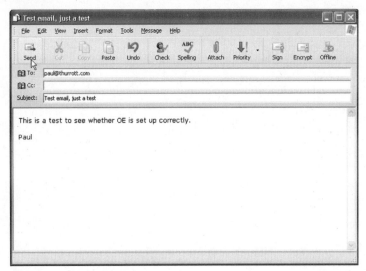

Figure 13-9: The New Message window lets you create e-mail to send to others.

Fill out your own e-mail address in the To field and then give the Subject field an appropriate subject, such as *Test e-mail, just a test*. Then add (or copy and paste) some text into the body of the message, which is the large white area at the bottom.

You can hit the Tab key to move quickly from field to field in the New Message window.

To send the message, click the Send button (or press Ctrl+Enter). If you configured OE to automatically send and receive e-mail at set intervals, the message should be sent immediately (if you're online; OE has to connect to your outgoing mail server to send the message). The message will arrive the next time you retrieve mail. You should notice the Outbox folder turning bold while the message is being transmitted to your outgoing mail server. After that, it's sent and moved to your Sent Items folder.

To make the e-mail message download more quickly, you can manually check mail by clicking the Send/Recv button after about ten seconds. This polls the incoming mail server and downloads any waiting mail, including the one you just sent.

Using the Address Book

Sending e-mail is fun, but it's unlikely you're going to be able to remember the e-mail addresses for all of your friends, family, coworkers, and other correspondents. For this reason, OE includes an Address Book feature that lets you store these addresses, along with other important information. To launch the Address Book, click the Addresses button in the OE toolbar. It's also available separately from OE; you can find it by choosing Start→All Programs→Accessories→Address Book.

The Address Book (shown in Figure 13-10) is a central location for managing e-mail addresses, along with their owners' corresponding names, addresses, phone numbers, and the like. If you're into this sort of organization, you can use this feature to manage all of your contacts.

When it comes to e-mail, the best Address Book feature might be the Nickname feature, which lets you save time by typing shorter, more familiar names into the To field of new e-mails. Before discussing the Nickname feature, you need to understand how OE, by default, uses an *address completion* feature when you're typing a name for someone to receive new e-mail. Say you have three e-mail contacts named John Thurrott, Joseph White, and Jonathan Thurrott. Even if you don't assign nicknames to each contact, you can just type their names. But these names all start with *jo,* so you'll have to type that much before the address completion feature can kick in. As soon as you begin typing a name, the To field changes, showing you the first name that matches what you are typing. So, if you begin by typing j, John Thurrott appears first. As you continue typing more letters, the name may change to reflect what you are typing. Once you get to third letter, if you press s, the name changes from John Thurrott to Joseph White. If this is the name you want, simply tab to the next field and OE will complete the To address for you with the name chosen.

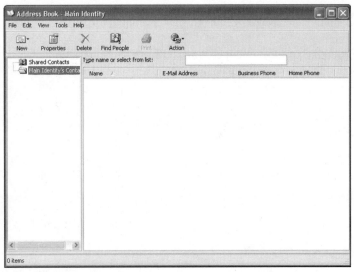

Figure 13-10: The Windows Address Book is a central location for managing your e-mail contacts.

Instead, the Nickname feature lets you address e-mail in a more personal (and condensed) nature. So I might provide the nickname *dad* to John Thurrott, *mrwhite* to Joseph White, and *bro* to Jonathan Thurrott. That way, I can just type *bro* in the To field when I need to send my brother Jonathan the latest Web story about a Celtics game or whatever. When you use the Nickname in the To field, OE will not show the full name until you either press the Check Names button or send the email. Then right before the email gets sent, the name will appear replacing the Nickname that was entered. If you are using Nicknames, it is always best to press the Check Names button just to ensure the mail will get sent to the person whom you wish to receive it.

To add a nickname, create a new contact by clicking the New toolbar button in the Address Book (or by typing Ctrl+N). Then in the Name tab, type a nickname for the contact in the Nickname field.

If you get an e-mail and want to save the sender's e-mail address, simply right-click the sender's name in the Outlook Express Inbox and choose Add Sender to Address Book. This generally grabs the first and last name and e-mail address. You can open up the Address Book later to add other information, such as a nickname.

 You can send plain text e-mail to some of your contacts automatically. Let's say you've ignored my warnings about using HTML e-mail and you've settled on a beautiful Hawaiian sunset picture as the backdrop for all of your outgoing e-mail. Aside from the shame that you will bring on yourself and your family, you may find yourself facing the ire of e-mail curmudgeons (like me). If this is the case, you can choose to always send certain contacts e-mail in plain text format, even if your default choice is HTML e-mail. To do this, open the contact in the Address Book and check the Send E-Mail Using Plain Text Only option.

Understanding E-Mail Security

Like any other connection to the outside world, e-mail is a potential conduit for danger. That may sound dramatic, but the single easiest way to spread computer viruses is through e-mail, and most of the problems revolve around how trusting people are, not some subtle technical issue.

If you receive an e-mail *attachment* (a file that is sent through e-mail) from someone you don't know, delete the attachment. It's that simple. Almost any type of e-mail attachment can harbor a virus these days, from Word documents to executable (EXE) files and HTML documents. Even if the attachment is from someone you know, you should be careful.

The most obvious thing you can do to protect yourself is to run a virus scanner such as Norton AntiVirus or McAfee VirusScan. Both products include an e-mail component that scans each incoming e-mail for viruses on the fly, and they offer the safest environment you can have while still receiving attachments.

In short, don't trust attachments, especially those sent from unknown sources.

STAYING UP-TO-DATE

The other proactive step you can take is to make sure that XP's Automatic Updates feature is turned on so that you will automatically receive any security-oriented critical product updates from Microsoft. You can configure Automatic Updates by right-clicking My Computer and choosing Properties. Then navigate to the Automatic Updates tab and ensure that the first option, Download the Updates Automatically and Notify Me When They Are Ready to Be Installed, is chosen.

Regularly visit the Windows Update Web site for other important system updates. I recommend visiting this site, available from within Help and Support, on a weekly or biweekly basis.

USING THE JUNK MAIL FILTER

Another problem facing e-mail users is *spam,* e-mail messages that advertise products and services you will never want or need (often sent from anonymous or nonexistent hosts). Outlook Express includes a decent Junk Mail filter that blocks e-mail from *specific addresses* or *entire domains* (for example, every address in the wesendspam.com domain).

To block a sender with the Junk Mail feature, select an offensive message and choose Message→Block Sender. A dialog box appears, noting that the sender has been added to your blocked senders list and that subsequent messages from this sender will be blocked so you never have to deal with them again. You can also opt to delete all other messages from that address from the current folder (typically the Inbox).

Want to block an entire domain (in other words, every user from thurrott.com, instead of just paul@thurrott.com)? Choose Tools→Message Rules→Blocked Senders List from the Outlook Express menu bar. This displays the Message Rules dialog box with the Blocked Senders tab open, as shown in Figure 13-11. Then click Add and type in the name of the domain you'd like to block. *Voilà!*

 Oops! What if you mistakenly block a sender from whom you really want to receive e-mail? Open up that Blocked Senders List again, as described in the preceding section. You can remove any mistakenly blocked addresses or domains from there.

Working with Usenet Newsgroups

Usenet newsgroups are one of the oldest Internet services and among the most popular. Newsgroups are hosted on *newsgroup servers* and accessed through a *newsgroup client,* such as Outlook Express. This makes OE relatively unique, by the way, because it supports both e-mail and newsgroups inside a single application. Only a few other programs, such as Netscape 6/Mozilla Mail, combine news and mail.

Newsgroup servers can be open to the *public,* like msnews.microsoft.com, which is used by Microsoft to provide peer-to-peer support for its products. Or they can be *private* and secured with a password (like privatenews.microsoft.com, which is used by beta testers to provide feedback for Microsoft's beta products). After you configure a newsgroup server into OE, you can access that server, subscribe to newsgroups you find interesting, check out the latest threads, and make your own postings, which can be read by anyone accessing the server. The coming sections take a quick look at this process.

Figure 13-11: The Blocked Senders list can contain both domains and individual e-mail addresses.

CONFIGURING A NEWSGROUP ACCOUNT

The process of configuring a newsgroup account is similar to that of creating a new e-mail account. In OE, choose Tools→Accounts to display the Internet Accounts dialog box. This time, you click Add and then choose News to launch the Internet Connection Wizard.

In the first step, add your name, which will be auto-inserted for you if you've already added an e-mail account to OE. Then insert your e-mail address. This, too, will be auto-filled, but you might want to think twice about supplying your real e-mail address here. If you'll be accessing a private newsgroup server – one that requires you to log on – then it's probably okay. But the public newsgroups are a breeding group for nefarious activities, and one of the common practices is for spam senders to collect e-mail addresses from such places so that they can repopulate their lists with new victims. So you've got two choices here. You can provide a bogus address, though that will prevent legitimate correspondents from reaching you. Or you can add some text to your e-mail address that will fool the spam makers but provide a clue to other users that you're simply trying to stop spam.

The most common way to do this is to add the text NO_SPAM somewhere in your e-mail address. So, instead of paul@thurrott.com, you might use paul_NO_SPAM@ thurrott.com or paul@NO_SPAM_thurrott.com. And if you see such an address somewhere on a newsgroup server, then you'll know that you have to remove that text before you can e-mail that person.

In the next step, you have to supply the name of the newsgroup server. I'll be using msnews.microsoft.com for this example because it's a public newsgroup server that almost anyone can access, but your ISP will probably have its own newsgroup server that is open for a much wider range of interests. If you have to log on to such a server, check that option and supply the information in the next step.

Otherwise, there's not much else to do. After you've completed the wizard, you can customize the account properties as you did with e-mail, though there isn't as much of a reason to do so with a newsgroup account. After you create a newsgroup account, it appears in the Outlook Express Folders list. And OE asks you if you'd like to download a list of the newsgroups from the server you just set up. Choose Yes.

As of this writing, Microsoft's public newsgroup server lists over 1,500 newsgroups, which you can see in the Newsgroup Subscriptions dialog box, shown in Figure 13-12. This dialog box lets you view all newsgroups, subscribed newsgroups, and any new newsgroups that might have just come online recently. If you click Reset List, OE will download the master newsgroup list again from the server.

Figure 13-12: Microsoft's public newsgroup server is for product support only, but your ISP will have more interesting choices.

 If you need to access the master newsgroup list again, simply right-click the newsgroup server name in OE's Folders list and choose Newsgroups.

Here is the lowdown on how to navigate a newsgroup:

◆ **To subscribe to a newsgroup:** Move through the list of available groups under the All tab and double-click one that interests you. An icon will appear next to the newsgroup's name, indicating that you have subscribed.

Then repeat this for each group to which you want to subscribe. When you're done, click OK, and the groups will appear under the newsgroup server name in the Outlook Folder list.

♦ **To display the contents of a newsgroup:** Simply select it from that list. The list of the postings in that group appears in the message pane windows on the right side of OE, as shown in Figure 13-13.

♦ **To read a message:** Click the message, and it appears in the preview pane as would e-mail. And you can double-click individual messages to view them in a separate window, again like e-mail.

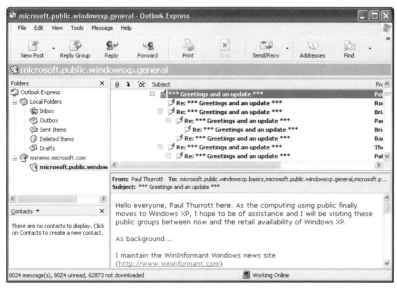

Figure 13-13: Newsgroup threads are similar to e-mail discussions, except that they can include numerous people and seem to veer off-topic on a regular basis.

WHAT TO DO WITH NEWSGROUPS

If it's not obvious, newsgroups supply a unique service to Internet users: They provide a place for people with similar interests to come together. Though e-mail might provide nice one-on-one conversations, newsgroups can be a great place to make those connections happen in the first place. You'll find groups dedicated to technical topics such as Microsoft products, Linux, and chemistry, but most newsgroups are actually dedicated to a far more diverse set of interests, including cats, cars, astronomy, knitting, reading, movies, exercise equipment, sports teams, celebrities, and almost any other topic you can imagine, including sex, of course. It's all out there.

When you find groups that interest you, you can peruse the threads, reading each posting. You can make your own posts (starting a thread) or reply to an existing post in the group, which will add a new post to an existing thread. Or you can reply to individuals via e-mail if you'd like to follow up with them privately.

In any event, there's a vast body of knowledge out there on the Internet, and not all of it is found on Web sites. If you're interested in finding people with the same interests as you, newsgroups are where it's really at.

Finding People on the Internet

In addition to e-mail and newsgroups, you can also use OE to find people through the Internet, using Web-based White Pages similar to the local phone books you receive at home. Unlike e-mail and newsgroups, this feature is better hidden.

To find someone on the Internet, follow these steps:

1. Click the small arrow next to the Find button in the OE toolbar and choose People (or just type Ctrl+E). The Find People dialog box, shown in Figure 13-14, is displayed.

2. In the Look In drop-down list, choose a place to look. This can be your Address Book or Active Directory (the native directory services infrastructure provided by businesses using Windows Server), or one of several Internet-based White Pages. Select one of these three default choices:

   - Bigfoot Internet Directory Service

   - VeriSign Internet Directory Service

   - WhoWhere Internet Directory Service

3. Add whatever information you have to the Name and E-Mail fields. You can also use the Advanced tab for partial name searches.

4. Click Find Now to search.

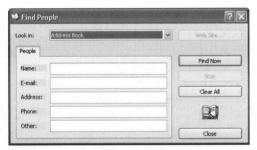

Figure 13-14: Find works with a variety of services, including your Windows Address Book, Active Directory, and several Internet White Pages.

Unfortunately, finding people isn't normally very easy. A search of my name, for example, displays five out-of-date e-mail addresses, none of which could be used to contact me today, as shown in Figure 13-15.

Figure 13-15: It's no substitute for a good private eye, but you can sometimes find an old chat room buddy this way.

Using MSN Hotmail

Microsoft's Hotmail service, which is technically called *MSN Hotmail*, is the world's largest Web-based e-mail service, with over 100 million users. Before Web-based e-mail became popular – it's offered by many other companies, including Yahoo! and AOL – e-mail required access to an application such as Outlook Express. But Web-based e-mail can be read on any Web-connected device, including Windows PCs, of course, but also Macs, Linux machines, PDAs like the Palm and Pocket PC, and even set-top boxes like WebTV. For this reason and its simplicity – you don't need to configure much – Web-based e-mail has taken off. And no service has exploded in use like Hotmail.

Of course, Web-based e-mail isn't as elegant as using an application like Outlook Express. You get a limited amount of storage (2MB), though Microsoft will sell you more for a small yearly fee. This can be a problem if you get a lot of attachments. And you have to deal with a Web-based interface, which often doesn't resemble a true Windows app, meaning you'll have to learn a whole new way of doing things.

But still Hotmail is pretty easy to use, and given its global availability, it's hard to beat the convenience.

Creating a Hotmail Account

To create a new Hotmail account, point your Web browser at www.hotmail.com. This loads the Hotmail Web site, which lets you log on to your existing account or sign up for a new account, as shown in Figure 13-16. Click the link at the top titled Sign Up for a FREE E-Mail Account (or similar; note that Web sites frequently change designs).

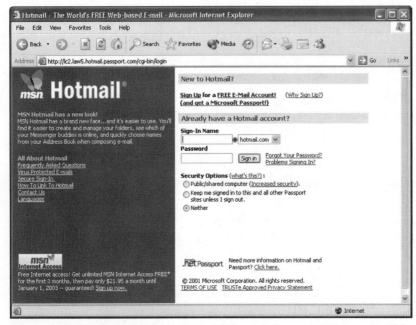

Figure 13-16: The Hotmail Web site is one of the most frequented sites on the Web.

There's no need to walk you through the entire sign-up process, but basically you provide information about yourself (name, address, and so on) and pick a username and password. Because Hotmail is so popular, all the obvious usernames like *paul*, *steph*, and *mark* are taken, so you'll have to be a bit creative. Whatever username you choose comprises the first half of your new Hotmail e-mail address. So if you chose the username *pthurrott*, for example, your full Hotmail e-mail address would be pthurrott@hotmail.com.

Before you sign up for a Hotmail account, consider the following warnings:

◆ **.NET Passport:** Every Hotmail user is automatically a .NET Passport user as well. Passport is Microsoft's .NET technology for supplying single sign-on capabilities, and it has come under fire, rightly or wrongly, from a variety of privacy special-interest groups. Check out Chapter 13 before signing up.

◆ **Opt out of automatic services:** By default, your new Hotmail address will be added to services like the Hotmail Member Directory and the Internet White Pages. *Do not allow this.* Like Usenet, these services are used by spam makers to get lists of valid e-mail addresses. On the Hotmail sign-up page, be sure to uncheck the options that join these groups.

Already signed up for Hotmail but neglected to uncheck those services? No problem — you can opt out after the fact. Here's how: Log on to Hotmail and click the Options link near the top of the page. Then click the Member Directory link under Your Information and uncheck Please List Me in the Hotmail Member Directory and click OK. Now, you need to visit the Internet White Pages site, which is hosted by InfoSpace. Navigate to `www.infospace.com/info.hot/redirs_all.htm?pgtarg=pplea` and enter your information. If you're listed in the Internet White Pages, this site lets you remove your information.

But the reality is that Hotmail is a great service, and as discussed earlier in the book, most XP users are going to want an account.

Logging On to Hotmail

To log on to your new Hotmail account, just visit the Hotmail Web site again and log on with your username and password. If you're checking your e-mail from the library, school, work, or some other public place, you can click the Public/Shared Computer security option, which prevents your logon information from being cached. If you have new mail, you are automatically taken to your Hotmail Inbox, shown in Figure 13-17. Otherwise, you're sent to the Hotmail Home page.

Hotmail utilizes the "shark fin" tabbed user interface that is now used by most MSN Web properties. Each tab brings you to a new location, such as the Inbox, Message Composition window, or Address Book. You can also access Hotmail options, get Help, and visit other MSN Web sites.

Sending and Receiving E-Mail

If you're not already in the Inbox view, click the Inbox tab. This view displays all the messages in your Hotmail inbox and includes options for managing e-mail. You can delete messages or groups of messages, move messages to other folders, block senders, and read messages.

To read an e-mail message, simply click the sender, who is listed under the From column. This displays a new page in the browser, with just that message showing, as shown in Figure 13-18.

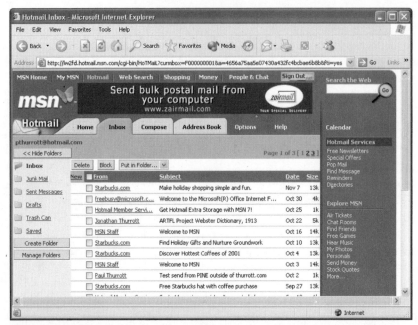

Figure 13-17: The Hotmail Inbox organizes the messages you've received at your Hotmail account.

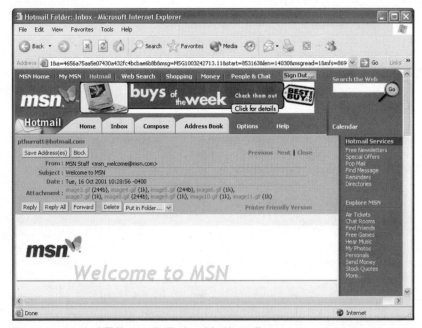

Figure 13-18: An HTML e-mail, displayed in Hotmail.

Here, you can save the address in your Address Book, reply to the message, forward it to another user, delete it, or move it to a new folder, among other tasks.

To compose a new message, click the Compose tab. This display will be familiar to anyone who has seen an e-mail program before, though it's self-contained in the browser window. Likewise, you can access your online Address Book by clicking the Address Book tab.

Blocking Senders and Handling Junk E-Mail

Like Outlook Express, Hotmail offers a nice Block Senders feature, which is especially handy given the low storage capacity you get on this Web-based e-mail system. You can manually choose to block certain senders at any time, and Hotmail can be configured to automatically move suspect e-mail to a Junk E-Mail folder, which is automatically emptied on a regular basis (every 14 days) as well. You access both of these features through the Hotmail Options page.

Clicking Block Senders displays a list of the e-mail addresses and domains that are already blocked, while providing a text-entry box so you can add your own manually. But it's easiest to do this through the Inbox view: Just check the box next to the message or messages from users you'd like to block and click the Block button.

For junk e-mail, you can choose the level of protection (High, Medium, Low, or Off) and whether junk mail is held temporarily or deleted automatically. My Hotmail Inbox tends to fill up with junk rather quickly, so I have mine set to High and immediate deletion, but you should experiment a bit before going for the final solution.

Using Hotmail with Outlook Express

Even though Hotmail is Web-based, you can still access it through Outlook Express like any other e-mail account, though there are a few obvious differences. Because Hotmail is a free Web service, Microsoft has elected to add an ugly Web banner ad to Outlook Express when you access Hotmail through that application. And because Hotmail normally stores your messages on Hotmail's servers, you have to deal with a weird second set of folders: You have your local e-mail folders (Inbox and the like) as always, but the Hotmail folders are separate. The nice thing is that you can drag messages from the Hotmail folders to your local folders, saving space on the server and providing a backup.

To set up OE with your new Hotmail account, you follow these steps:

1. Launch OE and choose Tools→Accounts to display the Internet Accounts dialog box.

2. Click Add and then choose Mail to launch the Internet Connection Wizard.

3. Supply your name and then your new Hotmail account e-mail address. Click Next to get to the next step, shown in Figure 13-19. The wizard automatically chooses HTTP as the server type and grays out the incoming and outgoing server names because it knows how to natively deal with this type of account. Click Next to proceed.

4. Supply your account name and password, if you want one, finish the wizard, by clicking Next and then Finish. Close the Internet Accounts dialog box, by clicking the Close button. A new Hotmail node is added to the OE Folders list, and you're asked whether you'd like to download the folders from the mail server you added. Choose Yes. OE then connects to Hotmail, examines the folders you're using on the server, and then displays them in the Folders list under the Hotmail node, as shown in Figure 13-20.

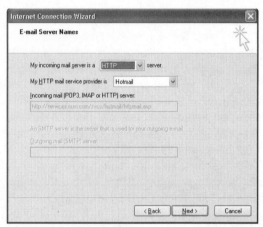

Figure 13-19: Outlook Express knows how to work with Hotmail, so you don't have to enter any server information.

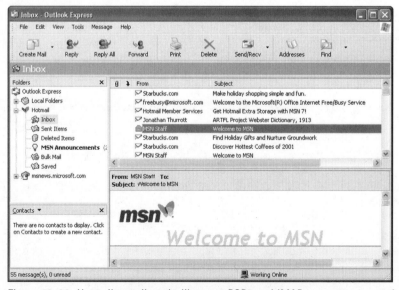

Figure 13-20: Hotmail e-mail works like most POP3 and IMAP accounts, except that you have to deal with a different, Web-based folder structure.

If you click the Inbox link under Hotmail, your Hotmail Inbox is displayed in OE. Then you can perform any option you'd normally perform in OE, such as creating and sending mail and replying to mail.

 Curiously, the one thing you don't get is your Hotmail Address Book. It's not listed in the Folders list, and it's not available through the normal Address Book.

Another thing you can do — and this is unique to Hotmail on OE — is move messages from the server down to your local folders. To do this, display the contents of your Hotmail Inbox (or other folder) in OE, select a message or group of messages, and then drag them over to a folder (like Inbox) under Local Folders. A Moving Messages dialog box briefly appears (or not so briefly, depending on the number of messages you selected). This is great for backing up important messages, but remember that after they're off the server, you won't be able to access them from Hotmail's Web interface anymore.

Chapter 14

Communicating with Windows Messenger

IN THIS CHAPTER

◆ See what's new with the latest Windows Messenger

◆ Understand how to use Messenger for managing your contants, your emails and for instant communication

◆ Use Messenger for communicating to friends not onlu talking to them but seeing them as well

◆ Sharing other applications and notes with Messenger

IT IS UNIQUELY IRONIC that personal computers and the Internet, created largely by loner geeks with little communications skills, would become such useful conduits for interpersonal communications. Before the World Wide Web and the Internet explosion, users of UNIX, VMS, and other similar systems became well acquainted with *chat* applications that would one day evolve into an industry of their own. Working at one of the first Internet service providers in Phoenix, Arizona, in the mid-1990s, I spent long hours conversing with friends and coworkers through *talk,* a command line application that allows two UNIX shell account users to send text messages to each other in a dedicated environment. The tiny talk application was crude, unfriendly, and generally of little interest to casual users, but it offered me one of my first experiences with peer-to-peer communication over the Internet. Using Windows 95 at the time, one or more command line windows could be open while running other applications in the background, so talk was also one of my first experiences with multitasking online. Like many people, I was quickly hooked.

But talk wasn't destined for greatness. Instead, early Windows and Macintosh GUI applications that allowed individuals to chat via text windows paved the way to what we now call *Instant Messaging (IM),* a popular Internet feature that is making its way beyond the PC and onto other connected devices, such as cell phones and PDAs. Windows XP includes an excellent IM, *Windows Messenger,* which extends the market for text chatting into new areas, including

◆ Voice and video chats

◆ File transfer

◆ Application sharing

◆ Remote help services

A Look at Instant Messaging

Instant Messaging isn't hard to understand at a conceptual level. One user opens an IM application and attempts to start a chat session with another user. If that second user is online and accepts the chat request, a similar window opens for the second user, and both users can send and receive messages. Unlike *stateless* network connections (such as the Web and e-mail) IM connections remain truly connected; in some cases, text appears as soon as the other user types it. (Newer programs replace this feature with status text that simply identifies the other user as *typing a message;* this lets you know that the other person is still working on something, but gives that person time to collect his or her thoughts without your seeing his or her work in progress.) Instant messaging is like a text-based telephone call, except you don't receive sentences until they are complete.

 IM, not e-mail, is responsible for the text emoticons we now take for granted. The :) smiley face and other similar text-based shortcuts arose out of a need to express feelings in text using the fewest possible keystrokes.

Microsoft's integrated IM system is *MSN Messenger.* This system differs from the other IM systems in a few key areas:

◆ It is tied into the *Passport* authentication system. Microsoft ties together authentication for its many Web services. For example, MSN Messenger users, as Passport users, also get a free Hotmail e-mail account. Messenger can then alert users when new Hotmail e-mail has arrived.

◆ Because MSN Messenger integrates with the Windows user interface, users get a more seamless experience.

This sort of integration is what landed Microsoft in court a few years ago. But it's hard to deny the benefits of integration, especially if you use these services.

Introducing Windows Messenger

Because of its varied functionality, Windows Messenger offers users much more than a traditional IM client. Instead, Windows Messenger (just *Messenger* for short) is a full-featured real-time communications client that includes presence and notification features and integrates XP with Microsoft's ever-expanding .NET ("Dot Net") platform.

From Pow-wow to Messenger

Instant Messaging as we know it now began with Internet-enabled applications such as *Pow-wow,* an early chat client that allowed people to chat together in real time using text messages. Shortly thereafter, other ISP's starting offering ways of instantly communicating to other members. These ISPs usually reserved this feature for chatting inside their own environments; for instance, AOL users could chat only with AOL users. But as the Internet became more popular, it became obvious that a wider standard was needed. Rather than interoperate, the early players all went their own routes, trying to establish the dominant chat platform.

The first popular IM application was *ICQ* (named after the infamous ham radio term "I seek you"). ICQ was swallowed by AOL, which had also created its own Internet-enabled chat program, AOL Instant Messenger (AIM). Other popular choices include Yahoo! Instant Messenger (Yahoo! IM).

By late 2000, the IM market was beginning to settle down. The big players, including AIM/ICQ, Yahoo! IM, and MSN Messenger, dominated the market. Most had added features for exchanging files and working with certain mobile devices in basic ways, and some had even added voice chat capabilities. But there were still two technical issues or problems that needed to be corrected:

- ◆ The IM market was still *fragmented.* Competing IM applications could not interoperate with IM applications from other vendors

- ◆ *Advanced real-time communications,* such as audio/video chat, were hard to come by.

Sensing a need, Microsoft began reworking its products to overcome these limitations.

Attempts at interoperability fell short. Microsoft figured out a way to let its MSN Messenger users communicate with AOL IM users in 1999, but then AOL shut its doors, accusing Microsoft of hacking its system. Microsoft found a way through again and was then shut down again. In an early 2000 agreement that lead to the merger of AOL with Time Warner, AOL agreed to open its instant messaging client to competing IM products. As of this writing, that still hasn't happened.

Microsoft's other efforts toward extending the Messenger platform are far more successful. The Windows XP version of Messenger offers access to a much wider range of services, audio and voice chatting capabilities, application sharing functionality, and a host of other useful technologies. Built on an open new line protocol called the *Session Initiation Protocol* (SIP), the next version of Messenger was designed as a platform in its own right. And although that might have gotten Microsoft competitors and the U.S. Justice Department in a tizzy, it's a boon for users.

Sounds pretty technical? Don't worry; it's not really confusing. First, the real-time communications phrase refers to Messenger's core functionality: letting users communicate live, in real time. This includes IM, yes, but also audio chat, one-to-one videoconferencing, file transfer, application sharing, and remote whiteboarding features. Second, Messenger's presence and notification features mean that you can use Messenger to keep track of your online contacts: So when a friend comes online, you can be notified of that. The reverse is also true: When you log on each morning, for example, your contacts can optionally be notified as well. Third, Messenger users can automatically or manually provide information about their activity as well: If you step away from the computer for a while, Messenger will report that you are away. These features are configurable by both sides, so you can determine whether your contacts receive this presence information about you, and you can configure whether you receive notifications about them.

To make all of this come together, Microsoft reengineered Messenger with the new open line *SIP* (Session Initiation Protocol) protocol. This protocol is complicated and not necessary for you to understand. Just be aware that SIP is how Messenger is able to do its work.

Previous versions of Messenger for non-XP Windows versions do not use SIP. Users with older Windows versions must update to the latest Messenger for many of the new communication features, such as audio and video chatting. If you want to collaborate with these users from an XP machine, make sure they're up-to-date.

Updating Windows Messenger

Windows Messenger hasn't sat still since Windows XP was released in October 2001. Earlier that year, Microsoft decided to ship a basic version of Windows Messenger — version 4.0 — in the box with XP. But it would also release an updated Messenger client on the day that XP shipped — October 25, 2001 — bumping the version number up to 4.5 and adding a slew of new features, including improved usability with a contact grouping functionality and nicer looking emoticons, support for .NET Alerts, and the ability to subscribe to PC-to-phone services.

Messenger has been updated since then with several MSN add-ins, such as

- ◆ E-mail integration with alerts for new Hotmail messages
- ◆ Chat integration, including celebrity chats
- ◆ Mobile-text messaging on cell phones and pagers
- ◆ Profile creation and viewing
- ◆ Daily links

The Messenger add-in functionality is open so third parties can create their own add-ins. And businesses can customize the Messenger phone-dialer feature to route computer-to-phone calls through their chosen service provider, lowering long-distance phone bills. Windows Messenger 4.6 also included enhancements to Help, error messages, the conversation window, and other areas. We will be using this version, 4.6, if you wish to follow along.

 TIP   I recommend that you download the latest Messenger client from Windows Update and stay up-to-date with the technology because it's improving all the time and newer versions are bound to be available by the time you read this. The Windows XP/.NET Integration features discussed in Chapter 11 also require you to have the latest version (4.6 at the time of this writing).

 TIP   For more information about the latest version of Windows Messenger, visit the Microsoft Web site: messenger.msn.com/.

Figure 14-1 compares the Windows Messenger version that shipped in XP with an updated download.

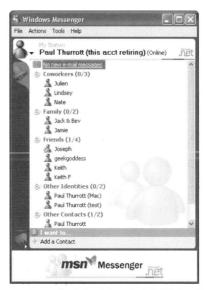

Figure 14-1: Windows Messenger 4.0, on the left, shipped with XP, but it's been updated to include more features; Messenger 4.6 is shown on the right.

Working with Messenger

Windows Messenger can work with your .NET Passport account to automatically log on to that service and provide simple notifications whenever any contact logs on.

Chapter 11 explains how you can integrate your .NET Passport account with Messenger.

Notifications appear in a "slice of toast," as Microsoft calls it, a small square window that slides up from the lower-right corner of the screen, as shown in Figure 14-2. Typical notifications include messages about contacts logging on, new Hotmail notifications, and .NET Alerts, including stock quotes, MSN Calendar schedules, and Expedia travel arrangements.

Figure 14-2: Messenger notifications appear on a "slice of toast" that slides up from the bottom of the screen.

If you want to work with Messenger, simply double-click the Messenger icon (the icon that resembles a small green man) in the system tray next to the clock. This opens the Windows Messenger main window, shown in Figure 14-3.

From this main window, you can perform tasks like these:

◆ View and access your contacts – both online and off

◆ Access a list of common tasks (Add a Contact, Send an Instant Message, and the like)

◆ View your .NET Alerts

◆ Change your online status

.NET Alerts and Messenger configuration are covered in Chapter 11; the next few sections in this chapter look at your contacts and what you can do with them.

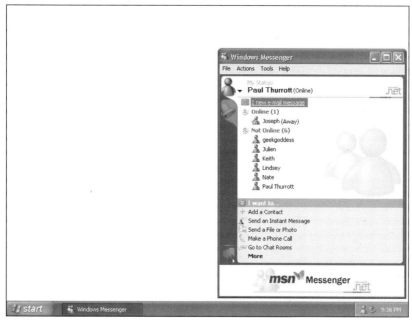

Figure 14-3: The main Windows Messenger window provides a starting point for all of your real-time communication needs.

Configuring Messenger

The first thing you should do is configure Messenger. You do this from the Options dialog box – shown in Figure 14-4 – that you can open by choosing Tools→Options from the Messenger main window.

The Messenger Options dialog box has six tabs of configuration options:

- ◆ **Personal tab:** Here, you can configure the name that your contacts will see when you log on. By default, this is set to your username, but you can change it to read almost any valid text string. You can also edit your online profile, which is stored on Microsoft's .NET Passport servers. This profile maintains personal information that appears to other users. Personal information like state, country, and zip code, as well as whether other users can contact you via e-mail. This tab also contains an option for changing the font used during text-based chat sessions.

- ◆ **Phone tab:** You can type in phone numbers where your contacts can reach you. If you have a compatible mobile device, such as a Smart Phone, you can configure this device to work with Messenger.

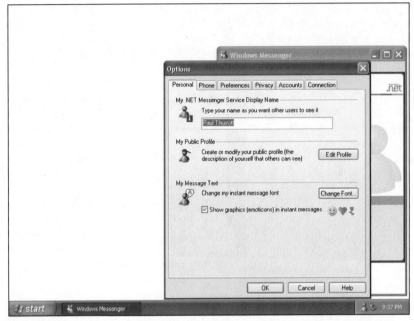

Figure 14-4: The Messenger Options dialog box provides numerous configuration capabilities.

 Any numbers you enter on the Phone tab will be publicly visible. I recommend that you leave these entries blank.

◆ **Preferences tab:** This tab contains a number of important options.

- You can determine whether Messenger starts when Windows starts, whether it can run in the background (or "as a service," in Microsoft-speak), and how many minutes of inactivity cause you to be marked as *away* (the default is five minutes) when your contacts check your online status.

- An Alerts section lets you configure alerts functionality (not to be confused with .NET Alerts), such as whether you are alerted when your contacts come online, when someone requests an instant message, or when an e-mail arrives.

- You can configure the folder used to store files that are transferred to your PC from other Messenger users.

♦ **Privacy tab:** You determine who can see your actual online status and who can start chat sessions with you. By default, all of your contacts can do this, but you can selectively block any users from seeing when you're online or starting conversations. Privacy is key online, so be sure to block users accordingly.

♦ **Accounts tab:** You can determine whether you're signing in with a .NET Passport account (typically a Hotmail or MSN e-mail address, as you will typically be doing with XP) or through another communications service, which is generally the case with businesses.

♦ **Connections tab:** You can enter proxy server information if you're using Messenger at work. On your home network, you should just leave the I Use a Proxy Server option unchecked.

After Messenger is configured, you can manage contacts, check e-mail, and perform other tasks.

Managing Contacts

If you're into chatting, one of the first things you'll likely do when you start Messenger is add some contacts. Your contact list will be friends, family, or coworkers who have .NET Passport accounts (typically Hotmail or MSN users) and might want to chat with you.

ADDING A CONTACT

To add a contact, choose Add a Contact from the task pane in the main Messenger window, or choose Tools→Add a Contact. Either way, the Add a Contact dialog box, shown in Figure 14-5, appears.

Figure 14-5: When adding a contact, you can choose to manually enter an e-mail address or search for the person.

Here, you can either *add a contact by e-mail address* or *search for a contact*.

Adding a contact by e-mail address is straightforward: enter the address, then click Next to continue and Finish to complete adding the e-mail address.

Searching for a friend is a bit more involved. Follow these steps:

1. Select the Search for a Contact option. You are prompted to supply whatever information you might have about this contact, including first and last name, country of origin, and a location to search, such as the Hotmail Member Directory or your local address book. Enter the information you know and click Next.

   If your search works, you will see the search results: a list of contacts that match your search criteria. However, you may run into problems, such as no results, too many results (such as when you try looking for *Bob Smith* in the United States), or the like. Try to add or remove details from the search screen for until you find the person you're looking for.

2. When the person you want is listed, select the correct name from the list and click Next. Messenger will attempt to add that user to your Contacts list. There are three possible outcomes to the attempt:

   - If the user doesn't have any restrictions on being added, the person is added to your Contacts list immediately.

   - The user might not be added until they respond to an e-mail from MSN that requests permission. When the user responds to the e-mail, the user is added to your Contacts list.

   - An error message might report that the user doesn't want to be contacted. In this case, you can't add the user to your Contacts list.

After you've added a contact to your Contacts list, that person appears in the Messenger main window. If that person is online, his or her name appears under the Online heading, as shown in Figure 14-6.

RECEIVING REQUESTS FROM CONTACTS

If someone else attempts to add you to his or her Contacts list, you see the dialog box shown in Figure 14-7. You have a couple of options to respond:

◆ To allow the person to see when you're online and start chat sessions, select Allow.

◆ To prevent the user from adding you or contacting you again, select Block.

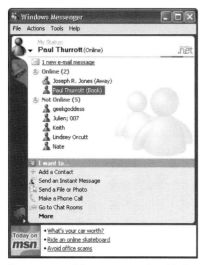

Figure 14-6: After a contact is added to your Contacts list, that person's name is shown in the Messenger main window.

By default, contacts that can view your online status are added to your Contacts list.

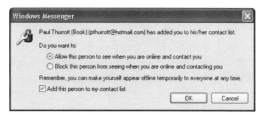

Figure 14-7: When other users try to add you to their Contacts list, you receive a chance to allow this request or block that user from accessing your presence information.

Checking E-Mail from Messenger

By default, Messenger alerts you when you receive an e-mail address at the Hotmail, MSN, or other .NET Passport address that's associated with your XP logon.

This notification appears in the lower-right corner of the screen and can be clicked; if you do so, an Internet Explorer window opens to the unread e-mail message. Figure 14-8 shows this.

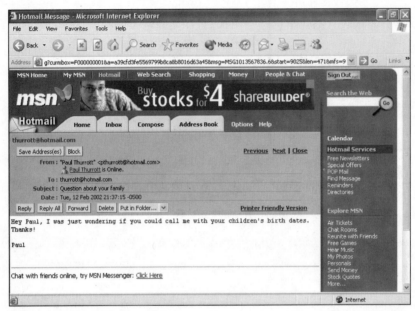

Figure 14-8: When Messenger alerts you about a new e-mail message, you can click the notification and automatically load the message in IE.

If you ignore the "toast slice" notification, it disappears from the screen after a few seconds. To check your mail after that, either click the e-mail hyperlink at the top of Messenger's main window, or right-click Messenger's system tray icon and choose My Email Inbox.

Sending an Instant Message Request

If you'd like to initiate an instant message, double-click the name of the person you'd like to chat with in the main Messenger window. This opens a Conversation window, as shown in Figure 14-9.

When you start typing, the other user is prompted to join your IM session with a notification window that displays the text you just typed. When the other user clicks that window, the Conversation window appears on the user's system, and you're free to chat.

The other user is not notified of the IM request until you type in a message. Simply opening this window does not make anything happen on the other user's machine.

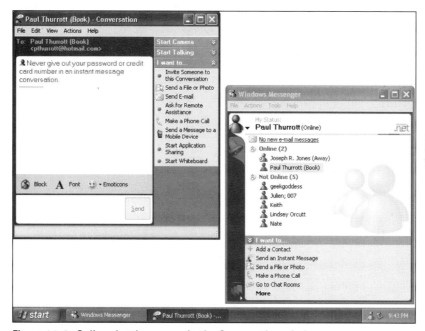

Figure 14-9: Online chatting occurs in the Conversation window.

Changing Your Online Status

Though Messenger will automatically change your online status to *Away* when more than five minutes transpires without any activity on your PC, there are times when you'll want to manually specify an online status so that you're not interrupted. Messenger includes a number of options, including Online, Busy, Be Right Back, Away, On the Phone, Out to Lunch, and Appear Offline. To access these choices, display the main Messenger window and click the down arrow next to your name, as shown in Figure 14-10. Simply select the status you want your contacts to see.

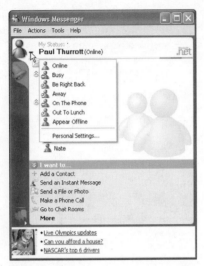

Figure 14-10: You can manually change your online
status with a single click of the mouse.

Using Messenger for Audio Chat

Text chatting is fun, but Messenger offers far more compelling options than that.
The first is audio chat, which lets you speak into a microphone and use the PC and
your Internet connection like a free-long-distance phone.

Starting an audio chat is identical to starting a text chat, or IM session. First,
double-click the contact you'd like to chat with, displaying the Conversation window. Now, click the Start Talking link in the right side of the Conversation window.

If you haven't yet tuned your audio or video hardware, the Audio and Video
Tuning Wizard, shown in Figure 14-11, appears next. This wizard steps you
through the process of optimizing your microphone and video capture devices (if
present) so you can use them with Messenger.

First, the wizard lets you specify which video camera, if any, you want to use.
Then it configures the microphone. You select the microphone (input) and speakers
(output) you'll use during Messenger audio and video chat sessions.

TIP   Typically, a USB-based headset gives the best results, but you can use any
PC microphone and your normal speakers.

Figure 14-11: The Audio and Video Tuning Wizard helps you configure microphones, speakers, and video input devices for use with Messenger.

After the microphone and speakers are configured, your audio chat request is relayed to the other person. Unlike text chats, audio (and video) chats must be *accepted* by the receiver, as shown in Figure 14-12. If the other person clicks the Accept link, the chat begins.

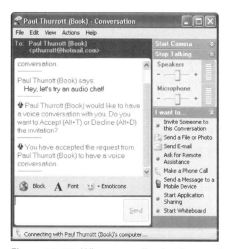

Figure 14-12: When an audio chat is accepted, you can adjust the volume of the speakers and microphone using these small built-in control panels.

You can still chat using with text during an audio chat session. To stop the audio chat, simply click Stop Talking in the Conversation window. Either user can end an audio chat at any time.

Using Messenger for Video Chat

Video chat is very similar to audio chat in that you start a normal conversation first. Then you click Start Camera to begin the video display. Again, the audio and video hardware need to be configured first, and the other user has to accept the request. You can combine video and audio chat to get the full experience, and it's possible for either user to have only a subset of the full capabilities (for example, one user could use audio chat only, while the other might only have video capabilities, or both audio and video).

When Messenger's audio and video chat comes together, you're doing something the phone companies say is impossible, and you're doing it over the public Internet without any long-distance charges. Audio and video chatting, shown in Figure 14-13, really is the next best thing to being there.

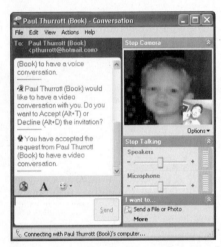

Figure 14-13: With the videoconferencing features of Windows Messenger, two people can play like the Jetsons.

Sending and Receiving Files with Messenger

Back in the early days of the Internet, one of the primary tools used by many people was File Transfer Protocol, or FTP, which allowed them to log on to computer servers, browse lists of files, and download particular files or groups of files. FTP still exists today, though many people transparently access this feature through their Web browsers without realizing it. But in many instances, you'll just want to send a single file to an individual, and there's no need to involve a server in this transaction. With Windows Messenger, you can instantly send any file to any of your contacts.

To do this, start a conversation and choose Send a File or Photo from the Sidebar on the right of the Conversation window. This displays the Send a File dialog box, shown in Figure 14-14, which is really just a standard File Open dialog box in disguise. Navigate to the file you'd like to send, select it (and make sure it's not some 190MB video file, please), and click Open.

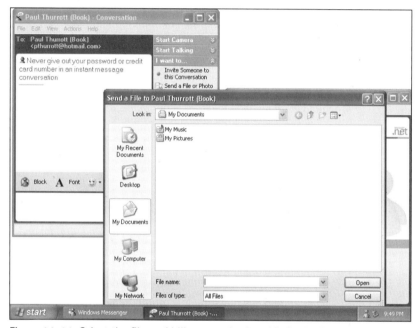

Figure 14-14: Select the file you'd like to send using this Send a File dialog box.

File transfers, like audio and video chat, need to be accepted by the other person. So your contact will see a request to initiate the file transfer. This request will describe the name of the file, the size and expected transfer time of the file at 28.8 Kbps, and options to accept or decline the file, as shown in Figure 14-15.

If the request is accepted, the transfer begins. When it's complete, both people are alerted to the transfer completion, and the receiver is prompted to the file's location on his or her system. Click the hyperlink, shown in Figure 14-16, to open the file.

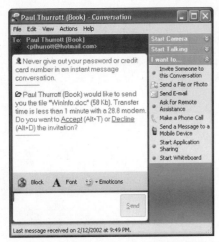

Figure 14-15: The receiver gets enough information about the file that you're trying to send to decide whether to accept the request.

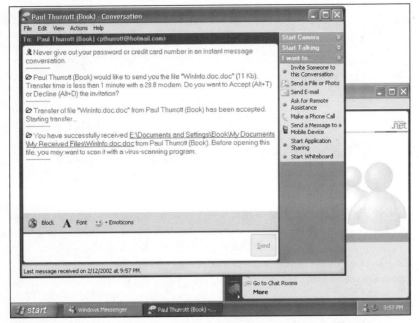

Figure 14-16: When a file is successfully delivered, the receiver can click this hyperlink to open the file.

Other XP Collaboration Features

In addition to text, audio, and video chatting, and file transfer capabilities, Windows XP includes other useful collaboration features. Most of the features are made available through Windows Messenger, so I focus on those here.

Application Sharing with Messenger

Chapter 17 discusses XP's Remote Desktop features, which allow XP users to remotely access their XP desktops when they're at another computer. Microsoft has built a related feature into Messenger called *Application Sharing,* though this feature is limited to a single application, rather than the entire desktop.

Why might you want to share an application? Perhaps you are collaborating on a document and want to edit it live, even though the other individual is far away. Or perhaps the other person doesn't have the application that's used to access a particular document type, so you want to temporarily give that person access to the application remotely. Either way, you can accomplish this through Windows Messenger.

As with other Messenger features, you first begin a conversation with the person that you will be application sharing with. Then launch the application you'd like to share – perhaps Microsoft Word or Excel. Then click the Start Application Sharing link in the Conversation window Sidebar. This sends an invitation to your contact, who accepts or declines the request.

If the invitation is accepted, the Sharing Session window opens, followed shortly by the Sharing window, as shown in Figure 14-17. These windows are your control panels for the application sharing session. They're also important because they give you the ability to close the session at any time, which could be important when you give another person remote access to your system like this.

In the Sharing window, select the application you'd like to share and then click the Share button. When I do, a window called *Paul Thurrott's programs* (the name is based on my Messenger profile) opens on the other person's PC and displays the contents of your desktop. Here's the catch: The other person can access only the program you shared (see Figure 14-18), and if you cover that application with other windows, it will be hidden from the other user.

If you'd like the other person to have (temporary) control of your desktop, you can click the Allow Control button on the Sharing window. And you can click Close on the Sharing Session window to end the whole session.

Using the Messenger Whiteboard

Another related feature is the Messenger Whiteboard, which allows two Windows Messenger users to share a common whiteboard, similar to the Microsoft Paint application, where both people can simultaneously scratch out ideas using text and graphics.

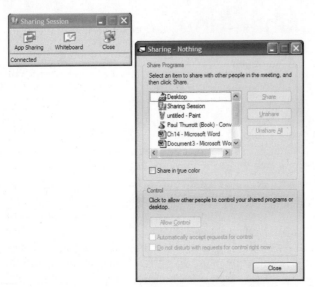

Figure 14-17: The Sharing Session and Sharing windows help you manage which applications you'll share with the connected user.

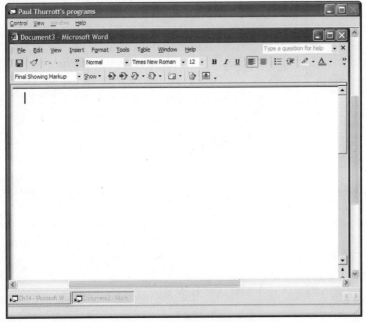

Figure 14-18: On the receiving end, the shared application can be accessed through the Programs window.

This feature is very similar to application sharing, except that the only application you'll share is the Messenger Whiteboard. Here's how: Open a conversation and click Start Whiteboard on the Conversation window's Sidebar. If the other person accepts the request, the Whiteboard window, shown in Figure 14-19, appears. This application presents text and graphical tools, all of which can be used simultaneously by either user.

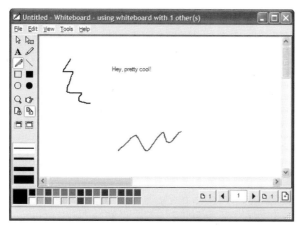

Figure 14-19: Two people can access the whiteboard simultaneously; here, the leftmost line is being drawn by the person who started the session, while the rightmost line is being drawn by the person who accepted the session.

Curiously, although you can save your whiteboard diagrams, they are not saved in native Bitmap (BMP) format; they're saved in a format called *NetMeeting Whiteboard* (NMW). Whiteboard diagrams are always saved on the system of the person who initiated the whiteboard session.

What to Do When Messenger Features Won't Work

Frustrated because that file won't transfer, or you can't initiate a video chat? The biggest problem with Windows Messenger is that its most exciting features — audio and video chat, file application sharing, and whiteboarding — require that the other user is accessing his or her contacts list through Windows Messenger as well; MSN Messenger often won't work. If certain Messenger features don't work with certain contacts, maybe they're not using Windows Messenger. Over time, many of these features will be ported to future versions of MSN Messenger, but at the time of this writing, there are still a lot of incompatibilities.

The other obvious problem you might run into is far more technical. Because Windows Messenger relies on the new SIP protocol, many existing networking hardware devices simply don't work. If you're connecting directly to a cable modem or DSL modem with your XP box, you're all set because XP includes the networking plumbing to enable SIP-based communications.

But if your home network is sealed off from the outside world by a pre–Universal Plug and Play (UPnP) home gateway or router, you're probably going to be out of luck. That's because these devices don't know how to work with SIP and its dynamic use of port forwarding: Older devices can only use static port forwarding. The solution, sadly, is to upgrade. Some devices will eventually allow for (free) software upgrades to allow this functionality, but many will not. The good news is that networking hardware is relatively cheap these days. So if you're in the market for a new gateway, make sure you get one that's UPnP compatible.

This topic is covered more completely in Chapter 5.

Chapter 15

Web Publishing

IN THIS CHAPTER

◆ What are web folders and how do you access them

◆ Publishing or building web pages with the enhanced Web Publishing Wizard

◆ Host your own web server with Internet Information Services (IIS)

FOR PEOPLE WHO WANT to be heard, no phenomenon is more exciting than the recent explosion of the World Wide Web ("Web"). In addition to the obvious benefits for students and other researchers, newshounds, and online shoppers, the Web has also opened up a new era of personal publishing that promises to outstrip even the importance of the printing press. Today, it's possible for anyone to use the Internet as a personal pulpit or remote storage area. And Windows XP, predictably, includes features that help you take advantage of this technology.

Ever since Windows 95, Microsoft has been integrating various Web publishing tools with Windows, including a "light" version of its FrontPage Web editor that is no longer available and shell integration with remote Web sites. In XP, these shell tools have been refined into something call Web Folders, and they're easier to use than ever before.

More intriguingly, XP Professional Edition includes a personal Web server, which makes it possible to experiment with your own live Web site. Internet Information Services (IIS 5.1), as this feature is now called, is a real Web server, too, though it's license is limited to only ten inbound connections so that users don't attempt to use XP on production Web sites.

You find out about both of these exciting Web publishing features in this chapter.

Working with Web Folders

Web Folders debuted with Internet Explorer 5 and Windows 98 Second Edition (SE) in 1999, providing Windows users with the capability to connect to Web Distributed Authoring and Versioning (WebDAV)–compliant servers using the familiar My Computer–style shell interface for the first time. WebDAV is a set of extensions to the Web's HTTP protocol that allows users to collaboratively edit and manage files on remote Web servers.

Adding this kind of technology to the Windows shell has precedent. Previously, Microsoft created the ability to connect to network shares on the local area network (LAN) through the Network Neighborhood (later renamed My Network Places), for example. Web Folders simply extends this capability to remote Web servers.

In previous Windows versions, however, Web Folders were somewhat of an add-on, and a Web Folders icon appeared in the root of My Computer, which was pretty cluttered up with icons back in the Windows 9.x/Me days. Today, Web Folders are just integrated directly into My Network Places, so you can create shortcuts – or *network places,* as they're annoyingly called – that connect to network shares, FTP sites, or WebDAV-compatible Web sites; they're all the same to XP and, thus, to the user. Microsoft makes things easy like that.

The company also makes sure that its various products and services work together: As you might expect, Web servers built with Microsoft technology (that is, FrontPage-oriented Web sites) are automatically WebDAV-compatible, so they can be accessed directly from the XP shell. And many of Microsoft's MSN-based online communities are also WebDAV based.

TIP Don't be lulled into thinking that WebDAV is some proprietary Microsoft technology that's available only to Windows users, because it's not. WebDAV was created by the WebDAV Working Group, which includes Microsoft and a number of other companies. And high-profile companies such as Apple Computer use this technology with their own products. If you've heard of Apple's iTools, for example, its iDisk component is implemented with WebDAV technology. You can hit such sites from Windows XP if you have the right permissions. Likewise, Windows-based WebDAV servers can be accessed from Apple's Mac OS X products, or other WebDAV compatible clients. Isn't it nice when we can all get along?

Understanding WebDAV

WebDAV – Web Distributed Authoring and Versioning, remember – is a network protocol at heart. It was designed to overcome the stateless connection model typically used on the Web, where a connection is made, information is transferred, and then the connection is broken. Consider what happens when you load a Web page: The Web browser sends a request to a Web server, and if it's accepted, the Web server returns images, text, and other information back to the browser. But after the request is fulfilled, the connection is severed. There's no continuity at all on the Web; it's just a series of browsers and servers passing in the night.

WebDAV doesn't completely overcome the limitations of HTTP – the Hypertext Transfer Protocol – by providing a fully stateful connection between a WebDAV client and a WebDAV server. But it does overcome the biggest problem with HTTP when it comes to remote file access: With WebDAV, it's possible to obtain exclusive or shared access to remote files, as needed, so that another user doesn't, say, overwrite a file you're working with. This feature enables WebDAV servers to be used for collaborative purposes, where multiple users can access shared file servers remotely over the Internet.

There are other WebDAV features, but file locking – where files can be marked as in use exclusive or in shared mode – is the big one.

TIP Interested in WebDAV? You can find out more on the World Wide Web, naturally! I recommend the WedDAV Working Group's Web site: www. webdav.org.

Connecting to Remote WebDAV servers

As previously discussed, Web Folders are the primary interface in Windows XP for WebDAV-capable servers. However, before you can connect to such a server, you need to find one. Conveniently, Microsoft lets Passport users – including any Hotmail or MSN e-mail users – publish private and public online communities on its MSN Web properties, so you can create one of those.

To get started, log on to your Passport account through Windows Messenger if you haven't already. And if you're not sure what Passport is, check out Chapter 11 for more information.

CREATING AN MSN COMMUNITY

Creating your own MSN Community site via Web Folders is a pretty straightforward process, but there's a catch. This process – and the catch – are detailed in the following steps:

1. Open up My Network Places and click the Add a Network Place option under Network Tasks. This displays the Add Network Place wizard, shown in Figure 15-1. Click Next to continue.

2. In the second phase of the wizard, shown in Figure 15-2, you can choose a service provider. By default, XP offers two choices here: MSN Communities and Choose Another Network Location. Choose MSN Communities and click Next.

3. After the wizard downloads information from the Internet, you're presented with a list of one or more choices, depending on whether you've configured any MSN Communities sites previously. If you haven't, you see just one choice, Create a New MSN Community to Share Your Files, as shown in Figure 15-3.

   Otherwise, you might see a number of choices, as shown in Figure 15-4. Hotmail and MSN e-mail users often see a choice called My Web Documents (Personal), for example.

Select Create a New MSN Community to Share Your Files and then click Next. (MSN users are prompted at this point to select a Shared or Personal community. Select Shared if you see this option.)

Figure 15-1: You can use the Add Network Place Wizard to create shortcuts to LAN resources as well as WebDAV and FrontPage-compatible Web sites.

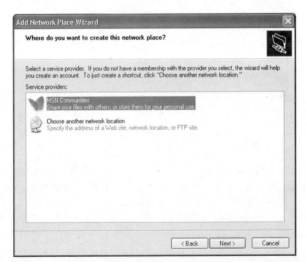

Figure 15-2: In the second phase of the wizard, you can choose between free MSN Communities or other types of network locations.

Figure 15-3: If this is the first time you've run the wizard, you'll probably see only this single choice.

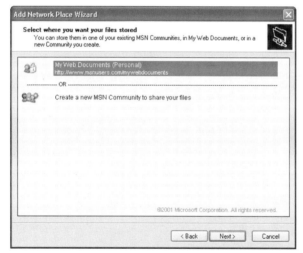

Figure 15-4: At other times, you might see a list of MSN Communities from which to choose; the list is different for various Passport account users.

4. In the next phase of the wizard, shown in Figure 15-5, you must pick a name for your community, supply your e-mail address, and agree to MSN's Code of Conduct. Note that MSN Community names must be unique, so you'll be prompted to try again if you choose one that's already being used. Click Next to continue.

5. In the next step, you can optionally enter a plain English explanation of the community, choose a language, and decide whether the community will be accessible to the public. Make the appropriate selections and click Next to continue.

6. Now, the wizard displays the Web address, or URL, for your new community and offers to add a shortcut to that address in your Internet Explorer Favorites list. Again, click Next.

7. In the next step, the wizard offers you the option of changing the location of the default Documents and Pictures folder, two folders that MSN creates for all of its Communities by default. That is, all non-image files will be uploaded to the Documents folder by default, and all image files will be uploaded to the Pictures folder. Change these settings if desired and click Next.

8. Now the wizard is complete. It notes that you have successfully created a new network place and offers to open that network place when you click Finish. Click Finish to close the wizard.

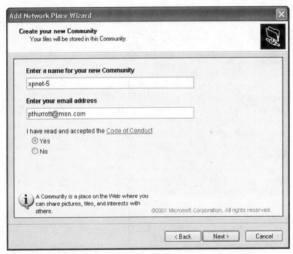

Figure 15-5: You can enter a name for your new Web community and the e-mail address at which you can be reached for administrative issues.

And then . . . nothing happens. Despite the explicit promise, no network place is created. However, your actions have at least created the MSN Community. This is evidenced by the e-mail you will receive shortly welcoming you to MSN Communities. This e-mail is sent to whatever e-mail address you configured in Step 4.

MAKING A NETWORK PLACE

So what happened? Clearly, this is a bug in XP. But all is not lost; you can still create a network place that points to your new MSN Community. Here's how:

1. In My Network Places, click Add a Network Place again and launch the Add Network Place wizard; click Next to proceed.

2. In the service provider phase, select the Choose Another Network Location option and then click Next.

3. In the next phase, enter the Internet address of your new MSN Community. This is available in the e-mail you just received, and it will resemble http://www.msnusers.com/*your_community_name*. Click Next to continue.

4. In the next step, you can enter a name for your new network place. This can be anything you'd like, such as *My MSN Community* or whatever. Be creative. Go nuts. When you're done, click Next to continue.

5. Again, the wizard is completed. But this time, it actually creates a new network place, as shown in Figure 15-6. Ah, progress.

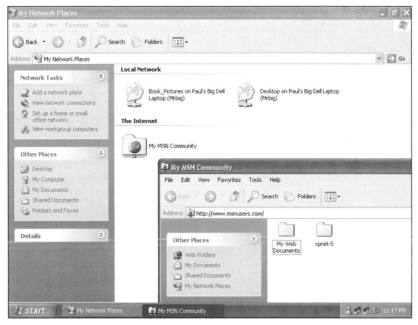

Figure 15-6: After you've created a network place, you can access it by using a standard Explorer view.

ACCESSING YOUR NETWORK PLACE

After you've created a network place, you can access it like any other local folder or shared network folder, albeit more slowly. You can create a shortcut to the network place on your desktop or other location, drag and drop files and folders between the network place and your local machine, and perform most of the other file and folder actions you've come to expect in Windows. Here are a few examples:

- ◆ To rename the network place, simply select it and press F2, and then enter any name you'd like.

- ◆ To open the network place, simply double-click it and wait a bit. Eventually, the contents of the place (just a folder named *Documents* by default) is displayed, and then you can drag files and folders in and out, delete files and folders, and even edit documents that are placed in the online community.

- ◆ One thing you can't do, interestingly, is use the network place's folder icon as a drop target. If you attempt to copy a file this way, you get an error message. That's because you can't write to the root of the MSN Community. But if you open up the folder, you can drag and drop files into the Documents folder.

But network places are online resources, and you can also access your new MSN Community with Internet Explorer. To do so, simply type the correct URL into the Web browser (such as `http://www.msnusers.com/your_community_name`); you'll see something similar to the window shown in Figure 15-7.

If you click the Documents or Pictures links on the left, you're presented with a file listing that includes any files you might have uploaded to the Community. For example, in Figure 15-8, an image named `capture.jpg` was uploaded to the Pictures folder.

MSN Communities are a pretty cool thing for Microsoft to give away for free, so they're something worth looking into if you've never given them much thought or, more likely, never knew that they existed.

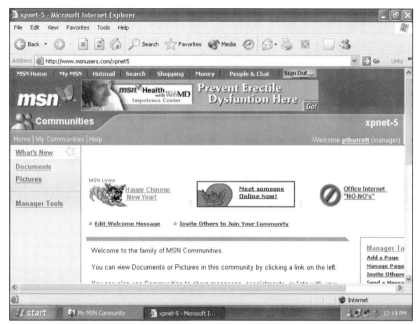

Figure 15-7: You can access the Web version of the MSN Community via any Web browser.

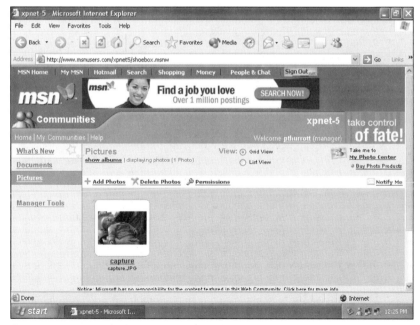

Figure 15-8: Image files are shown in thumbnail view and uploaded to the Pictures folder by default.

Using the Web Publishing Wizard

After you've set up a WebDAV server of your own – such as an MSN Community – you can use XP's Web Publishing Wizard to easily copy documents and images to the Web. The Web Publishing Wizard doesn't get a lot of face time in XP; it's basically hidden in a single task pane choice, depending on which My Computer window you're viewing. But it's a simple and elegant way to upload documents and images to WebDAV-compliant Web servers.

The next few sections discuss the wizard in the context of MSN Communities because anyone can start one (and you just did, if you've been following along in this chapter). And because the wizard works slightly different if you're uploading images or other kinds of documents, I discuss both instances in the next few sections.

Publishing Documents to the Web

When you use the wizard to publish non-image documents to an MSN Community, they are copied to the Documents folder in that community. Here's how it works:

1. Using My Computer, navigate to the file(s) or folder(s) you'd like to upload and select it. For this example, I'll use a single text file found in the My Documents folder, but you can obviously upload any file you'd like.

2. In the File and Folder Tasks section of the task list on the left, select Publish This File to the Web, as shown in Figure 15-9. (If you're publishing a folder, select Publish This Folder to the Web.) This launches the Web Publishing Wizard; click Next to proceed.

3. In the next phase, you can change your file selection if there are multiple files or folders in the folder in which you've already selected an item to upload. As shown in Figure 15-10, you can now select certain files and folders, select all items, or clear all items. When you're done, click Next to continue.

4. Next, you can choose the service provider. Microsoft provides two default choices: Xdrive Plus (an online storage solution) and MSN Communities. However, more might be available if you received XP with a new computer. Select MSN Communities and then click Next.

5. Now, you see a dialog box similar to the file storage location phase of the Add Network Places Wizard. But this time, the network place you previously created is available, in addition to any other applicable MSN Communities you've created or joined and the default choice of Create a New MSN Community to Share Your Files. This dialog box is shown in Figure 15-11. Select the community you just created and click Next.

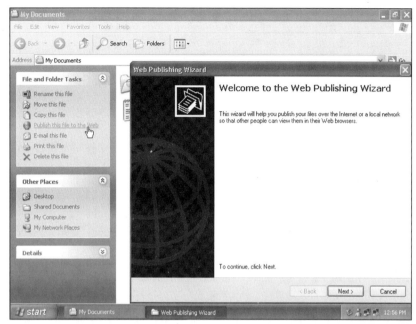

Figure 15-9: The Web Publishing Wizard is pretty well hidden in XP, but it's a surprisingly simple way to upload documents and images if you know where to find it.

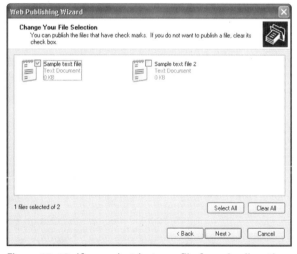

Figure 15-10: If you select just one file for uploading, the wizard gives you the option to select other files in the same directory as well.

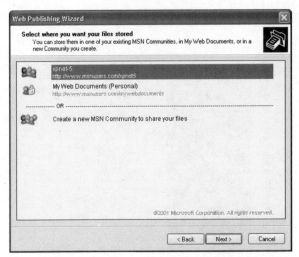

Figure 15-11: Now that you've created an MSN Community,
it will appear in any wizard that accesses MSN Communities.

6. In the next phase, you can choose to accept the default locations for documents and image files (Documents and Documents/Pictures, respectively)
   or publish your files to custom locations in the community. Click Next to
   continue.

7. At this point, your files are copied, as shown in Figure 15-12.

   When the upload is completed, you receive a success notification. Click
   Next to continue.

8. Now, the wizard is complete. Click Finish, and your MSN Community site
   is loaded in Internet Explorer. Navigate to the Documents folder to view
   your newly uploaded file, as shown in Figure 15-13.

If you select the file, it loads in your browser or in the appropriate application if
necessary.

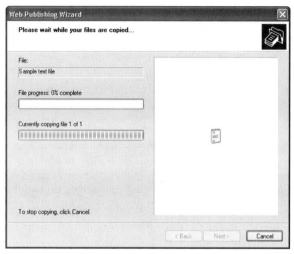

Figure 15-12: During the file copy phase, you can get pre-file progress reports because Web copying is a lot slower than local file copying.

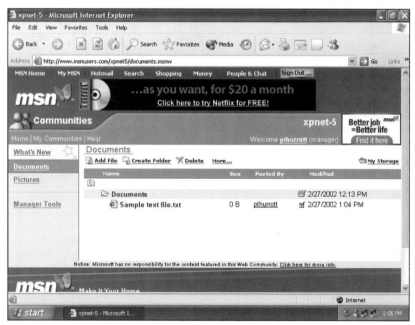

Figure 15-13: Non-image files uploaded to an MSN Community are placed in the Documents folder by default.

Publishing Images to the Web

The process for publishing images to your MSN Community with the wizard is almost identical to the instructions in the preceding section with three differences:

◆ Images files are automatically uploaded to Documents/Pictures, not Documents, by default.

◆ After you've selected the upload location, you are presented with the window shown in Figure 15-14. This lets XP automatically resize your image(s) to fit within certain sizes (such as Small [640 x 480] or Medium [800 x 600]), which is convenient if you'd like to eventually create some sort of online image slide show. You can uncheck the Yes, Make Them All This Size option if you'd like the image(s) to be uploaded without first being converted.

◆ As the images are uploaded, you can see a preview of each image, as shown in Figure 15-15.

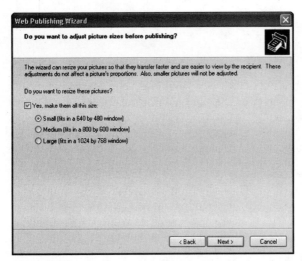

Figure 15-14: When you upload images through the wizard, you are given the option to automatically resize them as they upload.

As before, when the wizard is completed, it loads your MSN Community in Internet Explorer. Now, navigate to the Pictures folder, which includes thumbnails of each image you've uploaded. Click a thumbnail to view any image full-sized.

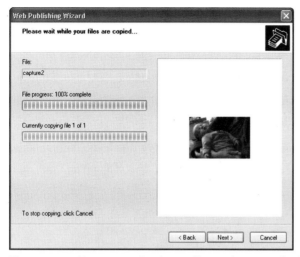

Figure 15-15: You can preview image files as they are uploaded.

Using Internet Information Services 5.1

Microsoft includes a full-featured version of its Internet Information Services (IIS) Web server in Windows XP Professional that lets you develop and test professional Web sites locally on your own PC.

 Internet Information Services is only included with XP Pro. XP Home Edition users are out of luck. You can either upgrade to Professional Edition or try one of the new non-IIS Web servers that run on XP. One good choice is Apache, the most popular Web server on the planet (www.apache.org).

In businesses, the XP Pro version of IIS can be used for publishing small intranet sites that don't get many users. (Windows 2000 Server or Windows .NET Server products would be more appropriate for actual production Web sites, of course.) This is also a useful feature for home users who want to learn or work locally with Microsoft's Web server technologies, including:

◆ IIS: The core Web server product, which also includes File Transfer Protocol (FTP) functionality for file sharing.

◆ **Active Server Pages (ASP):** Microsoft's pre-.NET technology for creating programmable Web applications that use server-side VBScript and JavaScript scripting and can integrate with server-side software components written in a variety of programming languages.

◆ **FrontPage authoring:** IIS includes the FrontPage Server Extensions, which allows any FrontPage-compatible Web page editor to connect to the server and access files and folders using an interactive environment that's similar to WebDAV but more proprietary to Microsoft. If you're a FrontPage user, IIS is a great way to develop sites locally and then publish them to a remote site. In fact, that's exactly what I do with the Web site for this book at www.xphomenetworking.com.

Windows 2000 (Server family and Professional) shipped with IIS 5.0, but the version in Windows XP Professional is slightly enhanced, so the version number was bumped up to 5.1. In Windows .NET Server, which is due to ship in late 2002, IIS 6.0 is included. This IIS version includes a number of significant enhancements, but of course, that's way beyond the scope of this book. To find out more about IIS 6, please visit my SuperSite for Windows: www.winsupersite.com.

Installing IIS

IIS isn't installed by default, so if you'd like use this component, you need to install it first. As always, there are a variety of ways to do this, but here's the easiest way:

1. Insert your Windows XP CD-ROM and wait for the Welcome to Windows XP window to auto-run. If it doesn't, open My Computer and double-click the CD drive icon to launch the Welcome window.

2. Select Install Optional Windows Components to launch the Windows Components Wizard, shown in Figure 15-16.

3. Scroll down the Components list and find Internet Information Services (IIS). Select this option (don't check it) and click the Details button. This launches the dialog box shown in Figure 15-17.

The following options are available, along with advice about which components to install. The goal here, incidentally, is to install as little as possible, because a Web server represents yet another target for hackers. Also note that most ISPs specifically forbid their users from running Web sites off their accounts, though your use of IIS for testing is probably acceptable. Just check your ISP's Usage Policy to be sure. Here are the options in the current dialog box:

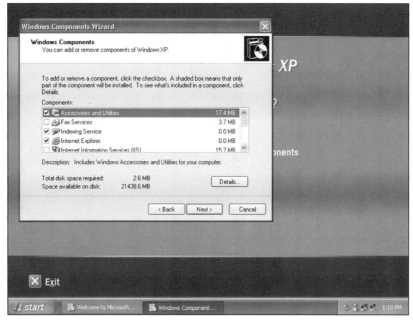

Figure 15-16: To install IIS on Windows XP, you need to access the Windows Components Wizard; this component is never installed by default.

- **Common Files:** This option installs required IIS program files, so be sure to check it.

- **Documentation:** If you're looking for more information about IIS, Web publishing, and related technologies, then select this option. I usually leave it off, although I installed it the first several times I installed XP.

- **File Transfer Protocol (FTP) Service:** If you don't think you'll be using this feature, then I recommend leaving it off. FTP is a prime candidate for hack attacks, and there's no reason to leave yet another port open on your machine, unless it's not connected directly to the Internet (in which case, only users on your local network would be able to hit the FTP site anyway).

- **FrontPage 2000 Server Extensions:** A requirement for users of FrontPage, Visual InterDev, or Visual Studio .NET, this set of technologies enables FrontPage-based Web site authoring and management. I use this feature all the time because I'm a heavy FrontPage user, but if you don't own one of the aforementioned Web development tools, leave it off. If you do check this option, the Internet Information Services Snap-In and World Wide Web Service options are automatically selected.

- **Internet Information Services Snap-In:** This is a required component and is preselected when you choose to install the FrontPage 2000 Server Extensions. This option adds an entry to the Computer Management console, which is discussed in the next section, allowing you to administer IIS via a GUI front end.

- **SMTP Service:** This component allows users hitting HTML forms on your Web site to send e-mail to internal e-mail servers. As such, this feature is rarely of use in a home setting, and I recommend leaving it off.

- **World Wide Web Service:** This is the core Web server technology in IIS and must be selected.

4. Click OK after you've selected the components you'd like to install, and then click Next in the Windows Components Wizard. The wizard then installs the appropriate components.

5. Click Finish to complete the wizard.

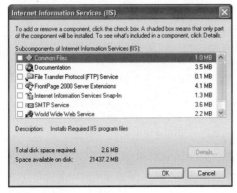

Figure 15–17: IIS consists of many parts, only some of which you need for a basic functioning Web server.

TIP If you installed Windows XP via a network share or other non-CD-based method, you can still get to the Windows Components Wizard by navigating to the Control Panel and selecting Add or Remove Programs. Then click the Add/Remove Windows Component option on the left of the Add or Remove Programs dialog box.

Administering IIS 101

After the Windows Components Wizard is completed, nothing obvious seems to happen. If you peruse the Start menu, for example, you won't see an IIS reference, unless you've enabled the System Administration Tools to appear in the Start menu (see "Accessing Management Tools from the Start Menu," later in this chapter). However, a number of things have actually happened behind the scenes, in addition to the installation of the Web server components:

♦ **A new directory structure:** A `C:\Inetpub` directory structure has been created to house your Web site and, optionally, FTP sites. You can actually change the location in which your files are stored, but the directory structure here must remain for some bizarre reason; it'd be nice if you could store the programmatic components in `C:\Program Files` and the actual Web site files in your My Documents folder, but it just doesn't work like that.

♦ **IIS management console:** A new IIS management console has been created. This is covered in the next section.

♦ **New node in Computer Management:** That new IIS management tool is also available as part of the wider Computer Management console. You also find out about this shortly.

The next few sections take a look at the various ways in which you can access the IIS Management tools.

ACCESSING MANAGEMENT TOOLS FROM THE CONTROL PANEL

On a stock Windows XP system, the simplest (but not fastest way) to access the IIS management tools is through the Control Panel. Navigate to the Control Panel and then select Switch to Classic View from the Control Panel tasks list in the left side of the window. This displays the classic Control Panel view, which includes an Administrative Tools icon. When you double-click this icon, XP's Administrative Tools are displayed, including Internet Information Services, as shown in Figure 15-18.

This isn't a very elegant method for accessing IIS management, however. But you can always create a shortcut to the tool on your desktop.

ACCESSING COMPUTER MANAGEMENT

The IIS management console is also available as part of the Computer Management tool, which is incredibly useful for a variety of reasons. However, it's also one of the most hidden features in Windows XP. To access this tool, open the Start menu, right-click My Computer, and choose Manage. (You didn't know about that one, did you?)

This displays the Computer Management console, shown in Figure 15-19. You can find a lot of good stuff in there, so you might want to spend some time checking it out.

Expand the Services and Applications node to reveal the Internet Information Services console. This is probably the quickest way to access the IIS management tools, and it's the route I recommend for power users. But if you're into cluttering up your Start menu, there's another choice, as described next.

Figure 15-18: The XP Administrative Tools are well hidden for some reason, but you can access them through the Control Panel if you know where to look.

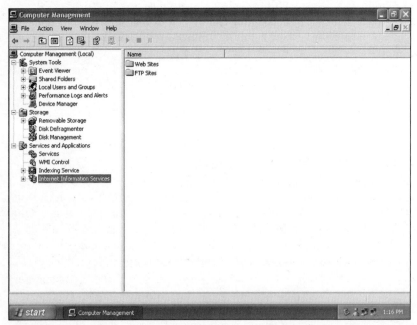

Figure 15-19: Computer Management offers links to the IIS administration tools and a whole lot more.

ACCESSING MANAGEMENT TOOLS FROM THE START MENU

By default, Windows XP ships with a Start menu that's configured the way that Microsoft thinks it should be. But give the company some credit; the Start menu is also highly configurable, and you can control how it looks and works to a large degree. One of the many items you can choose to display there are the Administrative Tools, which includes the IIS management console. Here's how:

1. Right-click the Start menu and choose Properties. This displays the Taskbar and Start Menu Properties dialog box.

2. Making sure that the Start Menu (and not Classic Start Menu) option is selected, click the Customize button to display the Customize Start Menu dialog box, shown in Figure 15-20.

3. Click the Advanced tab. The display now resembles Figure 15-21, where a list of configurable Start menu items is available.

4. Scroll down the list until you see System Administration Tools (it's the last option). You have three choices here:

   ■ Display on the All Programs menu

   ■ Display on the All Programs menu and the Start menu

   ■ Don't Display This Item (the default)

   The first option, obviously, adds an Administrative Tools option to the All Programs menu, which is available from the Start menu. This is actually a submenu (or folder), which includes a number of tools, including the IIS management console you're trying to access.

   The second option adds an Administrative Tools node directly to XP's new Start menu, right below the Control Panel option, as shown in Figure 15-22. You can open this submenu to reveal various administrative tools.

5. After selecting the appropriate option, click OK to close the dialog box.

However you choose to do it, you should now have an easy and obvious way to access the IIS management console. And that means that you're now ready to manage IIS.

ACCESSING THE IIS MANAGEMENT TOOLS

Open up the IIS Management tool (or, in the case of Computer Management, expand the left-sided nodes to reveal Services and Applications and then Internet Information Services), and you see a window similar to Figure 15-23. When you expand Internet Information Services, you see a folder node for Web sites and, if you installed this service, one for FTP sites.

Figure 15-20: To view the XP Administrative Tools in the Start menu, you need to customize the Start menu first.

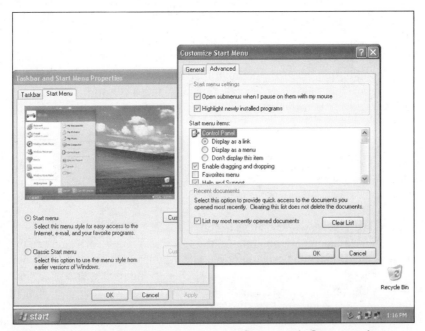

Figure 15-21: On the Advanced tab, you can configure certain Start menu items, including the XP Administrative Tools.

Figure 15-22: After they've been added, you can access an Administrative Tools submenu directly from the Start menu.

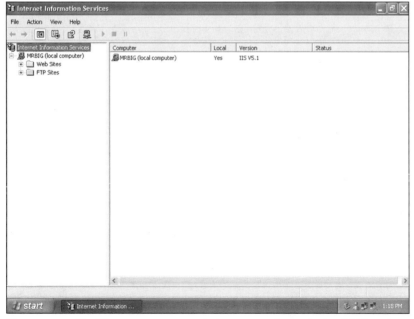

Figure 15-23: The IIS management console lets you configure the local Web and FTP sites.

Expand the Web sites node, and a node called Default Web Site is displayed. To manage and configure the site, right-click the Default Web Site name and choose Properties. This launches the Properties dialog box for the site (see Figure 15-24), which is the central management point for IIS. As you can see, this dialog box contains numerous options.

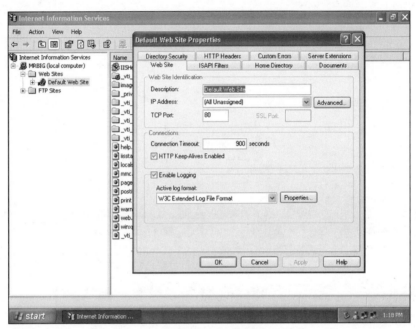

Figure 15-24: The Default Web Site Properties dialog box is your central location for IIS Web site management.

Frankly, on a personal Web site, you don't need to do much with this dialog box. You can use the Directory Security tab to set up a variety of security-related options, including whether anonymous users (the norm on the Internet) can access this site. This is particularly useful if you really intend to just test sites locally and not allow external access.

Local Web Serving

Interestingly, Microsoft sets up a default Web site for you. To view it, open up IE and enter one of the following URLs into the Address bar:

```
http://localhost
http://machine_name    (machine_name is the name of your XP-based PC)
```

Either way, you should see a default site. You can add files and folders to this site in a variety of ways, including with FrontPage. But if you don't use this tool, you can also just drag files and folders directly into the `C:\Inetpub\wwwroot` directory structure. It's even simpler than a Web Folder, and you don't have to wait.

On that note, you can also create a Web Folder that points to your local Web site if you'd like. Just run the Add Network Place wizard, select Choose Another Network Location, and type in one of the two preceding URLs as the Internet or network address.

Part IV

Remote Access

Chapter 16

Getting Help with Remote Assistance

IN THIS CHAPTER

♦ Help! Help! Receiving help from anywhere

♦ Learn the different ways (applications to use) to ask for help

♦ Controlling and helping others

♦ What to look out for when connecting through the internet and firewalls

REMOTE ASSISTANCE IS ONE OF the more exciting and powerful new features in Windows XP. It allows you to request help from other people, such as system administrators at work or friends and family in consumer settings, using any network including the Internet. With Remote Assistance, the person you're requesting help from can chat with you, view your screen, and with your permission, even control your system.

This feature is extremely valuable in an office environment because the IT department can help users with their problems without having to be physically at the PC that's having trouble. But this feature is also extremely useful for home networks. For example, if you need help, the person helping you remotely can actually see what's happening on your PC screen and even show you how to solve your problem by temporarily taking control of your PC. Or if you're the one helping a friend or relative remotely, you can see exactly what the other person is talking about.

This chapter reveals the different features of Remote Assistance, how to start Remote Assistance, how to use a Remote Assistance session, and important considerations you need to keep in mind when configuring Remote Assistance.

Getting Help Remotely

Throughout the years, various remote control solutions have been marketed, such as AT&T Research Lab's Virtual Network Computing (VNC), Computer Associates' ControlIT, Microsoft's Systems Management Server (SMS), and Symantec's pcAnywhere. These tools are primarily targeted towards businesses, not consumers. Windows XP marks the wide-scale introduction of this technology to average consumers with Microsoft's implementation of Remote Assistance and Remote Desktop (which is available only in Windows XP Professional Edition). Remote Assistance and Remote Desktop are both based on Microsoft's Terminal Services technology, which was introduced in Microsoft Windows NT 4.0 Terminal Server Edition. This technology allows computers to connect remotely to other computers over a network and view and interact with the other systems' desktops.

Remote Assistance allows you to view a remote computer screen (or someone else to view your computer remotely), chat with the other party involved in the Remote Assistance session via audio or text, send files back and forth, and give control of your computer screen or take control of the other person's computer screen.

Remote Assistance requires the helper and the helpee to be using Windows XP. You will be unable to receive help if you're using Windows Me, 2000, or older Windows versions. And you will be unable to help users of older versions of Windows with Remote Assistance if only you are running XP. Future versions of Windows, however, such as Windows .NET Server, will support Remote Assistance.

Sending and Accepting Invitations

You can start a Remote Assistance session a number of different ways: with Windows Messenger, with e-mail, and even with a file. The person requesting help must initiate the Remote Assistance.

Curiously, a system administrator cannot initiate a help session with a user, which is a major omission. Hopefully, this will be fixed in a future release.

Sending an Invitation via Windows Messenger

One of the easiest ways to start Remote Assistance is via the Microsoft Windows Messenger chat client, which is included in Windows XP. Windows Messenger is a real-time text, audio, and video client. In Windows Messenger, you can connect with other people by using Windows Messenger or MSN Messenger. These people sometimes are referred to as *buddies* or online contacts. (Windows Messenger is explained in more detail in Chapter 13.)

You can request help from a Windows Messenger buddy three different ways. The first two ways involve the actual Windows Messenger client and the third way involves the Remote Assistance interface in Windows XP's Help and Support Center.

REMOTE ASSISTANCE VIA YOUR BUDDY LIST

You can request a remote assistance session with someone in your Windows Messenger buddy list by right-clicking that person's name and selecting Ask for Remote Assistance, as shown in Figure 16-1.

Figure 16-1: Asking for help via a buddy list.

The individual from whom you're requesting help is prompted with your request. The prompt appears in a new chat session that opens automatically. The other user receives instructions on how to accept or reject your request, as shown in Figure 16-2.

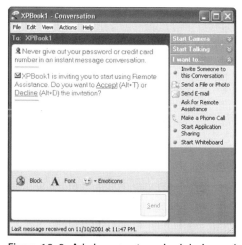

Figure 16-2: A help request received during a chat session.

Unlike other invitation methods, requests via Windows Messenger do not include a session password or invitation timeout. These features are discussed in the next section.

REMOTE ASSISTANCE INSIDE A CHAT SESSION

This method is similar to the preceding method. The only difference is that you click the Ask for Remote Assistance button inside a chat session, as shown in Figure 16-3.

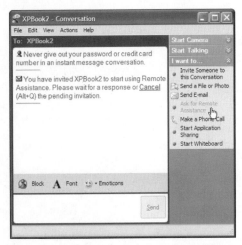

Figure 16-3: Asking for help in a chat session.

WINDOWS MESSENGER VIA THE REMOTE ASSISTANCE SUPPORT CENTER

Another place to start a Remote Assistance session with a Windows Messenger buddy is via the standard Remote Assistance Support Center in Windows XP's Help and Support Center. Follow these steps:

1. Open Windows XP's Help and Support Center, which is located in the Start menu under Help and Support.

2. Open the Remote Assistance option, shown in Figure 16-4.

3. Select the Invite Someone to Help You option.

4. As shown in Figure 16-5, you now see a list of your Windows Messenger buddies in the Windows Messenger area. Select the user you'd like to invite and then invite that person by clicking the Invite This Person option. At this point, the same thing happens as in the scenario in the preceding section: The person from whom you're requesting help is prompted with your request.

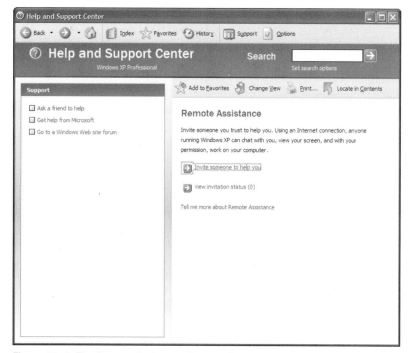

Figure 16-4: The Remote Assistance Support Center.

Sending an Invitation via E-Mail

Another way to send an invitation is with e-mail. This process takes place in the Remote Assistance Support Center and includes a few more steps than the Windows Messenger option. When you send an invitation via e-mail, you have the option of adding a detailed explanation to your request, adding an expiration time for your invitation, and requiring a password for connection.

TIP   To send an invitation via e-mail, you must use a Windows MAPI e-mail client, such as Microsoft Outlook Express or Microsoft Outlook. If you use a Web-based e-mail service, such as Hotmail or Yahoo! Mail, you should use either the Windows Messenger or File method discussed elsewhere in this chapter.

To send an e-mail invitation, follow these steps:

1. Go to the Remote Assistance support center via Windows XP's Help and Support menu.

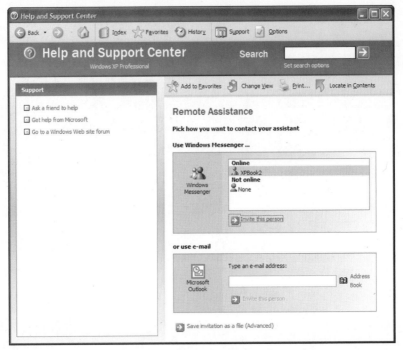

Figure 16-5: Select the person you want to invite via Windows Messenger.

2. Select the Invite Someone to Help You option.

3. On the next screen (refer to Figure 16-5), type in an e-mail address or select an e-mail address from your address book. When you're finished, select the Invite This Person option (see Figure 16-6).

Figure 16-6: Using e-mail to send an invitation.

4. As shown in Figure 16-7, at this point you can provide some information about your request so that the person to whom you're sending the request understands a little bit about your computer problem. When you're finished, click Continue.

5. On the next screen, shown in Figure 16-8, you can set an expiration time for your invitation (minutes, hours, or even days). Set a reasonable

expiration time based on how long you think it will take the person to respond. It's fairly easy to send out a new e-mail invitation in the future, and setting a reasonable expiration time will help prevent the invitation from being used at an indefinite date in the future.

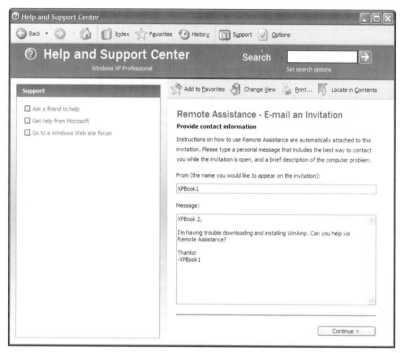

Figure 16-7: Providing contact information in an e-mail invitation.

6. You also have the option to require a password for the Remote Assistance session. I strongly recommend that you use a password to secure the Remote Assistance session because this provides basic security for a feature that opens up your system to the outside world. This password is not sent to the person from whom you're requesting help. You must provide the password to the individual in a separate e-mail or via telephone. If you're working with someone on Remote Assistance on a continuous basis, it is probably a good idea to set up a general password to use for all Remote Assistance sessions, perhaps one that is rotated regularly.

7. When you're finished, click the Send Invitation button.

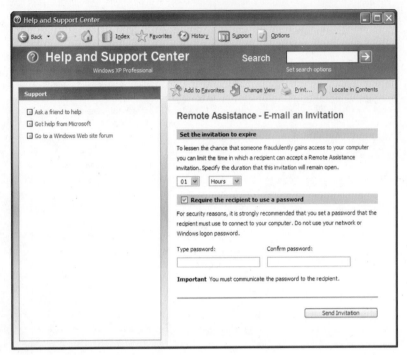

Figure 16-8: Setting session details.

Sending an Invitation via a File

If you decide not to use Windows Messenger or e-mail (or you're using Web-based e-mail or another non-MAPI e-mail client), you can send an invitation as a file. To create an invitation as a file, follow these steps:

1. Go to the Remote Assistance support center via Windows XP's Help and Support menu.

2. Select the Invite Someone to Help You option.

3. In the next screen that appears (refer to Figure 16-5), select the Save Invitation as a File (Advanced) option.

4. As you can see in Figure 16-9, sending an invitation via a file is similar to sending an invitation by e-mail. You are asked to give the name you'd like to appear on your invitation and set an expiration date. Go ahead and set this information and then click Continue.

5. You now have the chance to set a session password (see Figure 16-10). I recommend that you do so. Again, remember to communicate this password to the individual from whom you're requesting help! When you're finished, click Save Invitation.

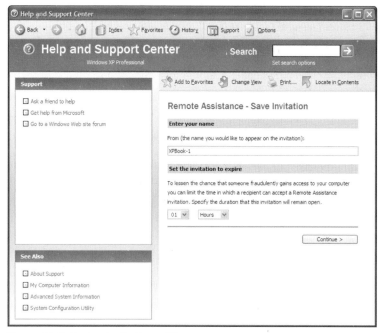

Figure 16-9: Saving invitation settings.

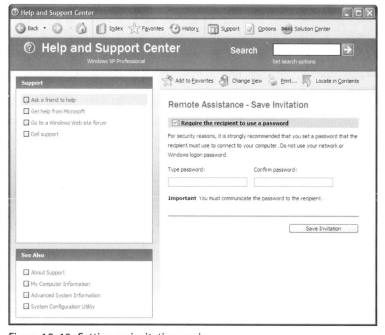

Figure 16-10: Setting an invitation session.

The Save As dialog box appears, select a location where you want to save the file. The tool saves the invitation as a text file. You can now provide this file to the individual from whom you're requesting help. As you can see in Figure 16-11, the Remote Assistance support center shows you where your invitation is saved. When you are ready to send this invitation, simply attach it to an email to the person who you wish help from.

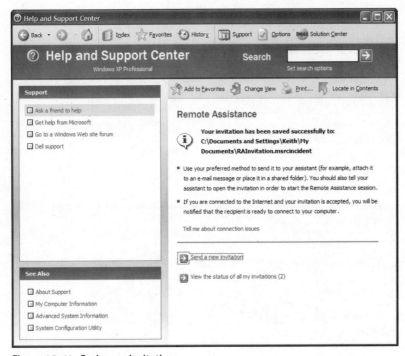

Figure 16-11: Saving an invitation.

Using Remote Assistance

After you've successfully sent off your Remote Assistance invitation, it's time to actually use Remote Assistance. Remote Assistance consists of two different parts: the interface for the person receiving help and the interface for the person giving help. Remote Assistance adds the word *Expert* to the name of the person giving help, so for this discussion, I'll use that name for the person giving help. I'll refer to the person receiving help as the *User*.

Remote Assistance for the User

For the User, the Remote Assistance user interface is pretty simple. After the Expert accepts your Remote Assistance request, you are prompted with a dialog box asking you if you'd like to start the Remote Assistance Session. Figure 16-12 shows the Remote Assistance window that appears.

Figure 16-12: The Remote Assistance window.

After you've approved the Remote Assistance session, a chat/control dialog box appears on your screen, as shown in Figure 16-13. You control all the aspects of your session with the options on this screen. You can chat with the Expert via text and audio (similar to the way these features work in Windows Messenger), exchange files, allow the Expert to take control of your PC, and disconnect the session. This last option is provided as a safeguard; if you're sitting there watching the Expert fix a problem on your system and don't like that he begins mucking around in your My Documents folder, or whatever, you can cut him off at any time.

Figure 16-13: The Remote Assistance user interface.

Remote Control of Your PC

At any time during a Remote Assistance session, the Expert can request to take control of your system, or you can request that the Expert take control of your system.

Remote Assistance makes it easy for you to manage the remote control session. You can watch the Expert control your system and easily exit out of the session by pressing the Esc key on your keyboard or any key combination that includes Esc key (see Figure 16-14).

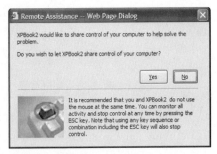

Figure 16-14: Remote Control acceptance.

When you're done with the Remote Assistance session, click the Disconnect button to end the session.

Remote Assistance for the Expert

The Remote Assistance user interface for the Expert is similar to the interface for the User, but it provides the Expert with a window in which she can view the user's screen (see Figure 16-15). The Expert can watch the user attempt to perform some sort of option or, optionally, take control of the user's desktop and manipulate it through the window.

From this interface, the expert can chat with the user via text and audio, send and receive files, and take control of the user's system.

Configuring Remote Assistance

Remote Assistance is built into Windows XP and doesn't require any special configuration or installation. However, you need to consider a few important things when you're trying to use Remote Assistance.

Address Issues

Most Internet service providers (ISPs) automatically and randomly assign IP addresses for dial-up customers. If you send out a Remote Assistance request, disconnect from the Internet, and reconnect before you've had a chance to take part in a Remote Desktop Session, it's possible – even likely – that your address will change. If this happens, you need to resend your invitation so that the Expert can reach your machine remotely.

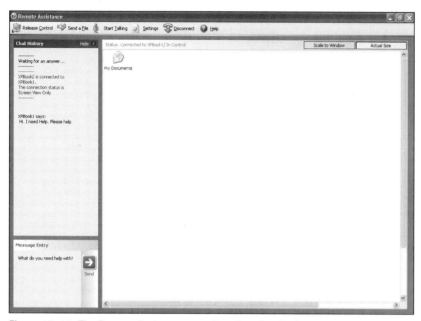

Figure 16-15: The Remote Assistance user interface for the Expert.

Thankfully, resending an existing invitation is fairly easy. In the Remote Assistance support center, you can check the status of your invitation requests by clicking View Invitation Status. Then on the next screen, you can click the Resend button for any particular invitation request, and your party will receive a new updated request. You can see the Remote Assistance Invitation status in Figure 16-16.

Firewall Issues

Another common issue with Remote Assistance concerns *firewalls*, the hardware or software that protects internal networks from the outside. (Windows XP ships with a basic software firewall called Internet Connection Firewall, ICF, that is automatically installed on the outgoing network connection.) Remote Assistance uses port 3389 to connect. If you are behind a third-party firewall product, such as BlackICE Defender or ZoneAlarm, or using XP's built-in Internet Connection Sharing (ICS) feature, this may be an issue. Note that ICF is Remote Assistance savvy, however, so if you've got XP on either end of a Remote Assistance request, all should be well.

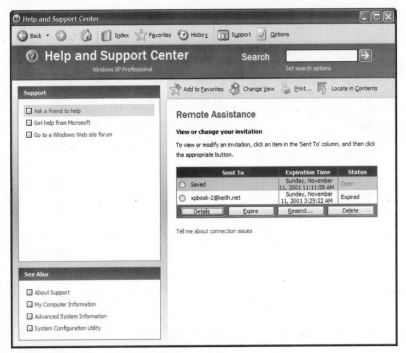

Figure 16-16: The Remote Assistance invitation status.

If your system is inside a corporate network and you are unable to connect to someone on the Internet with Remote Assistance, you should talk to your Network Administrator for help. Home users should check out Chapter 6, which takes a closer look at firewalls such as ICF and how they work with XP services such as Remote Assistance. This chapter also discusses Internet Connection Sharing, port forwarding, and other related issues.

Chapter 17

Using Remote Desktop

IN THIS CHAPTER

- ◆ See how to turn on and configure remote desktop
- ◆ Where or where are the clients? Learn where they can be found on the CD and how to install them
- ◆ Understand the options available and how to configure them for maximizing your remote access

IN 1998, MICROSOFT RELEASED its first version of a remote desktop tool alongside a then-new version of its Windows NT operating system dubbed Windows NT 4.0 Terminal Server Edition (TSE). This tool allowed businesses to buy scalable, expensive servers with which many users could connect simultaneously and remotely run application programs independently of each other by using relatively cheap PCs called *thin clients*. These thin clients were, in many cases, older or inexpensive systems that were repurposed as terminals. And because the server actually executed all the programs the user accessed, the configuration or speed of the thin client systems didn't matter much. All the client had to do was relay screen display information from the server.

With Windows 2000, Microsoft extended this technology to systems administrators with Terminal Services for Remote Administration. With this feature, administrators can manage servers remotely by interacting with the system as if they were on the console in front of the system. A subset of the overall Terminal Services feature, Terminal Services for Remote Administration allows only one user connection, so the server doesn't have to be specially set up for multiple connections.

With the release of Windows XP Professional in 2001, Microsoft extended this technology to the desktop with the inclusion of Remote Assistance (discussed in Chapter 16) and Remote Desktop.

Remote Desktop is only in Windows XP Professional. XP Home users are outta luck.

Remote Desktop is essentially a single-user version of Terminal Services optimized for desktop. Remote Desktop allows XP Pro users to connect to a PC from anywhere by using a Remote Desktop or Terminal Server client.

TIP Firewalls and routers may block you from connecting to Remote Desktop over the Internet because they are blocking the port that Remote Desktop uses. To see what port Remote Desktop uses, see the section titled "Connecting from the Internet," later in this chapter.

When you connect to your PC remotely, the experience is similar to when you're sitting in front of your PC using it interactively. You get your normal desktop, and you can use all the programs on your PC, albeit with a few small differences.

In this chapter, you find out how to configure, connect to, and use Remote Desktop.

Configuring Remote Desktop

Remote Desktop is installed by default in Windows XP Professional. However, it is not enabled by default. To enable Remote Desktop, you must have administrator-level access to your system. After you're logged on to an account with administrator access, follow these steps:

1. Navigate to the Control Panel and open the System item. The System Properties dialog box opens.

2. Click on the Remote tab and select the Allow Users to Connect Remotely to This Computer check box, shown in Figure 17-1. Then click Apply to make the change.

3. Click OK to close the System Properties dialog box. Remote Desktop is now enabled.

TIP You can access the System Properties dialog box more quickly by right-clicking My Computer and choosing Properties.

Any user with an administrator account automatically has access to Remote Desktop connections on that machine. But if you have non-administrative users to which you'd like to give Remote Access, you can add them to the list of acceptable users. You can also make this change through the Remote tab of the System Properties dialog box. Under the Remote Desktop section of the Remote tab, click the Select Remote Users button. This launches the Remote Desktop Users dialog box, shown in Figure 17-2.

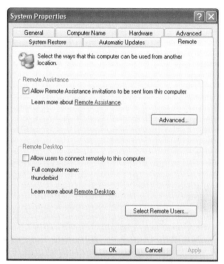

Figure 17-1: The Remote tab in the System Properties dialog box.

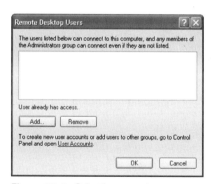

Figure 17-2: Selecting remote users.

This dialog box notes whether you already have access to connect to your PC remotely. In Figure 17-2, the user is logged on as the imaginatively titled account *User,* which is part of the Administrator group, so that person already has remote access. If you want to add more users, click the Add button and do so using the Select Users dialog box, shown in Figure 17-3. Click the Advanced button to search for users.

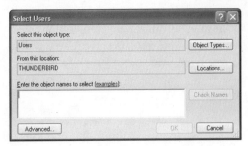

Figure 17-3: Adding remote users.

Installing the Remote Desktop Client

After Remote Desktop is enabled and configured, you should attempt to connect to the machine to ensure that Remote Desktop is working. Windows XP Professional already includes a Remote Desktop client, but if you're going to access your XP Pro box from a different operating system, you might need to install a compatible client. Windows XP Professional's Remote Desktop, like Windows 2000 Terminal Services, uses the Remote Desktop Protocol (RDP) to facilitate communication. So any RDP client will work with Remote Desktop, though only the Windows XP Professional client offers certain advanced features. (These features are discussed in the "Connection Configuration Settings" section, later in this chapter.)

You can access the Windows XP Professional Remote Desktop client — called Remote Desktop Connection — by choosing Start→All Programs→ Accessories→Communications.

Remote Desktop Client for Windows 2000, Me, 98, and 95

The Windows XP Professional CD includes 32-bit clients for other versions of Windows, including Windows 2000, Millennium Edition (Me), 98, and 95.

To install the 32-bit client on another version of Windows, insert the Windows XP Professional CD in that system. When the Welcome screen appears, click the Perform Additional Tasks option and then select Set Up Remote Desktop Connection.

Remote Desktop Client for 16-bit Users (Windows 3.1)

A Remote Desktop client does exist for 16-bit users, but unfortunately Microsoft doesn't make it very easy to find. Windows 2000 Server ships with the 16-bit client, and the only way to get ahold of the client is via the client setup folder

(`%systemroot%\System32\clients`) in a valid Windows 2000 Server installation. Inside the client setup folder, you find a directory called `TSCLIENT\Win16` that contains the 16-bit client.

However, it's unlikely that many home users will have access to this product, so it's unclear how most people can get the 16-bit client. On the other hand, most users don't really need the 16-bit client.

Remote Desktop Client for Windows CE/ Pocket PC Users

Microsoft includes a Remote Desktop client for Windows CE Handheld PC Edition Version 3.0 users on the Windows XP Professional CD. The client is available on the CD in `VALUEADD\MSFT\MGMT\MSTSC_HPC`. Windows CE Handheld PC Edition Version 3.0 is based on Windows CE OS 2.11. Note that this client will *not* work on any other version of Windows CE.

Pocket PC users (2000 and 2002 versions) get a Remote Desktop client with the Pocket PC software CD that comes with those systems. Pocket PC integration with Windows XP Professional is discussed in more detail in Chapter 19.

Remote Desktop Client for Web Users

Windows XP Professional includes a Web-based Remote Desktop client as well. The client is an ActiveX control that requires Internet Explorer and Windows 95, 98, Me, 2000, or XP.

To add this client to your system, you must have Internet Information Services (IIS) installed, another feature that is unique to Windows XP Professional Edition. (IIS is discussed in more detail in Chapter 15.) You can add the Remote Desktop Web client to XP Pro by accessing Add or Remove Programs in the Control Panel. Click Add/Remove Windows Components, then Internet Information Services (IIS), and then World Wide Web Service. Click the Details button then select Remote Desktop Web Connection, as shown in Figure 17-4.

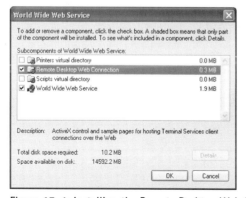

Figure 17-4: Installing the Remote Desktop Web Connection.

The Remote Desktop Web Connection adds the needed ActiveX control and some sample files to your Web site under the `/tsweb` directory (`http://yourweb-address/tsweb`). The Web files are located in your Windows directory under `\web\tsweb` (for example, `c:\windows\web\tsweb`). Figure 17-5 shows the default Web connection screen.

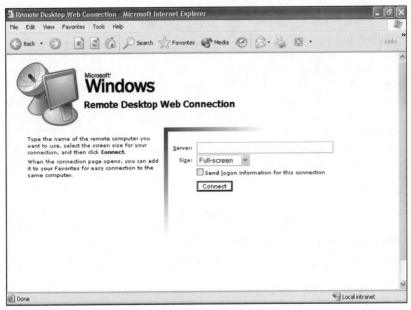

Figure 17-5: The Remote Desktop Web Connection.

The Remote Desktop Web client is a bare-bones, fairly limited client. The only two options you can configure are screen resolution and whether your logon information is sent automatically to the server when you connect. If you don't send your logon information on the Web page, you can enter it after you're connected. If you select a size other than Full Screen, the connection appears in a window on a Web page, as shown in Figure 17-6. And if you want to toggle to Full Screen mode, press Ctrl+Alt+Break. More screen resolution details are provided in the "Display Tab" section, later in this chapter.

Remote Desktop on Other Platforms

At this time, no Remote Desktop clients exist for other non-Microsoft operating systems, and it's unlikely that there ever will be. The RDP protocol used in Remote Desktop is based on technology that Microsoft licensed from a company called Citrix. Citrix makes a product called MetaFrame that competes with Microsoft's server-based Terminal Services products. One of the chief benefits of Citrix MetaFrame is the availability of clients for non-Microsoft platforms. But this is a server-only solution.

Figure 17-6: Remote Desktop on the Web.

TIP If you're interested in accessing a Windows XP Professional machine remotely by using Remote Desktop–like technology, check out AT&T's free VNC software. This software supports a variety of client types, including Linux, various versions of UNIX, and even Mac OS X. For more information, visit the VNC Web site at www.uk.research.att.com/vnc/.

Using Remote Desktop Connection

Now that we have covered all the clients. I hope you had time to choose one and install it. This section covers the detail on how to create and manage your connection to the remote desktop.

One User, One Connection

An important Remote Desktop concept is that only one user can use a Windows XP Professional PC at a time, either remotely or locally. So if another user is connected at the time you initiate a Remote Desktop session, you are asked if you want to disconnect that user. When you answer yes, the user is disconnected and sent to the Welcome screen, but his or her programs remain open, running in the background. (See Chapter 7 and Fast User Switching for more information.)

Creating a Connection

To start a Remote Desktop connection, open the Remote Desktop Connection application or the RDP client of your choice. In XP Pro, a Remote Desktop connection is pretty simple. As shown in Figure 17-7, the Remote Desktop client initially asks only for the name of the computer you want to connect to.

Figure 17-7: A simple Remote Desktop Connection.

When you click the Connect button, you're connected to the Remote Desktop with a minimal default setting. However, you can easily customize the connection by clicking the Options button in the Remote Desktop Connection dialog box, and I recommend that you do so.

Configuring a Connection

When you click the Options button, the dialog box expands to display five tabs: General, Display, Local Resources, Programs, and Experience. Any changes you make to the connection settings in any of these pages become the default settings for any future connections unless you save the connection options as a different Remote Desktop connection settings file.

The next few sections take a look at the various settings.

GENERAL TAB

The General tab (shown in Figure 17-8) allows you to enter information about the connection and optionally save the connection as a shortcut. It also gives you the ability to save the username, password, and if applicable, the domain, for the computer you are connecting to. If that information isn't provided before you connect to the Remote Desktop, you're prompted to log on after the connection is made.

When you're done setting up your options for the connection, you can save your connection as a Remote Desktop connection settings file, or shortcut. You can use this file in the future to connect to the Remote Desktop Connection with these same settings.

Figure 17-8: The General tab of the Remote Desktop Connection dialog box.

For security reasons, if you type in a password, it's not saved in the Remote Desktop file.

DISPLAY TAB

You can set the resolution and color settings for the Remote Desktop connection you are about make by using the Display tab (shown in Figure 17-9). The sizes are standard resolution sizes, where the smallest possible resolution is 640 x 480, and the largest is the resolution of the PC you are using interactively (this size is referred to as Full Screen). The default setting is Full Screen.

Remotely accessing your system can affect the layout of icons on your desktop. Say your XP Pro machine is set up to run at 1024 x 768, but you access it remotely using an 800 x 600 window. When this happens, your desktop icons and any open windows are moved to accommodate the new screen size. When you once again log on to the system interactively, you'll notice that these changes have persisted to the local session. D'oh!

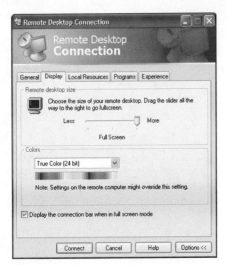

Figure 17-9: The Display tab of the Remote
Desktop Connection dialog box.

When you're in Full Screen mode, you have the option of displaying a connection bar at the top of the screen, as shown in Figure 17-10. The connection bar can auto-hide and includes buttons to minimize, maximize, and close the session. You use the thumbtack icon in the left corner to toggle between displaying and hiding the connection bar. The connection bar is displayed by default, and it's a nice visual reminder that you're in a remote, not local, session.

Figure 17-10: The connection bar in Full Screen mode
(with the connection bar toggled to stay on top).

Full Screen mode is discussed in more detail in the "Full Screen versus Windowed" section, later in this chapter.

 TIP Regardless of the Remote Desktop size, you can resize the window of the Remote Desktop client, just like you can any other window in Windows. The connection isn't resized, but the portion of the connection you see changes (see Figure 17-11).

Windows 2000 and Windows NT 4.0 Terminal Services support only 256 colors through remote connections, but Windows XP Professional's Remote Desktop feature supports many more colors, depending on the settings on your local computer and the settings on the computer to which you are connecting. The Display tab allows you to select a color setting for your connection, assuming you're accessing an XP machine. If you're connecting to a Windows 2000 or NT 4.0 system, the color settings are ignored. The default setting is the highest color setting supported by your PC.

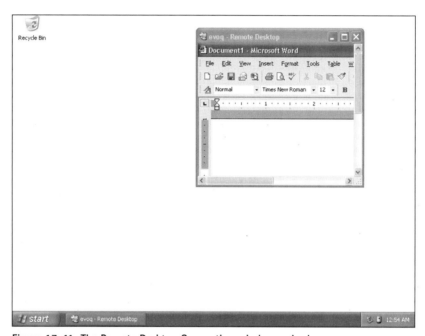

Figure 17-11: The Remote Desktop Connection window resized.

LOCAL RESOURCES TAB

With the Remote Desktop client, you can configure how different resources are handled. These options, available from the Local Resources tab (shown in Figure 17-12), include sound redirection, keyboard combinations, and access to local devices, such as printers and disk drives.

If the remote PC to which you are connecting has a sound card, you can redirect sound from the remote PC to your local machine. You have three options for configuring this feature:

♦ **Bring to This Computer (default setting):** The sound is redirected from the remote PC to your local PC.

♦ **Do Not Play:** The sound does not play on the remote and local PCs.

♦ **Leave at Remote Computer:** The sound plays out of the speakers of the remote PC only.

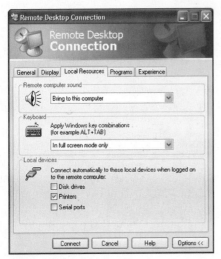

Figure 17-12: The Local Resource tab with the default settings.

Sound redirection is useful, but due to network speed issues, sound can be a bit slow and out of sync. To be able to hear system sounds is useful, but redirecting sound doesn't work all that well for listening to music files on the remote desktop. I recommend experimenting with this feature a bit and then deciding which setting to use.

If you've used Windows for a while, you're probably accustomed to using keyboard combinations such as Alt+Tab and anything involving the Windows key. You can choose to have these combinations work on the remote PC when you're connected to it. When you're connected, you can set up Windows key combinations in one of three following ways:

◆ **In Full Screen Mode (default setting):** Sets Windows key combinations to work on the remote PC when you're viewing the connection in Full Screen mode

◆ **On the Local Computer:** Leaves all Windows key combinations on your local PC

◆ **On the Remote Computer:** Redirects all Windows key combinations to the remote PC, regardless of whether you're in Full Screen mode

 Ctrl+Alt+Delete always defaults to your local PC and not the remote PC.

The last Local Resource configuration setting is the redirection of local devices. You can use some of the resources on your local PC on the remote PC while you're connected to it. The local devices you can redirect are disk drives, printers, and serial ports:

◆ **Disk Drives:** If you select Disk Drives, you can have your local PC's disk drives appear on the remote PC. This enables you to more easily transfer files back and forth between the two PCs. For example, my local PC is named Thunderbird. When I make a Remote Desktop connection, the drives from my PC appear in Windows Explorer on the remote PC as "*drive letter* on Thunderbird," as shown in Figure 17-13.

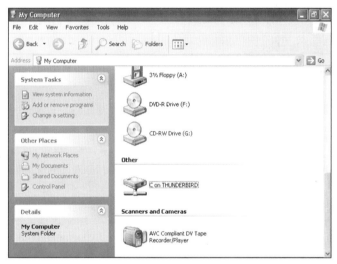

Figure 17-13: Drives in Windows Explorer on a remote PC.

◆ **Printer:** With the Remote Desktop client, you can print Web pages and other documents from a remote PC to the printer attached to your local PC. In order to do so, the system to which you are connecting must have the printer driver for your printer already installed (if both machines are Windows XP Professional, this will almost always be the case). The printer shows up in the Printer folder of the remote machine, as shown in Figure 17-14.

◆ **Serial Port:** Serial port redirection allows you to share the serial port on your local PC with the remote PC. This allows you to connect devices such as modems, bar code readers, and the like on your local PC and access them on your remote PC.

The only local resource enabled by default is printer redirection.

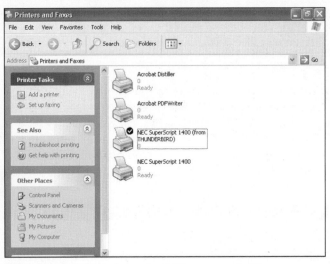

Figure 17-14: Printers from a local PC on a remote PC.

 When you make disk drives or serial ports available to the remote PC, you receive a Security Warning message when you connect. The message says that making those resources available to the remote system could be unsafe and advises you to proceed only if you trust the computer you are connecting to. Besides some unknown/undiscovered security problem in the Remote Desktop Protocol, there are no known risks with sharing local resources with the remote PC. The resources are available only while you are connected and are available only to your session. Bottom line: Make sure that you trust the system you are connecting to and sharing resources with, but this isn't something to be overly alarmed about.

PROGRAMS TAB

The Programs tab applies only to connections to systems running Terminal Services (see Figure 17-15). If you're connecting to a system running Remote Desktop (for example, Windows XP Professional), any settings on this tab are ignored.

If you're connecting to a Windows 2000 or NT 4 system with Terminal Services, you can have a program automatically launch when you connect. Whatever program you choose to run is the only program you can use while you're connected. For example, if you run Microsoft Word, after you exit Word, the Terminal Service connection ends.

Figure 17-16 shows a Terminal Services connection with just Microsoft Word running on the remote PC.

Figure 17-15: The Programs tab of the
Remote Desktop Connection dialog box.

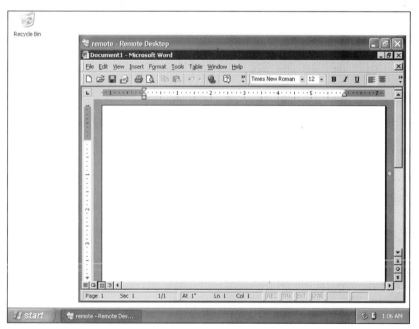

Figure 17-16: Terminal Services with only Microsoft Word loaded.

EXPERIENCE TAB

To help optimize your Remote Desktop connection, you can toggle certain visual
features in Windows by using the Experience tab (see Figure 17-17). The features

don't affect the functionality of your connection; they affect the way the connection appears visually. The features you can toggle include desktop backgrounds, showing the contents of window while dragging, menu and window animation, visual themes, and bitmap caching (which caches certain images to speed up the connection). Several different profiles exist, based on the speed of the network you use to connect to the remote PC; these profiles can help you decide which features to turn on or off. Here are the features enabled in each profile:

◆ **Modem (28.8 Kbps):** Bitmap Caching

◆ **Modem (56 Kbps):** Bitmap Caching and Themes

◆ **Broadband (128 Kbps–1.5 Mbps):** Bitmap Caching, Themes, Menu and Window Animation, and Show Contents of Window While Dragging

◆ **LAN (10 Mbps or higher):** Bitmap Caching, Themes, Menu and Window Animation, Show Contents of Window While Dragging, and Desktop Background

By default, the Remote Desktop client uses the Modem (56 Kbps) profile.

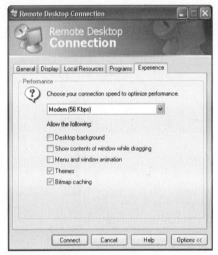

Figure 17-17: The Experience tab with the Modem (56 Kbps) profile selected.

FULL SCREEN VERSUS WINDOWED

You can display the Remote Desktop client in Full Screen mode by selecting Full Screen mode on the Display tab, or by selecting a smaller size than full screen (I call this *windowed mode* for the purposes of this explanation) and pressing Ctrl+Alt+Break on your keyboard. You can use the Ctrl+Alt+Break key combination to toggle between Full Screen mode and windowed mode. Windowed mode is useful if you're connecting to a remote PC to run one particular application and still plan on using your local system.

For example, say you don't have Microsoft Excel installed on your local PC but do have it installed on a remote PC. You can use Remote Desktop to connect to another PC in windowed mode and use Excel over the remote connection. As shown in Figure 17-18, the Excel window looks like any other windows on your PC. The only difference is that you have access only to local resources and the resources you've provided in the connection settings.

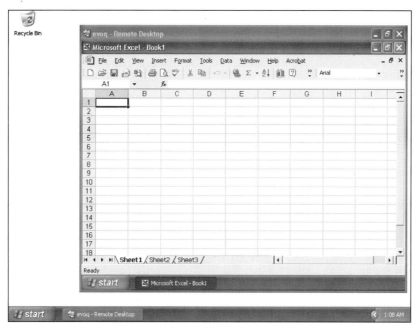

Figure 17-18: Excel open on the remote PC.

 You can copy and paste text between the remote PC and local PC by using standard key commands.

If you want to run everything from the remote PC, you should use Full Screen mode. Full Screen mode is useful if you're away from home and accessing a computer that doesn't have any of your programs or data.

Connecting from the Internet

Remote Desktop and Terminal Services use Port 3389. If you're using a home gateway device, such as a cable/DSL router, to access the Internet, look at the vendor's product documentation to see if it allows you to enable *port forwarding*. If you're connected to the Internet directly through Windows XP Professional and/or using Internet Connection Sharing in Windows XP Professional to get online, you can find more information about porting forward in Chapter 6.

Part V

Device Connections

Chapter 18

Laptops

IN THIS CHAPTER

◆ See how Windows XP excels in managing all the new power features of today's laptops

◆ Work easily with data files while you're out of the office and then seamlessly update the original files once you get back to work

◆ Learn how to secure your laptop with Window XP

◆ See what else Windows XP can do with all the new laptop integrated features

I'M NOT SURE HOW OBVIOUS THIS IS to the outside world, but one of the many metrics I track in my day job is PC sales, and over the past few years, sales of portable computers — called laptops or notebooks — have risen dramatically. In fact, mobile computer sales will likely surpass sales of desktop PCs sometime in the not-too-distant future. So don't be surprised if your next PC is a portable.

The reasons for this change are many. Laptops used to be about compromise, and users could choose a small, highly portable machine only at the expense of processing power and expandability. Or users might have opted for expensive desktop replacement machines that weighed a ton, inhibiting portability.

Recently, however, this has all changed. Laptops now feature powerful Pentium III and Pentium 4 processors that rival their desktop counterparts, as well as heaping amounts of RAM, 3D video cards, large hard drives, and other advanced features. And with prices dropping dramatically, the main complaint against portable computing is rapidly evolving.

It should come as no surprise that Microsoft has been going after the mobile market for some time. And since Windows 95, virtually every subsequent Windows version (with the exception of Windows Millennium Edition) has added crucial new mobile features. Naturally, Windows XP is the most proficient mobile operating system that the company has ever created.

In this chapter, you find out about the Windows XP features that are specific to portable computing. The two biggest mobile features are power management and offline content capabilities, followed by security features like the new Encrypting File System (EFS) and a host of other features that work together to make XP the ultimate mobile operating system.

Power Management

Power management functionality is available to any XP user, based on the underlying capabilities of the hardware, but it's never as important as on a laptop. For this reason, XP supports different settings for when your laptop is plugged in or powered by battery, providing you with more flexibility. And because XP supports the latest power management specification – Advanced Configuration and Power Interface (ACPI) – you can really fine-tune the power management capabilities of your system.

ACPI is a modern specification that takes power management control away from the underlying hardware and hands it off to the operating system. So you can configure when and if components such as the hard drive and display power down, when the system enters various low-power states, and in the case of a laptop, what happens when you close or open the system's display lid or press the power button.

ACPI power saver states include:

- ◆ **Suspend:** The suspend state provides the lowest level of power under which the PC is technically still on and operational. The monitor is turned off, the hard drive is spun down, and the CPU is placed into a nearly nonoperational condition.

- ◆ **Hibernate:** Hibernation writes the contents of RAM to the hard drive and powers off the system. When the PC is powered on, the system resumes from its previously saved state, which restores it to its pre-hibernate condition and takes a lot less time than a normal boot process. Laptop users should regularly use hibernation instead of turning off their PC.

You configure power management from the Display Properties dialog box. Here's how:

1. Right-click on a blank area of the desktop and choose Properties to open the Display Properties dialog box.

2. Navigate to the Screen Saver tab (shown in Figure 18-1), which includes configuration options for both the legacy screen saver and ACPI power management.

3. For security, configure a screen saver and set it to a low Wait period (10 minutes or less) so that the Welcome screen is displayed if anyone accesses the PC after the screen saver is initiated.

4. Then click the Power button to display the Power Options Properties dialog box, shown in Figure 18-2. This dialog box consists of several tabs, which are examined in the next few sections.

Figure 18-1: The curiously named Screen Saver tab is also the home to XP's impressive power management capabilities.

Figure 18-2: The Power Options Properties dialog box is your one-stop shop for power management configuration.

Power Schemes Tab

Windows XP supports a range of power schemes, which are built-in profiles designed around specific machine configurations such as Portable/Laptop, Always On, or Home/Office Desk. Each of these profiles fills a specific need and provides various time-based configuration options such as when to turn off the monitor or hard drives and when to enter Standby or Hibernation modes. And each of these options can be set differently, based on whether the PC is plugged in or powered by battery.

As nice as these built-in choices are, I don't think any of them are appropriate for regular laptop use. Fortunately, you can create your own profile. Simply select appropriate values for the various options and then click the Save As button and provide a name for the new scheme.

I recommend the following values, though you might want to experiment a bit:

When Computer Is:	Plugged In	Running On Batteries
Turn Off Monitor:	After 30 minutes	After 5 minutes
Turn Off Hard Disks:	After 45 minutes	After 10 minutes
System Standby:	Never	Never
System Hibernate:	After 1 hour	After 20 minutes

Alarms Tab

The Alarms tab lets you configure when and whether low and critical battery alarms are sounded. There's little need to configure these options beyond the default values, which specify text warnings when the batteries reach a 10 percent and 3 percent charge, respectively.

Power Meter Tab

The Power Meter tab provides an individual graphical display for each installed battery that displays remaining power. It also displays whether AC or battery powers the system.

Advanced Tab

The Advanced tab is, perhaps, the most important after Power Schemes. Here, you determine whether a power icon is displayed in the system tray (which I recommend), whether the system prompts for a password when it comes out of Standby (also recommended, if you use Standby), and how the system reacts when you close the lid of your mobile computer, press the power button, or press the sleep button (the exact options you see here are dependent on the capabilities of your system).

I recommend Hibernate for each of the last three options I just described. Properly configured, this tab should resemble Figure 18-3.

Figure 18-3: Your modern laptop has amazing power management capabilities — use them!

Hibernate Tab

The Hibernate tab determines whether your system can take advantage of the ACPI Hibernate feature. I strongly recommend enabling this feature on all portable PCs.

Accessing Content Offline

In addition to their obvious physical differences, mobile computers also pose some interesting procedural changes when compared to desktop computers. Specifically, laptops are often disconnected, physically, from the network and therefore will often not have access to the content and data that might be stored there. But because most laptop users try to get work done on the road in offline situations, Microsoft has provided some interesting offline content features in Windows XP that address these needs.

Offline Files and Folders

Offline Files and Folders stores network resources locally on your laptop in a hidden cache so that you can access them from the road.

Offline Files and Folders is an XP Professional feature that actually debuted in Windows 2000. Sorry, XP Home users can't do this.

The caching isn't brainless: If you edit an offline document, for example, or add a new document to an offline folder, the changes are replicated back to the source resource when you reconnect to the network. Likewise, if changes are made to the original file when you're gone, you will receive an option to correctly synchronize the data.

To enable this feature, however, you must first disable Fast User Switching, which generally doesn't make much sense on a laptop anyway. Follow these steps to disable Fast User Switching and enable the Offline Files and Folders feature:

1. Choose Start→Control Panel→User Accounts→Change The Way Users Log On or Off.

2. Then deselect the User Fast User Switching option and click Apply Options.

3. Open the Folder Options dialog box (the quickest path is to open My Computer and choose Tools→Folder Options) and navigate to the Offline Files tab. Click the Enable Offline Files check box, as shown in Figure 18-4.

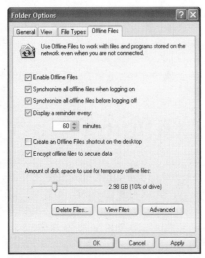

Figure 18-4: The Offline Files and Folders feature lets you cache network files and folders locally for use when you're on the road.

4. Here, you can also configure when offline files and folders are synchronized: The default is when you log off. But I recommend configuring this action to occur when you log on as well, especially if you'll be using this feature a lot. And choose the Encrypt Offline Files to Secure Data option for security reasons. When you're finished, click OK.

Now all you have to do is navigate to the network resource you'd like to cache, right-click, and choose Make Available Offline. This launches the Offline Files

Wizard, which steps you through the process of configuring the offline files and folders. You can choose to synchronize the offline files automatically every time you log on and off the computer (which I recommend). And the wizard allows you to set up various options, such as offline reminders and desktop shortcuts to the offline resources (see Figure 18-5).

Figure 18-5: The Offline Files Wizard lets you configure network resources for offline use.

When you complete the wizard, the files will be synchronized. Then you can set up other resources for local caching as well.

TURNING OFF INDIVIDUAL OFFLINE CACHING
To no longer cache a particular network resource locally, right-click it in My Computer and uncheck Make Available Offline.

REMOVING OFFLINE FILES AND FOLDERS
To remove the Offline Files and Folders functionality altogether, open up the Folder Options dialog box and navigate to the Offline Folders tab. Then uncheck the Enable Offline Files option and click OK.

Offline Web Pages

In addition to network resources such as documents, you can also cache Web content, which is probably a more common scenario for many home network users. To make Web pages available offline, you need to load them one at a time into Explorer, save them as Favorites, and choose the Make Available Offline check box, as shown in Figure 18-6.

To schedule the synchronization of offline Web pages or to perform a manual synchronization, open IE and choose Tools→Synchronize. This displays the Items to Synchronize dialog box, which displays a list of the offline Web pages you've configured. Click the Setup button to launch the Synchronization Settings dialog box, shown in Figure 18-7, where you can determine how and when offline Web synchronization occurs.

Figure 18-6: You can make your Internet Explorer Favorites available for offline use as well.

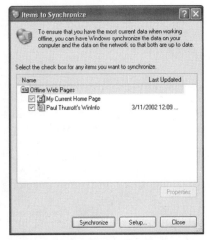

Figure 18-7: In the Synchronization Settings dialog box, you can configure offline Web pages.

 If you've already saved a wide range of Favorites and would like to make some of them available for offline use, you can do that as well. Simply open the Favorites menu, right-click on a Favorite you'd like to cache, and select Make Available Offline. You can also do this by opening the Favorites Explorer bar, which may be a more efficient method if you're repeating this several times.

 Before the Offline Files and Folders and Offline Web Pages features, there was *Briefcase,* a removable storage and network synchronization feature that debuted in Windows 95. Unbelievably, you can still access this anti-quated feature in XP, and it's actually a decent alternative for Windows XP Home users who are bummed out about not having Offline Files and Folders. I won't waste much time on it here, but check out XP's online help and search for *Briefcase* for more information.

Laptops and Security

Security is an important topic for any computer user, but it becomes all the more important when you're carting around all your personal data, as well as a potentially expensive piece of hardware. So you need to consider some issues that are above and beyond the obvious.

Password Protection

Ensure that your system is set up so that all users require passwords before they can log on and access the local resources. Then configure XP to return to the Welcome screen during idle moments so that an unattended PC can't just be accessed by someone walking by.

You configure this through power management, as described at the beginning of this chapter.

Enhanced-Security File Systems

XP users who want to prevent nefarious ne'er-do-wells from reading laptop files have a couple of file system options.

NTFS

The *NTFS file system* (New Technology File System) provides a minimal amount of security in the event that your portable system is stolen and someone gains physical access to the hard drive. The person can hook the hard drive up to another system and gain access to your files quite easily.

 If you have XP Home on your laptop, NTFS is the file system for you. It isn't the strongest protection available, but it's the most powerful option in XP Home.

EFS

For better security, the Encrypting File System (EFS), an XP Professional–only feature prevents other users from accessing data stored on your hard drive.

 XP Home users must upgrade to XP Professional to use EFS.

Here's how it works: If the drive is removed from the machine and connected to another machine, its encrypted contents will be unavailable. EFS is essentially a file or folder attribute that you can add to individual files, groups of files, or entire folders. If you encrypt a folder, future files that are saved there are encrypted as well, and as far as the user is concerned, the process is transparent: You will never see any side effects or delays.

TIP   Consider encrypting the My Documents folder and any other locations that contain important data, especially on portable systems.

Follow these steps to encrypt a file or folder:

1. Right-click the file or folder you'd like to encrypt and choose Properties. This displays the Properties dialog box for that item.

2. On the default General tab, click the Advanced button. This displays the Advanced Attributes dialog box, shown in Figure 18-8.

Figure 18-8: Encrypting files and folders is as simple as selecting the proper file attribute.

3. Click the Encrypt Contents to Secure Data check box and then click OK.

4. Back in the Properties dialog box, click OK. If you selected a folder previously, you are asked to confirm the encryption attribute change and decide whether it will be applied to only the current folder or also to all the folders and files it contains (the default).

5. Click OK, and the encryption is applied. If you have configured Folder Properties to display compressed or encrypted files and folders in a different color, the file or folder you just encrypted now displays its name with green text.

You can selectively reverse the process by following the same steps. Just deselect the Encrypt Contents to Secure Data check box in Step 3.

Other Mobile Improvements

In addition to the various features discussed earlier in this chapter, Windows XP supports a wide range of mobile-oriented features that bear some mention.

Automatic Multiple Network Configuration

Before Windows XP, users who took a portable computer home from work or to a remote office had to manually configure the network connection settings at each location. This could be a real pain, especially if the user had to make these changes each time the laptop was moved. It was even worse if one of the connection settings required the user to enter manual IP address, subnet, and Domain Naming System (DNS) information. The problem was so bad, and so common, that Microsoft fixed it in XP.

XP has a feature called Automatic Configuration for Multiple Networks. Instead of offering only a single network configuration profile for each network connection, XP offers two.

- One configuration, typically, looks for a DHCP server and attempts to configure the connection automatically.

- The *Alternate Configuration* can be hard-coded with IP address, subnet mask, default gateway, DNS server, and WINS server information.

When the system comes on, it will attempt to perform an automatic configuration. If the automatic configuration fails, the Alternate Configuration will be used.

You configure this feature through the TCP/IP properties for the network connection. To access it, open up Network Connections, right-click the correct connection and choose Properties, and then select Internet Protocol (TCP/IP) in the list of installed protocols and other items. Then click the Properties button to display the connection properties. You'll see the Alternate Configuration tab, shown in Figure 18-9.

Integrated Wireless Networking

One of the coolest innovations in Windows XP is its integral support for wireless networking. In fact, it's so cool, that I dedicate a whole chapter to the topic. If you're interested in wireless networking, head on over to Chapter 9 for more information.

Figure 18-9: Alternate TCP/IP Configuration is an innovative feature that helps users who move a laptop between two networking environments.

ClearType

Windows XP is Microsoft's first desktop operating system to support ClearType, a new display rendering technology that takes advantage of a hidden feature in digital LCD displays to accurately render text at three times the usual resolution. This can create a stunningly clear textual display on certain screens, though it seems to be a perception issue: Some people love it, and others don't.

You enable ClearType from the Display Properties dialog box. The quickest way to get there is to right-click on an empty part of the desktop and choose Properties. Then navigate to the Appearance tab and click the Effects button. This displays the Effects dialog box, shown in Figure 18-10. Select ClearType under the Use the Following Method to Smooth Edges of Screen Fonts check box.

I strongly recommend that you do not enable ClearType on a non-digital LCD display. Many people seem to think that ClearType is desirable on a standard CRT monitor. This is most definitely not the case: ClearType relies on a sub-pixel rendering technology that's accurate only on an LCD panel attached to the system via a digital interface. This type of connection is available on every laptop in production today and on many desktop-based LCD screens. For LCDs with analog connections or CRT monitors, ClearType just blurs text, causing eye strain and, possibly, long-term vision problems.

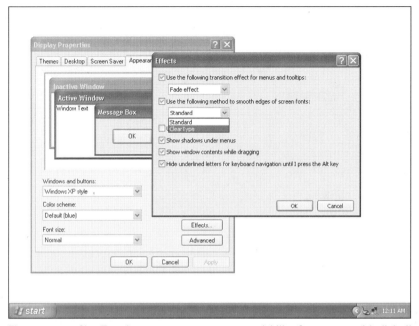

Figure 18-10: ClearType improves on-screen text readability for systems with digitally attached LCD displays.

DualView

Many mobile computers include a *DualView* display adapter that supports two different outputs:

◆ The built-in display screen

◆ An external monitor

   This can be especially beneficial for people who use their laptop as their only PC: Docked in the office, you can take advantage of an external monitor and use an external keyboard and mouse. On the road, you take advantage of the built-in screen. This feature is also good for presentations. In this configuration, your LCD display and an external display (typically an overhead projector) show the same image elsewhere.

Infrared Networking

Many portable computers include an IrDA (Infrared Data Association) port, a low-speed wireless connection that predates today's more common Wi-Fi 802.11b wireless standard. IrDA enables two compatible devices – such as laptops, printers, or portable devices – to communicate and exchange data. You might use an IrDA-equipped laptop to print to an IrDA-equipped laser printer, for example.

The biggest problem with IrDA is that it's directional: The IrDA ports on each device need to be lined up almost exactly, or no connection can be made. But assuming this isn't a huge problem, Windows XP automatically detects IrDA connections in a manner similar to previous Windows versions.

Fast Startup Features

Windows XP overcomes a huge problem that dogged earlier Windows versions: It comes to life a lot faster. Whether you're starting from a cold stop or coming out of a power management sleep state such as Standby or Hibernation, a Windows XP machine will beat any previous Windows version time and time again. This is because XP utilizes new Fast Boot technologies that reduce the number of items that execute when the system first comes on.

The coolest part of Fast Boot is that it also includes a component that watches what you do when you first start up your PC. So after the first several restarts, XP actually starts booting faster, thanks to subtle optimizations.

Mobile Processor Support

Windows XP natively supports power management features in new mobile processors from Intel Corporation, which support varying CPU speeds, based on whether the PC is powered via AC or batteries. In previous Windows versions, PC makers had to manually add this support.

Wake-on-LAN Networking Capabilities

Windows XP supports a relatively new networking feature that allows a suspended or hibernating notebook PC to be "woken up" when a network-related task needs to be completed. Then when the task is done, the machine returns to its previous state. This feature is most often used on corporate networks, where IT administrators might need to update networked PCs simultaneously, but it can benefit any networked machine.

Hardware Hot-Swapping

Because many portable machines include port replicators and docks, XP supports hardware hot-swapping. You can undock or unplug a laptop without generating excessive error messages like in previous Windows versions.

Chapter 19

Pocket PC

IN THIS CHAPTER

◆ Take a quick trip down Pocket PC history and then learn what features are available in the newest editions

◆ Work with synchronizing your pocket device with Windows XP

◆ See how to network your Pocket PC

A FEW YEARS BACK, I was attending a trade show in Las Vegas and repeatedly had to open up my laptop and wait for it to boot up so I could check the time and location of my next meeting. After a few days of this, I decided to get a portable Personal Information Management (PIM) system of some sort. I eventually chose a personal digital assistant (PDA) based on Microsoft's Pocket PC platform.

Pocket PCs offer the most power and versatility in this market, along with gorgeous color screens and serious multimedia capabilities. And beginning with the Pocket PC 2002 products, first introduced in late 2001, these devices also feature a streamlined user interface with pleasing high-color, high-resolution icons and other on-screen elements.

In this chapter, you find out about the Pocket PC and the various ways you can connect one to your home network, synchronize it with your desktop data, and take it on the road.

Introducing the Pocket PC

The Pocket PC platform is the latest iteration of Microsoft's Windows CE operating system for handheld devices. The line began rather ignominiously in late 1996 with the introduction of Windows CE 1.0 and Handheld PCs (HPCs), clamshell-like devices with a tiny chiclet keyboard, a stylus for selecting and pointing, and a black-and-white Windows 95–like user interface. The first few generations of the Handheld PC, code-named Pegasus, bombed big time in the market, although later versions added color capabilities, higher resolutions, bigger keyboards, and other features. The products virtually ceded the market to Palm and, later, Palm OS licensees such as Handspring and Sony.

But Microsoft had bigger plans. An offshoot from the HPC, code-named Gryphon, was in development before the first HPC shipped. This platform supported what proved to be the more popular configuration, a palm-sized device with a vertical color screen and a stylus for input. The first generation of this line, originally dubbed the Palm PC, shipped in 1998. However, Palm Inc. felt this name would cause confusion in the market, and the company sued Microsoft to get the company to change the name to something less similar to Palm's own products. Microsoft finally settled on Palm-sized PC.

Like the HPC, the Palm-sized PC saw limited success. Palm controlled the market, with Palm OS–compatible devices making up over 90 percent of handheld device sales. When Microsoft announced a new Palm-sized platform, dubbed the Pocket PC, in early 2000, few took notice. But when the Pocket PC launched in April 2000, it was clear that the company had gotten it right.

The Pocket PC featured a high-resolution color screen, like previous Windows CE–based handhelds. What set it apart from previous versions was a sudden and decisive move away from the old Windows 9x user interface, which was difficult to maneuver on a tiny Palm-sized PC screen. Instead, the Pocket PC moved its Start button to a more convenient location in the top-left corner of the screen, where users' hands didn't obscure it. The product's multimedia, connectivity, and Internet-browsing features were upgraded dramatically, as were its suite of Pocket Office applications, including Pocket Word, Pocket Excel, and Pocket Inbox.

And then something unexpected happened. Pocket PC devices began to sell out. Compaq couldn't make enough copies of its best-selling Pocket PC device called the iPAQ. And slowly, but surely, the Pocket PC began to eat away at Palm's market share, even as Palm moved to quickly ape the Pocket PC's multimedia features in its own products. But for the next few years, few Palm devices could keep up with Pocket PC devices, which offered more internal storage space, crucial for multimedia files. And during this time, Pocket PC devices and add-on components sold like gangbusters, especially Compaq's line of iPAQ devices, which featured a powerful Intel microprocessor, brilliant color screens, and a gorgeous industrial design.

The follow-up to the successful Pocket PC was Pocket PC 2002. Among other things, the Pocket PC 2002 platform supported a single hardware platform rather than a variety of hardware types as had previous renditions. Not surprisingly, Microsoft chose the Intel platform used by Compaq's best-selling iPAQ.

But Pocket PCs weren't just differentiated by the underlying hardware. They sported a beautiful Windows XP–inspired user interface, with high-color, high-resolution icons; pop-up balloon dialogs; a customizable Start page; improved Pocket Office apps and Pocket Internet Explorer; new connectivity options (including integrated Wi-Fi [802.11b] wireless networking); and other advanced features. And though the first generation of Pocket PCs arrived in late 2001 with the same 206 MHz Intel processor that powered the original Pocket PCs (which had been retroactively renamed to Pocket PC 2000), new devices featuring 400 MHz and 500 MHz Intel chips arrived in early 2002.

"Is that a PC in your pocket, or are you just happy to CE?" I asked in a 2001 WinInfo article (www.wininformant.com). The Pocket PC had come of age.

Unless otherwise noted, the operation and use of Pocket PC and Pocket PC 2002 devices are largely identical. For the screen shots in this chapter, I use a Pocket PC 2002 device, but Pocket PC devices operate in a similar manner. Don't be confused by minor differences in the user interface.

Unique Pocket PC Features

Compared to Palm OS–based devices and other similar Palm-top devices, Pocket PC– and Pocket PC 2002–based machines offer a number of unique features:

- **Windows-like interface:** The Pocket PC is like a Windows PC where it makes sense. It has a Start button like in Windows, but the button sports only a Windows flag logo, in order to save space. And as mentioned previously, the Start button is in the top-left corner of the screen where users can easily access it with a stylus. Throughout the interface, the UI is clean and simple, but still enough like Windows that any PC user should feel right at home.

- **Automatic application management:** In desktop Windows versions, the user must shut down applications. However, in a bid to make the Pocket PC simpler, applications are shut down automatically, if required. So as you switch from app to app, you don't need to worry about running out of memory; the device handles that task for you.

- **Single tap selection:** Because most Pocket PC users use a stylus to interact with their devices, the on-screen Pocket PC elements react to single clicks, rather than the more common double-clicks used on desktop PCs running Windows and previous Windows CE products.

- **Fast performance:** Compared to Palm devices, previous Windows CE–based products were relatively slow, with frequent "hour glass" cursor appearances. Beginning with the Pocket PC, this is no longer an issue, and despite the fact that most Pocket PCs feature high-resolution color screens, they have no problem keeping up with the speediest black-and-white Palm OS devices.

- **Multimedia features:** Out of the box, Pocket PC devices can play back popular MP3 and Windows Media Audio (WMA) formatted digital music files and even digital movie files.

- **Internet connectivity features:** All Pocket PC devices ship with a version of Internet Explorer, which includes offline features and decent Web site rendering compatibility.

- **Native Office document support:** Pocket PC devices ship with Pocket versions of Word, Excel, PowerPoint, and various Outlook components.

◆ **Wireless networking support:** Support for 802.11b wireless networking is available in every Pocket PC device. Just add a compatible PC card or CompactFlash-based wireless NIC, and you're online.

◆ **Microsoft Reader:** The Pocket PC ships with Microsoft's Reader software, which lets you read eBooks by using crystal-clear ClearType technology, which effectively triples the horizontal resolution of on-screen text.

◆ **Handwriting recognition:** Unlike the Palm OS, which forces you to learn a hieroglyphic-like *Graffiti* handwriting method for inputting text, Pocket PCs support a Transcriber application that performs handwriting recognition.

Changes to Pocket PC 2002

Introduced in October 2001, the Pocket PC 2002 includes or updates all the features found in the original Pocket PC and adds the following unique features:

◆ **Malleable user interface:** Based on the success of third-party Pocket PC applications that let users control the look and feel of the system, the Pocket PC 2002 supports user interface themes.

◆ **Instant messaging:** Pocket PC 2002 ships with a mobile version of Windows Messenger, Microsoft's real-time communications product.

◆ **Enterprise features:** Pocket PC 2002 has better support for enterprises, including VPN support and direct synchronization support with Exchange Server e-mail systems.

◆ **Emerging wireless technology support:** In addition to infrared and Wi-Fi support, Pocket PC 2002 devices support Bluetooth, a technology for personal area networks (PANs), and WAP (Wireless Access Protocol), a cell-phone-like textual Web interface.

◆ **Spell checking:** Pocket Inbox and Word now support spell-checking capabilities.

◆ **Graffiti support:** Pocket PC 2002 now includes the same Graffiti application used by Palm OS devices.

◆ **Improved system messages:** Pocket PC 2002 devices support balloon-window-like dialogs for various system messages, including reminders, a low battery warning, and volume controls.

Synchronizing with the Desktop

Like Palm devices, Pocket PCs are designed as desktop PC companions rather than PC replacements. Most users typically enter and manage data — such as contact information, scheduling data, task lists, and e-mail — on their PCs and then synchronize it with their Pocket PCs. On the Pocket PC end, you can enter information quickly by using a stylus and the device's on-screen virtual keyboard.

Say you enter a client's new cell phone number in your Pocket PC while traveling. When you get back to the office, you can synchronize the device with your PC to replicate the information in your Outlook Contacts module. Before PDAs, such a task would require pen and paper and a good memory. (How many times have you written down information on a scrap a paper only to misplace it later?) Now, you can automate the task quite easily.

The key here is ActiveSync, software that Microsoft supplies with each Pocket PC. You can download an updated version of this software from Microsoft's Pocket PC Web site (`www.pocketpc.com`).

TIP Microsoft constantly updates ActiveSync, fixing bugs and adding new features with each update. I recommend downloading the latest version rather than using the one that comes with your device. For example, the first version of ActiveSync 3.5, which ships with all Pocket PC 2002 devices, is incompatible with Windows XP and Office XP, despite claims to the contrary. Make sure that you have the latest version to avoid running into problems.

The ActiveSync application, shown in Figure 19-1, creates a *partnership* between your PC and your Pocket PC. The connection is usually hardware based, through a USB-based cradle or cable. Other connections are possible, including infrared, modem-based, or wired or wireless networking, but the first connection has to be physical via a USB connection.

Figure 19-1: ActiveSync creates a partnership between your desktop PC and a Pocket PC device.

The ActiveSync application is easy to use, and synchronization is largely automatic. You'll want to configure synchronization during installation or shortly thereafter. By default, your Pocket PC automatically synchronizes with the desktop, constantly, while connected. You can change this setting if you want.

Installing and Configuring ActiveSync

The first time you plug in a Pocket PC device, Windows XP should detect it automatically. If this doesn't happen, simply cancel out any Hardware Wizard tomfoolery and install the ActiveSync software, which clears up any compatibility issues.

SETTING UP ACTIVESYNC

During setup, ActiveSync attempts to determine the type of connection your Pocket PC will use for synchronization. Here is a rundown of the three choices, as shown in Figure 19-2:

◆ **Serial (COM port):** Serial connections are out-of-date and not typically used with Pocket PC 2002 devices (many XP-based PCs don't even include serial ports). A serial connection is also far too slow to transfer files – especially multimedia files – at an acceptable rate.

◆ **USB:** Most often, you'll be using USB.

◆ **Networking:** A networking connection is certainly possible, but your first connection between the PC and Pocket PC must be via one of the other two choices.

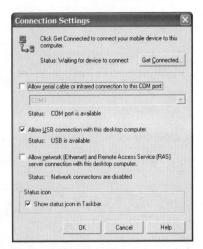

Figure 19-2: You have numerous choices for connecting to a Pocket PC device.

After the connection has been established, you can determine which items to synchronize on the Sync Options tab of the Sync dialog box, similar to Figure 19-3. (You can get to this screen by clicking the Options icon as shown in Figure 19-1.)

What you see in this dialog box is based on the applications that are installed on your PC. (You can add other Pocket PC/PC synchronization items later, including those for such products as Microsoft Money).

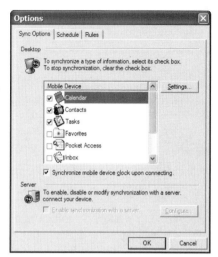

Figure 19-3: Which applications you synchronize will be based on your needs and the applications you have installed.

By default, ActiveSync is set up to synchronize with Outlook's Calendar, Contacts, Inbox, and Tasks, as well as Internet Explorer's Favorites list. I generally trim this down a bit and recommend that you do as well, depending on your needs. In my case, I don't access my e-mail on the Pocket PC, which would be disastrous for several reasons, the primary one being the sheer volume of mail I receive. And while I've experimented with Pocket Internet Explorer Web browsing, I don't see the need to store all my Favorites on the Pocket PC because most of the sites I visit aren't formatted correctly for the small display. (Pocket PC-specific versions of many sites are available. For this reason, I store only Favorites that point to Pocket PC-specific web sites on the Pocket PC).

After you specify which items you want to synchronize, ActiveSync attempts its first synchronization. At this point, you're asked how you want to synchronize. Here are the three conflict resolution options, which kick in when you've changed an item on the PC or the Pocket PC:

◆ **Leave the Item Unresolved.** Unresolved items are left unresolved, leaving different versions on the Pocket PC and PC. You are prompted to resolve these conflicts and can manually choose which version to replicate on the other device.

◆ **Always Replace the Item on My Device.** Conflicted items on the Pocket PC are replaced with information from the desktop. This is the way I have

ActiveSync set up, because I don't generally enter or change contact or scheduling information by using the Pocket PC.

◆ **Always replace the item on this computer.** The conflicted item is automatically replaced on the desktop PC with information from the Pocket PC.

 When you install a Pocket PC under Windows XP, a Mobile Device icon is added to My Computer. You can use this icon to navigate through the Pocket PC file system directly from My Computer in the same way that you'd access any local drive or network share.

FURTHER ACTIVESYNC CONFIGURATION

After ActiveSync is installed and the initial synchronization is complete, you can configure other features. I recommend that you do this because the default configuration is unsuitable for most people.

If you close the main ActiveSync window, a circular icon remains in the system tray (as shown in Figure 19-4). The color of this icon indicates the status of the application:

Figure 19-4: The ActiveSync tray icon changes color based on the status of the device.

◆ **Green icon:** The Pocket PC is connected and synchronized.

◆ **Gray icon:** The device is disconnected or is powering down.

◆ **Yellow icon:** A synchronization conflict has occurred.

When you click the circular icon in the system tray, you're presented with a list of choices: You can open the main ActiveSync window, for example, change the connection settings, or explore the Pocket PC device by using a My Computer–like interface.

From the main ActiveSync window, you can access various options through the toolbar or menu system.

SYNCHRONIZE To synchronize manually, click the Sync button or choose File→Synchronize.

GET CONNECTED When the device is unconnected, you can re-run ActiveSync's Get Connected Wizard (by selecting File→ Get Connected), which determines how the device connects to and synchronizes with the partner PC. The wizard polls the serial, USB, infrared, and networking capabilities of the PC and determines which are available for connecting to the Pocket PC.

This option is useful if you want to change the default connection type. For example, you might have to use USB for the initial connection but prefer to use infrared after that.

CONNECTION SETTINGS After you choose a connection type, choose File→Connection Settings to display the Connection Settings dialog box, shown in Figure 19-5. Here, you can select or deselect the types of connections that ActiveSync will poll. I use only USB synchronization, so I deselect serial, infrared, and network connections.

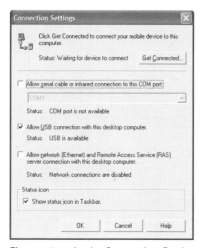

Figure 19-5: In the Connection Settings dialog box, you can deselect the connection types you won't be using.

You can also select an option to display the ActiveSync icon in the system tray. I recommend leaving this icon displayed.

OPTIONS A comprehensive set of options is available from the Options dialog box, shown in Figure 19-6. You can open this dialog box by clicking the Options toolbar button or by choosing Tools→Options.

Here is a rundown of the tabs in this dialog box:

◆ **Sync Options:** On the Sync Options tab (refer to Figure 19-6), select the check boxes for the items you want to synchronize. To set per-item synchronization options, select an item in the Mobile Device list and then click the Settings button. For example, when you select Calendar, you see the dialog box shown in Figure 19-7. Here, you can determine whether to synchronize all appointments or only certain appointments (such as those that occurred during a certain time range or meet certain criteria). Likewise, you can synchronize all Contacts or only those that are manually selected from a list or meet certain criteria.

♦ **Schedule:** The most important option in the Options dialog box is available from the Schedule tab, shown in Figure 19-8. Here, you determine how often ActiveSync synchronizes your PC data with the Pocket PC.

The default is laughably inappropriate for most people: When connected, the device synchronizes with the PC every five minutes. You can change that schedule, or synchronize only when first connected, or synchronize manually. I synchronize when first connected and then manually synchronize as needed.

♦ **Rules:** On the Rules tab, shown in Figure 19-9, you can do the following:

■ Configure the conflict resolution choices discussed in "Setting Up ActiveSync," earlier in this chapter.

■ Configure options for file conversions. Many document types must be converted before being transmitted to or used on the Pocket PC. ActiveSync generally sets up file conversions properly for you, so it's unlikely you'll need to change these settings.

■ Configure Internet Connection Sharing, which is referred to as Pass Through. If your device is connected to the computer, you can access the Internet through that connection.

Figure 19-6: The Options dialog box provides access to synchronization, scheduling, and rules settings.

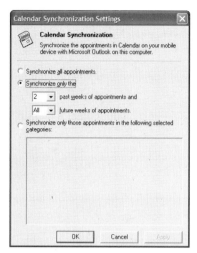

Figure 19-7: The Calendar Synchronization Settings box provides options for configuring synchronization for just this component.

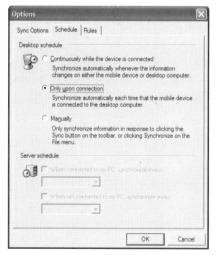

Figure 19-8: On the Schedule tab, you determine how and when the Pocket PC synchronizes with the desktop PC.

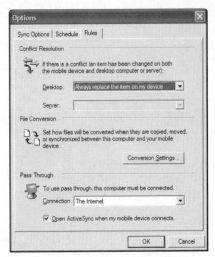

Figure 19-9: The Rules tab determines how conflicts are resolved and other similar options.

Synchronizing Files

Though you can copy files between the Pocket PC and its partner PC manually, ActiveSync also offers a more automated file synchronization feature. This feature is pretty basic and works much like the old Briefcase feature from Windows 95 (this was replaced in Windows XP with a more powerful feature called Offline Files and Folders, which is discussed in Chapter 18), but it does work. Here's how you configure this feature:

1. From the main ActiveSync window, choose Tools→Options to display the Options dialog box.

2. On the Sync Options tab, select Files from the list of sync items and then click Settings. This displays the File Synchronization Options dialog box.

   By default, you must use a specific folder for file synchronization. This folder is located at `C:\Documents and Settings\`*username*`\My Documents\PocketPC2002 My Documents` on your PC, and it synchronizes with the My Documents folder on your Pocket PC.

3. You can copy files into this folder or manually add files to be synchronized by clicking the Add button. It's generally easier to copy the appropriate files and folders into that folder via My Computer. Click Ok when you are all done adding folders and files.

Several things happen when you set up file synchronization. First, a shortcut to the new PocketPC2002 My Documents folder is created on your desktop. Then ActiveSync attempts to synchronize. As with the initial synchronization, you're presented with a Combine or Replace dialog box, which lets you determine how file conflicts are resolved. And from then on, any ActiveSync synchronization will include files and folders found in that new folder.

Networking a Pocket PC

Like PCs, Pocket PC devices can be networked using modems or wired or wireless network cards. Wireless networking makes the most sense for such a device, and many PC card 802.11-b-based network cards – usually designed with laptops in mind – will work fine with Pocket PCs that support PC Card expansion (the iPAQ offers this type of compatibility, for example). And a new generation of CompactFlash-based wireless NICs, designed specifically for Pocket PCs, was introduced in late 2001, making it easier for these palm-sized devices to connect wirelessly to a network and the Internet.

NIC compatibility varies from model to model. Before purchasing a card, be sure to check for Pocket PC compatibility and then follow the manufacturer's instructions for installing and configuring the card.

After the card is installed, you can connect to the network. In Pocket PC 2002, you follow these steps:

1. Choose Start→Settings→Connections on the Pocket PC device. The screen resembles Figure 19-10.

2. To configure the networking card, select Network Adapters and then select your adapter from the list that appears. In Figure 19-11, the wireless adapter is ORiNOCO Wireless Network Driver.

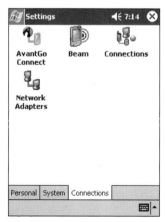

Figure 19-10: In the Connections screen, you can configure various device connections, including network adapters.

3. Click the Properties button. This displays the screen shown in Figure 19-13. Here, you configure the IP address information. Generally speaking, you will configure a wireless adapter to accept a dynamic IP address, as you would with a desktop PC. However, you can configure the network adapter with a static IP address; in this case, you need to configure subnet mask, default gateway, and name server information.

Figure 19-11: The Network Adapters screen lists the adapters that are configured for the system, which doesn't necessarily mean that all of these devices are installed.

Figure 19-12: The Network Adapter Properties screen is similar to the Properties dialog box for network connections in Windows XP.

On the Pocket PC, changing network adapter settings often require a soft reset before the new settings can take place.

To test your settings, load Pocket Internet Explorer and navigate to a live Web site. If the network is properly configured, you should be able to load a site, as shown in Figure 19-13.

Figure 19-13: Pocket Internet Explorer can display normal Web sites like this, but it works better with Web sites that are designed specifically for mobile devices.

Chapter 20

Using Palm Devices with Windows XP

IN THIS CHAPTER

◆ Understand the various Palm OS devices and the changes made to them

◆ Installing, Configuring and using Palm devices under Windows XP

IN THE EARLY 1990S, PC makers and other companies in the computer industry turned their attention to an emerging market for handheld devices, or personal digital assistants (PDAs), which some estimated would soon be worth billions of dollars. The first generation of these devices – most obviously represented by Apple's ill-fated Newton – exemplified the problems these companies would have bringing this market to fruition. The devices were large, heavy, and rarely as easy to use as the companies promised, and as a result, consumers stayed away in droves.

So when a tiny startup from California started approaching investors with a plan to introduce a new handheld device code-named Touchdown, it wasn't surprising that few were interested. But the company – Palm Computing – pushed on and released its first product, the PalmPilot, in 1996. It was an instant success, primarily because it avoided the problems of the past. The PalmPilot was small, simple, and inexpensive. And rather than try to adapt itself to a plethora of usage scenarios, the PalmPilot and its successors focused solely on personal information management, and they got it right the first time.

Today, Palm-compatible devices run on a large range of devices from companies such as Palm, Handspring, Sony, and others. The Palm OS, which powers these devices, is by far the most popular platform for handheld computing available today. Not surprisingly, Palm devices work well with Windows XP and provide XP users with a way to take their important personal information with them while away from the desktop. In this chapter, you find about out about these devices and how they work with Windows XP.

Introducing the Palm OS

Developed by Palm Computing, the simple Palm OS has powered Palm-compatible devices since 1996, when the original PalmPilot appeared. Though Palm and other companies that produce Palm OS–compatible products have constantly updated their hardware with new features, different ways of connecting with the PC, and more memory, the Palm OS has changed very little over the past several years. The reason for this is simple: When you do something right the first time, you only have to make incremental changes as necessitated by consumer demand and bug fixes. And the Palm OS is one of those rare instances where the technology worked right from the beginning.

The Palm OS user interface, shown in Figure 20-1, is simplicity itself. The main screen is a grid of simple buttons with intuitive icons and descriptive text. The most popular personal information management functionality – address book, date book, expenses, mail, memo pad, and to-do list – are available upfront (either as buttons on the device or on the main screen), along with other popular handheld functions, such as a calculator and city time display for travelers.

Figure 20-1: The Palm OS is based on simplicity and ease of use.

In addition to the user interface, which is activated via on-screen clicks with a stylus, most Palm-compatible devices feature an area below the display screen that users can command with the stylus as well. This area allows the user to draw simple strokes and use the bundled Graffiti application to enter texts and numbers, which appear on-screen (see Figure 20-2). Shortcut areas for the main screen, the menu, the calculator, and a search function are also available next to this scratchpad area.

Palm devices connect to the PC via serial cable, USB, or infrared connection, and synchronize with a PC-based PIM (Personal Information Management) package through an application called HotSync. You can initialize HotSync by pressing a button on the Palm device's synchronization base, through software on the Palm or PC, or at automated intervals.

For compatibility with leading PIM packages and other software, Palm developed a software technology called *conduits*, which convert information to and from Palm's internal format. The use of conduit software means that a Palm device can be programmed to work with virtually any software product. The devices ship with conduits for the most popular packages such as Microsoft Outlook and the like. If you don't already have a PC-based PIM, Palm provides one of those as well, called Palm Desktop. HotSync and Palm Desktop are covered a bit later in this chapter.

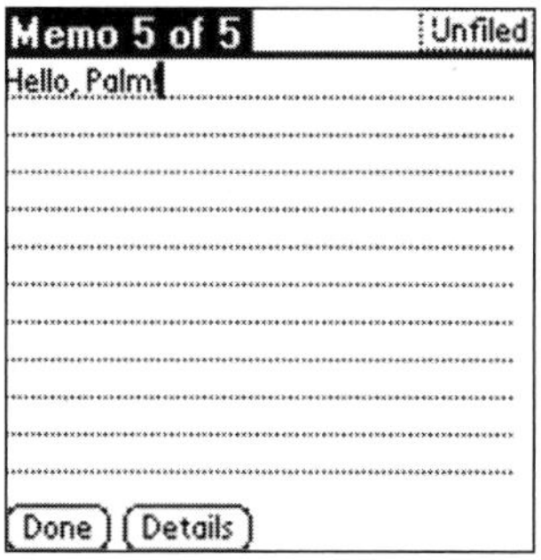

Figure 20-2: As you move the stylus across the device's scratchpad, characters appear on-screen.

Over the years, the Palm OS has been enhanced with various capabilities, but the core values of simplicity have never changed.

Changes to Palm OS 4.x and Beyond

In 2001, Palm introduced Palm OS 4. This OS version includes enhanced security with encryption features for securing your private data, support for 65,000 color displays, wireless e-mail and Internet capabilities, and other features. By late 2002, you should be able to purchase devices based on OS 5, which includes support for faster new processors and advanced, Pocket PC–like capabilities.

Palm OS 5 moves the Palm platform to the same Intel-based designs used by Pocket PC 2002 devices (see Chapter 19 for details). These devices feature multimedia capabilities, 802.11b and Bluetooth wireless networking support, and other advances, while retaining compatibility with the hundreds of thousands of Palm OS applications that are available today.

But wherever the Palm OS is headed, one thing remains true: It's the simplest and most popular platform for mobile computing. An investment in a device that runs the Palm OS today will pay off in the future. As long as the Palm OS system continues to grow and expand, you 'll be able to easily transport your important data onto your new Palm device. In some ways, this resembles Microsoft's strategy with Windows, where a completely different platform like Windows XP behaves and is compatible with previous Windows 9.x versions, which have very little in common with XP internally.

Looking at the Palm Device Players

Choosing a particular Palm device is not an easy task. Several companies license the Palm OS from Palm, and you can find popular devices from Palm, Handspring, and Sony in consumer electronics stores and other retail outlets. I provide an overview of these companies and their current wares here.

PALM

The originators of the original Palm are still in the game, and command a strong lead in not only the market for Palm-compatible devices but also in the wider market for handheld devices. Palm currently markets two basic product lines:

- The stylish m series, which is designed for home users, college students, and small office users
- The elite i series, which offers wireless e-mail and Web connectivity

Palm devices range in price from about $100 for a low-end m-series model to almost $500 for a top-of-the-line i-series, which also requires a service plan that costs $10 to $35 a month. The company has stayed true to the original Pilot design, so none of the Palm models feature integrated keyboards or other non-stylus input capabilities.

HANDSPRING

Handspring was founded by the original co-founders of Palm, and its long-term goal was to make wireless connectivity a reality. In 1998, the company launched a line of Visor products that it has enhanced over the years. The Edge model features a stunningly thin industrial design and vibrant color models dubbed the Visor Prism. The Visors are, by and large, standard Pilot-like devices that rely on a stylus for input.

Handspring's future is wireless, and in late 2001, the company announced its first *communicator* product, which it dubs the Treo. The Handspring Treo runs the Palm OS and includes cell phone functionality, a built-in keyboard, and wireless messaging and Internet capabilities. The Treo is the device Handspring wanted to build all along, and though the first generation features black-and-white screens, a color version is expected in late 2002.

Handspring's Visor line is bargain priced at about $150 to $300 for a color model. The Treo line is a bit more costly, of course, with prices ranging from $400 to $500, assuming you sign up for a wireless service. Wireless service runs about $20 to $100 a month, depending on the service plan you choose.

SONY

After an initial failed stab at the handheld market in the mid-1990s, Sony licensed the Palm OS in late 1998. The company's Palm-based Clié products haven't disappointed, combining Sony style with a wealth of multimedia features never before seen on Palm-compatible devices. The Sony Clié product line includes a number of stylish black-and-white and color handhelds that resemble Palm and Handspring devices. What sets the Clié line apart from the competition are expansion capabilities through Sony's proprietary MemoryStick technology, video and music playback capabilities, TV remote compatibility, and even a built-in video camera in some cases.

In early 2002, Sony introduced its next-generation PEG-NR70 line, which features a flip-over built-in keyboard and a gorgeous color display that quadruples the resolution of most Palm-compatible devices. The result is a stunningly modern take on the Palm handheld, one that is sure to win Sony some awards down the road.

Style comes at a price, of course. Sony Clié devices range from about $200 for a black-and-white unit to $600 for the high-end PEG-NR70.

LOOKING FORWARD

The handheld market is changing all the time, of course, but the basics of using a Palm device are the same regardless of which model you choose. For updates on these companies and their Palm-compatible products, please visit the Web site for this book at www.xphomenetworking.com.

Using the Palm OS with Windows XP

Regardless of which Palm model you choose, you receive a version of the Palm Desktop and the HotSync synchronization software, which interacts with the device via a serial, USB, or infrared connection.

If you don't already use a PC-based PIM package, you could do worse than the Palm Desktop, which offers date book (shown in Figure 20-3), address book, to-do list, memo, and expenses components, along with a front end for Palm's software installation routine.

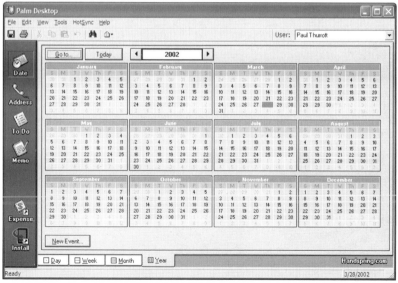

Figure 20-3: The bundled Palm Desktop application is a full-featured Personal Information Management package.

Synchronizing

You use the bundled HotSync application to synchronize data between your PC-based PIM and the device. Like ActiveSync on the Pocket PC, HotSync can resolve differences between the data stored on your PC and the data on your device based on criteria you specify (see Figure 20-4). For example, you can choose to overwrite the data in the handheld with the data on your PC.

Figure 20-4: You can customize how various types of data are synchronized between the device and your PC.

HotSync, shown in Figure 20-5, sits idle in your system tray until synchronization is required. Synchronization can be automated — it can occur at set intervals or in response to certain events — or it can be manual. For example, you can press the Sync button on your handheld's base unit to initiate a synchronization.

On the device itself, you can use the HotSync application, shown in Figure 20-6, to configure HotSync properties. This application is located in the System menu.

Figure 20-5: The HotSync application manages information synchronization.

Working with Palm OS Software

To install software on the Palm, you can use the Install Tool application that's provided with your device. Install Tool, shown in Figure 20-7, enables you to add new software to the device and remove existing software that you may no longer need.

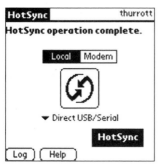

Figure 20-6: A version of HotSync is available on the Palm device.

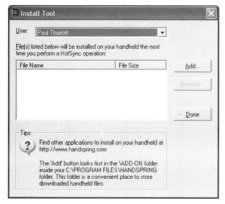

Figure 20-7: You use Install Tool to add and remove Palm OS applications.

Installing Palm OS Software

To install software on the Palm OS, follow these steps:

1. Launch Install Tool, which is generally located in your Start menu with your other Palm OS tools. (This location varies by device. For the Handspring device I use, Install Tool is located in a subfolder called Handspring under All Programs).

2. Click the Add button and navigate to a shell folder that contains a Palm installation program (file type *.prc), as shown in Figure 20-8. You may have received some free installable applications with your device, or you can download an application from the Web.

3. Select as many applications as you want to install at one time and click the Open button. The Install Tool lists all the applications that you have chosen to open, along with their corresponding file size. The file size is important to know because most Palm OS devices ship with relatively tiny amounts of memory.

4. Click Done. Install Tool then notifies you that the software will be installed the next time you perform a HotSync operation.

5. Trigger a HotSync by tapping the synchronization button on your Palm device's connection base. The software is installed during synchronization.

6. After synchronization is complete, pick up your Palm device and tap the Home button with the stylus. Then choose All from the menu to display all the applications on your device. The new application should be available from this list.

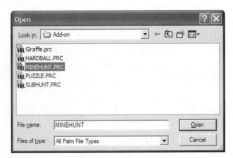

Figure 20-8: Palm OS applications are denoted by the PRC file extension.

For purposes of this example, I installed the MineHunt game that came free with my Handspring device, as shown in Figure 20-9. This game is virtually identical to the Minesweeper game that ships with most Windows desktop versions.

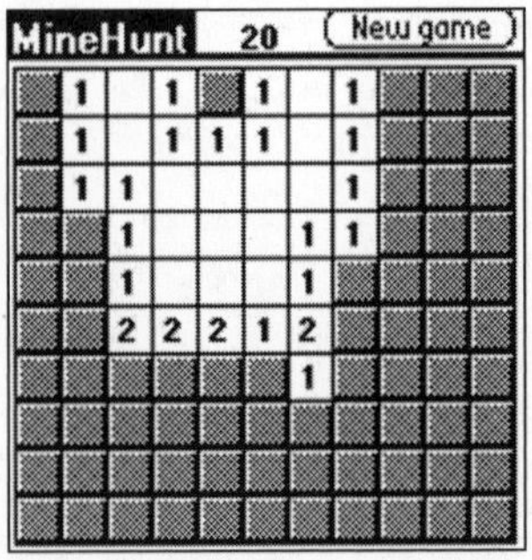

Figure 20-9: A Palm application that was added to the device with Install Tool.

Uninstalling Palm OS Software

To uninstall software on the Palm OS, follow these simple steps:

1. Launch Install Tool.

2. Select the application you want to uninstall from the list.

3. Click the Remove button.

Chapter 21

Other Devices

AS HOME NETWORKING TECHNOLOGIES become cheaper and more readily available, they're being applied to devices that have less and less to do with computing. Of course, networking technologies make sense for a certain range of connected devices, such as Pocket PCs and smart cell phones, because these devices often interact with a desktop PC. But many upcoming consumer electronics devices — some of which interact with the PC and others that do not — are being fitted with networking capabilities where appropriate, in order to better serve customers' needs.

Currently, dozens of connected devices are on the market, including portable audio players, digital audio receivers, TV photo viewers, and the like. Some devices that are aimed at a more technical crowd rely on a home PC, but others are designed to operate as the hub of a connected home, where no PC is expected or required.

Sometime in the middle to late 2002, Microsoft plans to ship an upgrade to Windows XP called Windows XP Service Pack 1 (SP1). This update will include dramatic improvements to the digital media and home networking capabilities of the operating system, allowing consumers to move many computing experiences out of the home office and into the den or other areas of the home.

This chapter takes a look at these exciting technologies, detailing what's available now and what will be coming in the near future.

Working with Connected Devices

A *connected device* is any consumer electronics device that can be connected in some way either to the outside world via an Internet connection or to your home computer, by using networking or other connection technologies. A wide range of such devices are available, and more are on the way, despite some early notable failures, such as the Sony eVilla, the Compaq MSN Companion, and the 3Com Audrey. These early failures provided consumers with simple access to a subset of the features found on a full desktop PC and were designed to replace, rather than supplement, a PC. They provided access to Internet features such as Web browsing and e-mail access, but offered no local storage and often included slow dial-up connections rather than broadband support.

Today's connected devices take a different approach. Some of these devices work with your existing PC. For example, digital audio receivers (DARs) use home networking technology to bring your PC-based digital music collection to any room in your home so you can listen to your music on a kicking home stereo rather than your PC's pathetic little speakers. And other connected devices move digital media functionality such as CD ripping and burning to other rooms in the house.

The most popular connected devices are portable audio devices, which enable you to copy digital music from your PC or home entertainment system and bring it with you on the road. Most portable audio devices are small enough to fit in your pocket and offer excellent battery life.

DIGITAL AUDIO RECEIVERS (DARS)

Capitalizing on the recent trend of users storing their CD collections digitally on their PCs, various hardware companies have released digital audio receivers (DARs). These devices make it relatively easy to output PC-based music to other rooms in the home by using home networking technologies such as Ethernet or HomePNA (phone-line-based networking).

DARs typically support both MP3 and Windows Media Audio (WMA) formats, which are the most popular audio formats. The receivers generally match home stereo components, and can work with a component stereo receiver or directly with self-powered speakers. Most models also include a large LCD display so you can view the on-screen menu and playing information such as song title, artist name, and track time. And most include a remote control so you can access your music from the couch.

NETWORKING DARS   To connect a DAR to your PC, you have to sort out the networking issues first. Unless your home is wired for Ethernet, you'll probably want to use HomePNA, which lets you move network data over your standard phone lines without disrupting your normal voice service. HomePNA networking requires that you install a HomePNA network adapter in the PC that stores your digital audio files.

Most DAR models include software that instructs the player where to find your music. The DAR can then access your music files and playlists across the network; they aren't copied to the device but instead played live over the network.

OVERVIEW OF THE PLAYERS   The most popular DARs are sold by SonicBlue, though the company also OEMs its products to PC makers such as Dell Computer. The devices feature a small form factor (its size and shape makes it easy to hold and use), 20 watt amplifier, stereo speaker and RCA connectors, and support for HomePNA and 10 Mbps Ethernet networks. The cost is the $220 to $300 range.

Gateway also markets a DAR, the Gateway Connected Music Player. This device fits better with most home stereo equipment than Dell's but lacks an amplifier. It's also more limited than Dell's in that you can't just point its software to your music. Instead, you must store your digital music in a specific folder. Gateway's DAR is about $300.

CONNECTED STEREO EQUIPMENT

In mid-2001, PC companies announced *connected stereo equipment*. Like DARs, these products look right at home in your living room with your other stereo components, though connected stereo equipment tends to include a much larger form factor than most DARs. These devices are a complete solution without a PC in your home, but most of them require an Internet connection of some sort.

Connected stereo equipment does away with the need for a PC by providing PC-like features – such as a hard drive, CD-RW drive, and Internet connectivity – wrapped into a box that's supposedly easy enough for any consumer to use. To rip your CDs, place them in the CD-RW drive; use the built-in Internet connection to download title, track, and artist information; and then write the songs to the local hard drive. You can also use the CD-RW drive to make audio mix CDs of your favorite songs, and some models even support USB connectivity so that you can connect portable audio devices. These devices use your TV set as a display and a remote control as an input device.

The big problem is expense. Most connected stereo equipment costs at least $1,000.

The first companies to jump into the connected stereo equipment market were Compaq and Hewlett-Packard, two old-school PC makers making their first tentative steps into other markets. SonicBlue is a newer entry into this market. Here is a brief rundown of devices from these three companies:

- ◆ HP's device is the Digital Entertainment Center (DEC). It has a 40 GB hard drive, dial-up Internet access, HomePNA or 10/100 Mbps Ethernet for an Internet connection, and a 4x/8x CD-RW drive. It accesses Internet radio stations and interoperates with portable audio devices through a USB port.

- ◆ Compaq's entry, the iPAQ Music Center, sports similar specs to the DEC and an identical price. It includes a 20 GB hard drive, CD drive, modem, HomePNA networking, and three USB ports.

- ◆ SonicBlue's Rio Central features a much larger LCD display than the competition, a 40 GB hard drive, a CD-RW drive with support for making audio mix CDs and MP3-format data CDs, PC connectivity options, support for Rio portable audio devices, and HomePNA networking support.

PORTABLE AUDIO PLAYERS

While companies struggle to find new markets for connected devices, the strongest market is for the device that started it all: the portable digital audio player. Portable audio players come in all shapes and sizes, including a dying breed of flash

RAM-based models, most of which ship with 32 to 64 MB of memory. This isn't enough storage for more than several songs, so alternatives are cropping up, offering higher storage capacities and better functionality. Some of these include

◆ **MP3/WMA CD-R:** Portable CD players that offer MP3 or WMA compatibility are an alternative to flash RAM-based players because they offer 700 to 800MB of storage per CD and blank CDs are cheap. Most portable CD players that offer this sort of functionality use the popular MP3 format only, but some WMA-compatible units are available as well. Units generally cost $80 to $150, and higher-end versions offer rechargeable internal batteries. Various car CD players offer MP3 and WMA compatibility.

◆ **Hard-drive-based portable audio:** New devices like the Apple iPod and SonicBlue Rio Riot are based on PC-like hard drives. Massive storage capacities make it possible to bring your entire collection on the road. Creative Labs was an early player in this market with its NOMAD Jukebox, featuring a 6 to 20GB hard drive wrapped in a large plastic shell. Apple Computer's iPod device – which features a 5 to 10GB hard drive, fast FireWire-based connectivity, and an elegant design that is easy to use – is not natively compatible with Windows, though various third parties are working to get around that limitation. The iPod's FireWire connection transfers music at speeds 40 times faster than USB, and it can store 1,000 to 2,000 MP3 songs at 160 Kbps, which is a fairly high encoding rate. These players are $250 to $500.

If you're looking into portable digital audio, look for something that integrates with XP's Windows Media Player, or just go with a CD player, which offers the best compatibility and cheapest prices.

The Future: Freestyle and Mira

Microsoft has looked at the emerging market for PC/living room integration and created some new PC-centric technologies that allow users to take the PC experience and move it into the living room. These technologies are code-named Freestyle and Mira:

◆ **Mira** is a wireless networking technology that enables a new generation of wireless computer displays that you can carry around the home and use away from the PC.

◆ **Freestyle** is a new user interface for digital media that's designed for TV sets.

These products will be introduced to the public in late 2002 when Microsoft releases Windows XP Service Pack 2 (SP2).

Home Networking, Mira Style

Mira combines the Remote Desktop feature from Windows XP with integrated wireless (802.11b) networking capabilities and a Windows CE .NET–enabled LCD display. Here is a brief description of its key features:

◆ The primary Mira display replaces your existing PC monitor and lets you work normally at your desktop, or you can carry the display to another room. You interact with the display by using a built-in stylus and an on-screen keyboard, much in the same way that Pocket PCs work today.

◆ Secondary displays, which work in tandem with a main display (possibly your current, non-Mira display), come in a variety of sizes and can be stored anywhere in the home. You might keep one in the living room or bedroom, for example.

◆ Mira is aimed squarely at home users, not the office, which Microsoft targets with its Tablet PC products. A Mira display uses about 32MB of RAM and a similar amount of ROM, runs Windows CE .NET, and uses a relatively low performance CPU, which keeps down costs and complexity. And unlike a Tablet PC, Mira displays do not include a hard drive or other PC-like components. In fact, Mira displays feature no moving parts.

Microsoft expects Mira to do for monitors what the cordless handset did for telephones, freeing consumers from their home offices and allowing them to enjoy the complete Windows XP experience, including full Web browsing, sending and receiving e-mail messages, listening to music, and editing and displaying digital images, from any room in their homes. Based on my testing of the technology, I think they've got a huge success on their hands.

Companies such as Fujitsu, LG Electronics, NEC, Philips, ViewSonic, and several others are working on a wide selection of Mira-enabled displays, including 15-inch and 20-inch primary displays and a variety of 8-inch and 10-inch secondary displays. Want one? Microsoft and its partners say that Mira-enabled devices will ship in time for the 2002 holiday season. Various companies will also offer more rugged Mira displays that can withstand drops, coffee spills, and even small children.

In the future, Mira technologies will be applied to other devices, including fold-down screens for under kitchen cabinets and next-generation TV sets.

Taking Digital Media into the Living Room with Freestyle

In the same way that Mira is designed for a new generation of display hardware, Freestyle is designed for a new generation of PC hardware that resembles stereo components and sits in your living room next to the TV. Freestyle-enabled PCs feature wireless keyboards and mice for normal PC input, and a remote control for interacting with the beautiful Freestyle software, shown in Figure 21-1.

Figure 21-1: Freestyle's Start screen is simple to use.

Freestyle-enabled PCs (that is, Windows XP SP1 machines) allow users to view home videos, music, and photos, watch DVD movies, and program Digital Video Recorder (DVR) capabilities through an on-screen program guide, like the one shown in Figure 21-2. The DVR enables you to watch, pause, and record live TV like you would with a TiVo, ReplayTV, or UltimateTV device.

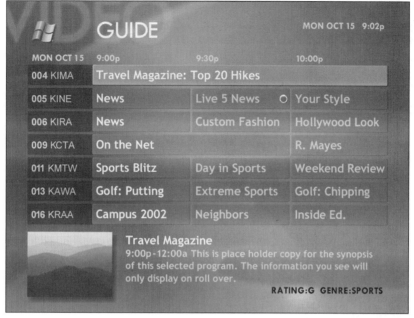

Figure 21-2: Freestyle's program guide integrates with cable and satellite TV systems.

Index

Symbols & Numbers